The New York Times

SUNDAY MORNING CROSSWORD PUZZLES
75 Giant Sunday Puzzles

Edited by Will Shortz

ST. MARTIN'S GRIFFIN ❧ NEW YORK

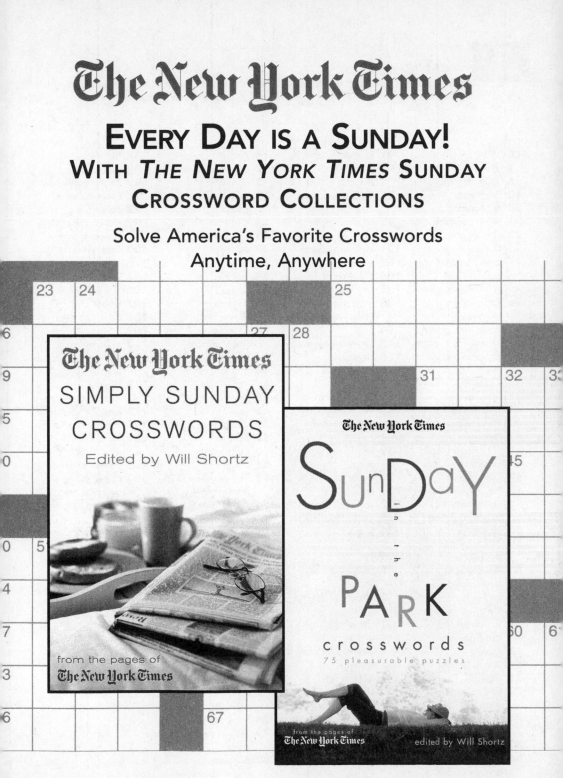

1 KNIGHTS ERRANT

ACROSS

1 Stud
6 Journal
13 Formative
20 Au courant
21 More often than not
22 Threefold
23 Unhappy author's complaint to an editor?
25 Full Italian pockets?
26 Train for the ring, in a way
27 Prefix with phase
29 "The X-Files" extras
30 Lance on the bench
31 How-to book for lovebirds?
37 Tribal drums
41 Joie de vivre
42 Parisian peeper
43 Brouhaha
44 "Quantum Leap" co-star
47 Even chance
52 Ice cream flavorer
55 Parrot's cry
56 Coupling device
58 Ninny
59 Broken plumbing in the basement?
63 Proscriptions necessitated by kosher law?
65 Historical records
66 Refrigerator device
68 Card game for three
69 It may be raw
71 Flipper
72 CNN offering: Abbr.
74 Nanking nanny
77 Take back
82 Covers up
86 Reprobate's choices on a hot day?
88 "Go ahead, shoot!"?
90 Candidate's concern
91 Executes
93 Stock or C.D.: Abbr.
94 She played Nora in "The Thin Man"
95 Maxima maker
97 Like virgin land
101 Missing a match
102 Mars, e.g.
104 It has body parts
105 City near San Jose
108 Most popular Halloween mask?
114 Bog
115 Often-twisted treat
116 Harmony
117 It may reveal some bugs
122 Bang source
125 What happened when I spilled coffee?
129 Like Rodeo Drive shops
130 Undo
131 Provide
132 Soft-shell clam
133 Order from Florida
134 Is quiet

DOWN

1 "Airplane!" actor Robert
2 "Return of the Jedi" critter
3 Haleakala Crater locale
4 Deodorized spot
5 Close by
6 Still drying
7 So far
8 Pilot's problem
9 Friend in the 'hood
10 Sharer's word
11 Inherited wealth
12 "One Flew Over the Cuckoo's Nest" novelist
13 Attack from the air
14 Significant stretch
15 11th-century date
16 Architect Jones
17 One of the Judds
18 Sen. Specter
19 Reason for a spanking, maybe
24 Inn array
28 Car trunk item
32 Badger
33 Wild bugler
34 Hook target
35 Loc. ___
36 Science
37 Indian drum
38 Cineplex ___ (theater chain)
39 No-brainer?
40 Run through
45 Receivable
46 Prunes
48 Tale of woe
49 Gouge
50 Sch. for midshipmen
51 Nudnik
53 They're likely to be honked at
54 Tree-trimming time
57 Elbe feeder
60 Former despots
61 Rubs out
62 Flicker?
64 ___-Roman
67 Most qualified to serve
70 Dirty
73 Prized
74 Abecedary link
75 "La Bohème" heroine
76 Santa ___ (hot winds)
78 Way to pray
79 Broken mirror, to some
80 Big name in snowmobiles
81 E-mail, e.g.
83 Splash catcher
84 Rather, informally
85 A heap
87 Reviews
89 Part of Y.S.L.
92 Styptic pencil, e.g.
96 Once called
98 Persian, e.g.
99 Handicapper's hangout, briefly
100 Tariff-eliminating pact
103 Winter coat
106 Flat provider
107 Chant
108 Phony
109 Blow
110 Have a hunch
111 Opera about a diva
112 Opener
113 Way too weighty
118 Romano sources
119 Some scrimmagers
120 No children's viewing
121 Some souvenirs
123 Easter entrée
124 Córdoba cry
126 Astronaut's outing: Abbr.
127 "Dawson's Creek" character Lindley
128 Part of many U.R.L.'s

by Bob Peoples and Nancy Salomon

ACROSS

1 Aged
9 Cry from Homer Simpson
12 Bugs
15 Hook deliverer
19 Romeo
20 Christian ___
21 Literary monogram
22 Chow chow chow
23 SPAETZLE
26 No haute cuisine
27 Ecological community
28 Seven up, e.g.
29 HOUSE
31 Pitcher Martinez
32 Record player
33 Fr. martyr, maybe
34 GROUCHY
40 Berlin-to-Leipzig dir.
41 Good thing to have in war
42 "The Karate Kid" co-star
43 Development areas?
47 Antiquated outburst
48 Academy newcomer
49 ORDINAL
55 Shake
56 California's ___ National Forest
57 Protractedly
58 Old telecommunications conglomerate
59 Panthers, e.g.
61 It may be needed for a change
65 Cry of disgust
66 SEALING WAX
71 William F. Buckley was one
72 Reply of affirmation
74 Inattention
75 20%, often
76 Drive down the fairway
81 Order to a band
82 Quash
83 DISDAIN
87 Two-time U.S. Open winner Hart
88 What prices may do
89 Megacorporation
90 Take off the stock exchange
91 Slip
92 "Moesha" broadcaster
94 TIMBREL
99 Run in front of U
100 It's rich in oil
104 See 60-Down
105 LONE WOLF
107 It may be jumped
108 Pulitzer winner Sinclair
113 Son of Venus
114 MESS
117 Romanian's neighbor
118 Word before second or hour
119 Protein source
120 They were striking in the Stone Age
121 Gridiron group
122 Gridiron gain: Abbr.
123 Gridiron goals, briefly
124 Détente documents

DOWN

1 Whipped cream serving
2 Rice-A-___
3 "No, No, Nanette" lyricist Harbach
4 Pronoun in a Hemingway title
5 Puppy pickup point
6 Gaucho's gold
7 One may be spotted in a gym
8 Revolution in square-dancing
9 Precise
10 E-mail address ending
11 Comedy club chorus
12 Flashy Chevy, for short
13 Cancer or Scorpio
14 Architectural tapers
15 Burkina ___
16 Bad treatment
17 12-Down, for one
18 Best players, usually
24 Big copper exporter
25 Eastern newt
30 Something to be shown
31 Annual tourn. holder
34 Heighten
35 Western accessory
36 Brother of Iphigenia
37 Feeling
38 Hot time in Québec
39 Pair
44 Pair
45 Magazin article
46 Molecular biology topic
47 Seat of Jackson County, Texas
49 Eden event
50 "___ be in England . . ."
51 MGM co-founder
52 Pastoral expanses
53 Most curious
54 Disquiets
56 Like some modern restaurants
59 Hawk or Hornet
60 With 104-Across, former voice of "This Week in Baseball"
62 Czar who succeeded Catherine I
63 Undemocratic tendency
64 Dorothy Parker delivery
67 Sounds from a sauna
68 Year the empress Octavia was murdered
69 Prefix with dermal
70 Ore site
73 Aqueduct of Sylvius, e.g.
77 Hue stronger than scarlet
78 Fu-___ (legendary Chinese sage)
79 Mozart's "L'___ del Cairo"
80 252 wine gallons
82 Part of mV
83 Software clients, collectively
84 Noted seafarers
85 Town near London, site of England's first paper mill
86 "All aboard!" area: Abbr.
87 Excellent, to a hip-hopper
90 Dress in
92 Old Mideast inits.
93 Like Top-Siders and khakis
95 They're not easily broken
96 Pizazz
97 Step off
98 Oceanside town north of San Diego
101 One side in an 1899 war
102 Entrepreneur's reading, maybe
103 One might get a cut
106 Celestial array
108 Meat approver, for short
109 Exam for jrs.
110 El alternative
111 S-curve
112 Top Untouchable
115 Turkey
116 Ending with butyl

by Frank A. Longo

3 NATURE CALLS

ACROSS

1 Spin doctor
6 Some TV's
10 Like some sketches: Abbr.
14 90%, say
18 Its walls withstand a lot of pressure
19 Novelist Ephron
20 The rain in Spain
21 Enough, for some
22 Pick up
23 Key material
24 Outlying district, briefly
25 Ginza glower
26 Never, in Nordhausen
27 When the American Academy of Arts and Sciences was founded
30 Cross with
32 ___ chi (martial art)
33 Eight in a row?
34 Hands-on defense?
35 Patriot, e.g.
36 Flip side?
38 Sorority letters
39 Social reformer Bloomer
40 14-Down's warning
41 Some annexes
42 No formal discourse
44 Lift, so to speak
45 Like sleep, ideally
47 Where sharks prowl
50 Linguist Chomsky
51 "The Christmas Song" co-composer
52 Mrs. Rabin
54 Winter time: Abbr.
57 Destroyers, in brief
59 "Gotcha"
60 ___ colada
61 Prefix with friendly
62 "Knight, Death and the Devil" engraver
63 Local forecast focus
66 Tawny thrush
68 Record's end?
69 Germs may grow in it
71 Blender sound
72 Oklahoma state tree
73 Surprise party admonition
74 Lock producer
75 Took a position in the service?
76 Scott Turow book
77 Kind of day, month or year
79 Least perturbable
82 Dog
87 "Howdy!" sayer
88 "Sula" novelist Morrison
89 Big clod
90 Famous getting-off spot
91 Water ___
92 "Right as the Rain" songwriter
93 P.I., e.g.
94 Stanza alternative
95 Trash can on a desktop, e.g.
97 Ceiling
98 Yawl look-alike
100 1956 Sinatra song
103 Traveller's rider
104 Tennis's Nastase
105 Like Dumas's mask
106 Actress Valli
107 Soul singer Thomas et al.
110 Some srs. take them
111 Seine tributary
112 Skater, at times
113 Brisk
114 Derisive laughs
115 Turndowns
116 Son of Seth
117 Age

DOWN

1 Blood brother
2 Spawn
3 Crime-solving couple of old radio
4 Skylit courts
5 "Harper Valley P.T.A." actress
6 Leaks
7 Saki's "The Chronicles of ___"
8 Frigid follower?
9 Refuse
10 Diamond legend
11 Unconvincing concurrence
12 Dogpatch possessive
13 Mr. Kotter's portrayer
14 Crossbreeding result
15 Two quarters
16 Dog that yips
17 Like some loan repayment plans
19 Concentrate, in a way
28 Durango dish
29 Neil Diamond's "___ Said"
30 Church dignitary's title: Abbr.
31 It flows through the Lake of Thun
37 Some college endowers
42 It may be stuck in an apple
43 Mortgagor, often
46 1,000-pager, e.g.
47 Part of 108-Down
48 "Tijuana Taxi" performer
49 "Star Wars" role
51 Kind of seating
53 Be clueless
54 No great endeavor
55 Almond
56 Peace Nobelist John ___ Orr
57 Juice bar stock
58 Justice Souter's appointer
63 Neighbor of Mauritania
64 Up
65 Streamlet
67 "James Joyce" author Leon ___
70 Place for pumps
72 TV exec Arledge
75 Former Polish capital
78 Sexless ones
79 It began after 1945
80 On ___ (without a contract)
81 Kind of support
82 Intoxicant
83 Iris features
84 Used, as an idea
85 Unaffected
86 Delhi wrap
88 Some vacuum tubes
91 Hairy
92 Magnet alloy
96 ___ Fraser of tennis
99 Hitchcockian
101 Dumas's musketeers, for example
102 Hate group
108 V-mail address
109 Dict. listing

by Jim Page

ACROSS

1 Flap
5 Billiard shot
10 Shipping worries
15 Push-ups strengthen them
19 New Rochelle college
20 Old road to Fairbanks
21 Fancy pourers
22 Server's edge, on the court
23 STATE FAILS BID FOR FEDERAL FUNDING
26 Falafel holder
27 Assign odds for
28 Attorney follower
29 Shocker stick?
30 Stevie Wonder's "___ Three Words"
31 STATE DESTROYED BY MOUNTAIN LIONS
35 Grp. concerned with clubs
37 Pink
38 "Von ___ Express" (1965 film)
39 Bossa nova's Mendes
43 It's left to an ox
44 Is behind
47 STATE TOURISM INCREASES AMONG ORDINARY FOLK
51 Wall Streeter's deg.
54 Of the same sort
55 Plus more: Abbr.
56 Pretty up
57 "___ Herr" ("Cabaret" tune)
58 Heap
59 One wearing pyjamas?
60 When all hands meet
61 Ostentatious
63 PARISIAN TEAM HANDILY DEFEATS ALL-STATE SQUAD
68 Wal-Mart and Walgreens
70 Connors contemporary
71 New coin
72 University offering
75 Symbol of goodness
76 Jazz pianist with eight Grammys
78 Alternative to Kodak or Fuji
79 Longtime Big Apple restaurateur
80 Poorly
81 CITY AGENCY DECEIVES STATE LEGISLATURE
85 Bestows, biblically
86 "The X-Files" extras, briefly
87 Search (out)
88 Toro competitor
90 Emphatic no
92 Routine perfection?
93 RELIGIOUS PILGRIMAGE UNDER WAY THROUGHOUT STATE
98 "___ Calloways" (Disney film)
103 Begin a revolt
104 Closes up, perhaps
105 Places for some pairs
107 A dime a dozen, e.g.
108 TRIBE MEMBERS HOLD RAUCOUS STATEWIDE CELEBRATION
111 River to the Fulda
112 Hall-of-Famer with 3,154 hits
113 Turning point?
114 French bean
115 It reproduces by spores
116 Actress Allgood and others
117 Acted (as)
118 "Nana" star Anna

DOWN

1 Pupils take part in it
2 Numbers holder?
3 Ludicrous
4 Shoemakers' leather strips
5 Like some names: Abbr.
6 Silky-fleeced animal
7 ___ Flow (British naval base site)
8 Intl. carrier
9 Starfleet Academy grad.
10 Irish Prime Minister Ahern
11 "The Seven Year Itch" co-star Tom
12 Far from base
13 Unlike a child
14 W-2 info
15 Thick-rinded fruits
16 Prolific patentee
17 Some ticket writers
18 Carroll quarry
24 Dresser-top item
25 Dumbarton ___ (D.C. estate)
29 Choreographer Tharp
32 Dragnet
33 In the ground, in a way
34 Quarterback Kramer
36 Wields a scepter
39 Have words, so to speak
40 City on the Humboldt
41 Drops from above
42 Become empty-handed?
43 Blueberry's family
44 Lopez of pop
45 Butter
46 Slithering striker
48 Suffix with arthr-
49 Momentous
50 Strapped
51 "A mighty fortress is our God," e.g.
52 Show ___
53 At-cost connection
57 Like some mus. keys
59 Poor Richard, really
60 Japanese-American
61 One with a great view of a zoo?
62 Thai tongue
64 Océano feeder
65 Tough, durable wood
66 Warm, sweetened wine drink
67 Heinie
68 Bears' home, briefly
69 Prince of the theater
73 Victor at Brandywine
74 "Phooey!"
76 Prompt
77 Mich. neighbor
78 A chorus line?
79 Round Table address
81 Irresistibly fascinating woman
82 In preference to
83 Kind of test
84 Nissan offering
85 Wonders of nature
88 El ___
89 Power groups
90 Parking meeters?
91 If not
92 Take on
93 Part of a Mideast palace
94 "Ten North Frederick" writer
95 Ratty place
96 Sack toter
97 Thrills
99 Some people can't take them
100 Inception
101 Play in the N.H.L.
102 Bad ___ (Lower Saxony city)
106 Scratched (out)
108 It doesn't air ads
109 Talk to a beat
110 John Lennon's middle name

by Con Pederson

5 POST-HOLIDAY BLUES

ACROSS
1 "Aw, shaddup!"
8 Unfit for detail work
14 Stew holders
20 Horizontal molding
21 Long-tailed finch
22 "Who'd like to volunteer?"
23 Start of a January lament
25 Yellowish-pink
26 ___ con Dios (Spanish farewell)
27 As to
28 Arab's greeting
30 Business card abbr.
31 Évian-___-Bains, France
34 It's a bust
36 Muscat money
39 Lament, part 2
46 Human rights agcy.
47 Aligned
48 Pops composer Anderson
49 Tabby talk: Var.
51 Short end of the stick
53 Big boo-boo
54 Long suits
55 Sandusky's county
56 Photo finish
59 Shipboard direction
61 Wool coat wearer
62 Coup ___
64 High, in Le Havre
66 Two- or four-seater?
68 Lament, part 3
73 Code of the samurai
76 Diamond figure
77 Must
81 "Deathtrap" writer Levin
82 Bird of prey
86 On the up and up
88 Wet septet
89 Ford classics, familiarly

91 Center of Los Angeles
93 First name in civil rights
95 "The Crucible" setting
96 Escalator feature
97 New York strip alternative
99 8 in a date: Abbr.
100 Lament, part 4
104 Taylor of "The Nanny"
105 How some losses are shown
106 Major 20's supplier?
107 # # #: Abbr.
109 Meadowlands contests
112 Modern ice cream flavor
114 Look ahead
118 "Sure thing!"
121 End of the lament
125 Kind of notebook
126 Up
127 It's enough to make you cry
128 What's left behind
129 Like Miss Congeniality
130 Shakes a leg

DOWN
1 Initials in 70's–80's comedy
2 "Field of Dreams" setting
3 Carhop's need
4 Marked down
5 N.Y.C. hoops contest
6 First person in Berlin
7 Garr of "Mr. Mom"
8 Olympics no-no
9 Dims
10 Be beholden to
11 Wonders
12 Little yipper

13 Webb Pierce song "___ Know Why"
14 Redeem
15 Information decoder, maybe
16 Olive ___
17 Follows
18 Fort with a fortune
19 Posted
24 ___ dos aguas (in doubt): Sp.
29 Lee side?
32 Art Deco designer
33 "Get lost!"
35 Allied jumping-off point of July 1944
37 Caution
38 Animal house
39 Put on
40 Car trunk item, maybe
41 Namely
42 It's hard to keep going
43 Athens's Temple of ___
44 Make piles, say
45 "Camelot" composer
50 Drew on
52 Failure
53 One of Alcott's "little women"
54 Woman of die Welt
57 ___ lepton (physics particle)
58 Jerk
60 Symbol like :-) or :-(
63 Classic Orson Welles film, with "The"
65 Abbr. sometimes used twice in a row
67 Rib
69 Vitamin bottle info
70 Campus location
71 Poetic preposition
72 "Blue-eyed" one in "The Tempest"
73 Crumbs
74 Like some legends

75 Boy's outfit with bell-bottom trousers
78 Lay into
79 Ryan's daughter
80 River named for an Indian tribe
83 On the fence
84 A hundred sawbucks
85 True-to-life
87 Island nation east of Fiji
90 Astrolabe plate
92 Gulf port
94 Broken, old-style
96 Seating section
97 It's due once a month
98 Delaware senator
101 Quiet
102 Storehouses
103 BMW, e.g.
107 Trading letters
108 "My bad"
110 ___ even keel
111 Math rings
113 Gadzooks, for one
115 Go downhill fast?
116 Simile part
117 Eliot ___
119 Kind of strap
120 Dig in
122 Legal conclusion
123 Actress Benaderet
124 Much of "Deck the Halls"

by Nancy Salomon

6 FALSE IDENTITIES

ACROSS

1 Skilled felon
5 "Hold on there!"
9 Hustles
13 Some engines
19 Sphere
20 Snake dancers
21 Fish with scarlet fins
22 Mark for greatness
23 He's got clout
25 She sews at home
27 Proscribed
28 Kind of commander
30 Air traveler's choice
31 The great Ziegfeld
32 He'll thank you kindly
35 Too heavy makeup
36 Prov. on Atlantic Time
37 Open court hearing
38 Equally irate
40 Range
41 Actual
45 Australian crop pests
47 Under, in a way
49 Conqueror of Northumberland, 954
50 Author Lessing
52 VCR button
53 Laundromat machine feature
56 Shirt style
57 Poe poem
62 Matches
63 Spoils
64 Opera libretto
65 "Oh, that's silly"
66 Kind of skirt
67 She's a softy
69 Start of a conclusion
70 New Age composer John
71 Propose at a meeting
72 Orthodontist's concern
73 Hardly a little angel

75 Uphold
77 Musical epilogue
78 Long-suffering
79 Start of a popular round song
80 Dinnertime annoyances
82 "Star Wars" figure, informally
83 Unsavory types
87 "Just a Gigolo" singer, 1985
88 The way ferries go
92 When pinned, it's a lock
93 Church tenets
95 Island with a 13th-century cathedral
97 Big Apple subway line, with "the"
98 Ally McBeal, e.g.: Abbr.
99 He's got a craggy face
104 Measure of conductance
105 Places to drill
107 "You go not till ___ you up a glass": Hamlet
108 "Do I ___ second?"
109 She plays her little game
112 She has a ghostly pallor
115 Early source of spices, with "the"
116 Challenge, metaphorically
117 Hoskins role in "Hook"
118 Scott Turow title
119 Relatives of the Omaha
120 Colorless, as writing
121 Brain tests, briefly
122 Renamed oil company

DOWN

1 It puts you off course
2 Asmara is its capital
3 Form of dynamite
4 Nero's successor
5 Victor's reaction
6 What students want to know
7 Watchful
8 Star in the sky?
9 Shade darker than chestnut
10 ___-Locka, Fla.
11 Garden perennials
12 Yiddish writer Aleichem
13 Provider for Pravda
14 Les États-___
15 Former Congressman Dellums
16 It's hard to photograph
17 Classic Bob Marley song
18 Rowed
24 Short report
26 Turner and others
29 Ran ragged
32 Well-related
33 Something flexible to wear
34 Bull: Prefix
35 She comes to a full stop
39 Yankee Jeter
42 He's getting a doctor's help
43 "Why, ___ delighted!"
44 Boys in the 'hood
46 She's holding things down
48 Cotillion V.I.P.
51 Operagoer's wear, maybe
53 ___ spell on
54 Showed obvious interest in

55 Like some whiskey
56 Crown
58 Much sought-after
59 Actor born Laszlo Loewenstein
60 Prepare to surf?
61 Missing money
63 Devastation
64 Second in a series
67 Put a lid on it
68 Centrally, at sea
71 Made kit calls
73 "Ciao"
74 007's school
76 Cartoonist Chast
77 Mask
78 Pebble Beach event
81 Quarterbacking locale?
82 Never ever
83 Suds maker
84 Suds
85 Independent land since 1991
86 Not so pleased
89 Dutch money
90 Alters an assessment
91 Big oil company, for short
94 "You're mine!"
96 Common threat
100 Harvest
101 "That's for sure"
102 Not used
103 Deep border lake
105 Newcastle's place
106 Emulates Pac-Man
110 Master of photog.
111 Year in Vigilius's papacy
113 Table part
114 "Rock 'n' Roll Is King" band

by Manny Nosowsky

ACROSS

1 Show bills
9 Pull an all-nighter
13 "___ the races!"
18 Gilbert & Sullivan operetta
19 Like some cold medicines
20 Water nymph
21 Most varicolored
22 Fingerprint, say
23 Links legend, informally
24 It begins "In the Lord I take refuge"
25 Member of Nixon's cabinet
26 Signed contracts
28 Notch
29 In an odd way
31 Fine threads
32 Star Wars letters
34 Tribal V.I.P.'s
35 Fake
37 Writer LeShan
38 Rush
40 Where "amo, amas, amat" is learned
41 Part of an act
43 Former head of Nicaragua
45 Rudolph Valentino, e.g.
47 Photo ___
50 This may prove one's innocence
52 Not a quick jaunt
53 Patsy Cline's "___ to Pieces"
55 Coventry Street locale
56 Intelligently planned progress
59 Comic Charlotte
60 Like some faithful friends
63 Like old jokes
67 Grandparents, e.g.
68 Bach, Beethoven and Brahms
69 Yodeler's perch
70 Film industry data
72 Defendant at law
74 Bring up
76 Villainous queen in "Titus Andronicus"
79 Think about
83 The Blues Brothers sang here: Abbr.
84 Potato chip feature
87 Heart line
88 Stop sign feature
90 ___ Way
92 Quarters
93 Father's wear
96 Palace ruler: Var.
97 Navigated
98 Century starter?
99 Actress Sobieski
101 Datebook
102 Animation sheet
104 Do well at craps
106 Some doters on babies
107 Popular citrus drink
110 Appliance maker
111 Opening remarks
113 Mix master?
115 Critic
116 Dispose of
117 Uniform's decoration
118 What a dummy!
119 Lip
120 Links

DOWN

1 Go-between, of sorts
2 Stops in London
3 Much-visited Web site
4 Street, in San Juan
5 Japanese cartoons
6 Way from Syracuse, N.Y., to Harrisburg, Pa.
7 Baseball figures: Abbr.
8 Congeal
9 Rude ones
10 Actor McDowall
11 Time-off time, maybe: Abbr.
12 Four-footed TV star
13 One way to stop
14 Travelocity.com info
15 Grand time?
16 Shadowed
17 German victory site, October 1941
19 When the ball drops at Times Square
22 River to Lake Champlain
25 Maximums
27 Narrow, in a way
29 Former N.H.L. rival
30 Chows down
32 Like show horses
33 "Oh, crumb!"
34 Horror film figure
35 Flew the coop, old-style
36 Bottom line?
39 Beliefs
41 Fishhook attachment
42 ___ a kind (pair)
44 Fab Four member
46 Gen. Robt. ___
48 Many a golf course hole
49 Generous slice of the pie.
51 1939 movie dog
53 Mint, e.g.
54 Guitar master Paul
57 Talks on Sun.
58 St. Columba's locale
60 Word with mail or rail
61 "Ah, me!"
62 It's in the back row, right of center
64 Stable worker
65 Future litigators' exams: Abbr.
66 Bruce's ex
71 Beethoven's violin piece in A, Op. 30
73 When some Wimbledon matches are won
75 Trickiness
77 Is self-reproachful
78 Poplars
80 Animal house?
81 "What's Hecuba to him ___ to Hecuba": Hamlet
82 Wall Street table heading: Abbr.
84 It's smallish, dresswise
85 Oklahoma city
86 Court addressee
89 Airline worker
91 ___ Lingus
93 Hitching posts?
94 ___ Brothers
95 Dress down
97 Fine restaurant no-nos
100 Soloist?
101 Spreads
102 Rustic digs
103 Pass over
105 Caesar and others
107 Like an N.B.A. team
108 Blazer's detail
109 Work units
112 Museum funder: Abbr.
113 Respected media inits.
114 Spanish treasure

by Elizabeth C. Gorski

ACROSS

1 Stock market figures
6 1994 Jodie Foster title role
10 Cribbage equipment
14 Macbeth or Macduff
19 Dunderpate
20 Lip balm ingredient
21 Part of a spread
22 Hornswoggles, with "in"
23 Community with its Christmas decorations up?
25 Gift-giver's comment after tying the bow?
27 Small group of carolers
28 Product made by Armor All
30 In stock
31 Out
34 Putt-putter
36 Native Missourians
40 Ends, as class
42 Noted pilgrimage site
44 Call
45 J.F.K. times
46 Kind of cheese
48 Way of life
50 1990 film autobiography "___: My Story"
51 Go (over)
52 Word with hand or home
53 Rote learning method
56 Hip-hop's ___ Kim
57 Played (around)
60 Hellish
62 Musical retrospective, maybe
64 Kind of jump
65 Island singer
67 Meeting reading
69 Relieves (of)
70 Who is stronger than Superman?
72 Tire reinforcement
73 Not seriously
75 Shows of joy
77 Gum arabic tree
80 Westernmost African city
82 To whom reporters report: Abbr.
85 Torrent
87 Nightclub
89 Curve enhancer
91 HBO competitor
92 Noncompromiser
94 Architect Saarinen
96 French 101 verb
97 P.G.A. champ Sutton
98 Combative sort, they say
99 Sicilian wine
102 Not work out
103 Spanish princess
105 1950's game fad
108 Extra pages, say
110 Certain buttons
112 Congo native
113 Taskmaster's cry
114 Stoppage
116 Eur. land
118 Slammin' Sammy
119 Christmas?
123 Money envelopes on a Christmas tree?
128 Carol singers
129 Take out
130 Island in the Tyrrhenian Sea
131 Milk symbol
132 Pastels
133 Sound of a leak
134 Difficult to fathom
135 Give back

DOWN

1 Sellout
2 A mean Amin
3 Ingredient in a Blue Pacific
4 Hors d'oeuvre servers, maybe
5 Caterer's supply
6 Expanding org.
7 "Do Ya" rock grp.
8 Stock market figures
9 Helped out, in a way
10 Irishman, informally
11 Seconded
12 Starbucks order
13 "___ Speaks" (Jane Roberts book)
14 Switch
15 Elephant seat
16 Financial fig.
17 P.T.A.-aligned org.
18 Clairvoyance, e.g.
24 Like most Christmas trees
26 ___ Paulo
29 Show pique
31 Israeli leaders?
32 Caused to go
33 Attempts at decorating a treetop?
35 One with a gift
37 Tree holder, in an indoor football game?
38 Like the rich and beautiful
39 Some mattresses
41 Tiny ___
42 Caused
43 N.L. Central team: Abbr.
47 Potato dish, in British slang
49 Researcher's staple
54 Actress Charlotte
55 Place to stay
58 Tokyo, once
59 Popular 80's daytime show
61 Bashes
63 Actress Joanne
66 Japanese competitor of IBM
68 Cartoonist Browne
71 Big Ten sch.
72 "The Autobiography of Miss Jane ___"
74 To's partner
75 Kidder
76 Scarf down
78 Yellowfin tuna
79 Trigonometry abbr.
80 ___ good turn (helps out)
81 Gillette product
83 Treat with contempt
84 Like some ancient markers
86 Is messy
88 Not pleased
90 Like a doctor's patients
93 Miami's Eden ___ Resort
95 Suffix with pay
100 Piedmont province
101 Kind of committee
104 Monster's nickname
106 Tolerates
107 Some French sounds
109 Part of Santa's team
111 Marino or Gabriel
115 Guides: Abbr.
117 First name in detective fiction
118 Parka closer
119 Agt.'s reward
120 Density symbol
121 Long time to wait
122 "You bet!"
124 White House nickname
125 Viper
126 Actress Peeples
127 Important

TREE

Counterclockwise: Holiday tune

by Bill Zais

ACROSS
1 Mountain cats
6 Haitian dictator's nickname
13 Site of thousands of flowers
18 Peace in the Mideast?
20 United way?
21 Little gander
22 Start of a verse about holiday fruitcake
25 1931 sudser about a washed-up prizefighter
26 Seurat's "___ Baignade"
27 Like some pitches
28 See 95-Down
29 Do
31 Literary monogram
32 Small piano
36 "A good servant but a bad master": Bacon
37 38-Across's milieu
38 Junk, e.g.
42 Brown bagger
43 Unhappy expression
44 Henley crew
45 Movie theater
46 More about that fruitcake
52 Luau fare
53 Cartoon frames
54 Pakistan's chief river
55 Uninspiring talk
56 Eminence
58 Tee-hee
60 Chic
61 Parallel
63 Wasn't paid up at the bar
65 Sanction
68 Cloisonné coating
70 English class activity
74 Mosque priests
75 Newsreel pioneer Charles
76 Embellish
77 Coroner's abbr.
78 Yet more about that fruitcake
83 Its playing fields are famous
84 They're black for witches
85 Oriental au pair
86 ___ doble (two-step dance)
87 Last word of "For He's a Jolly Good Fellow"
88 Ref's decision
89 Theatrical backdrop
91 Paint basecoat
93 Map abbr.
94 Inclination
95 Barrett of Pink Floyd
96 Adult's cry in a children's game
100 Kind of observatory: Abbr.
101 Parts of Middle Earth
106 Final words about that fruitcake
110 Mideast millionaires
111 Late
112 Kind of inspiration
113 Pair on a bike
114 Bloodshed
115 Makes out

DOWN
1 "Hey, you"
2 Slip acknowledgment
3 "If He Walked Into My Life" musical
4 Novelist Waugh
5 She had a choice in literature
6 "Hair" producer, 1967
7 Be in bed, maybe
8 Grand ___ ("Evangeline" setting)
9 Attraction
10 Like lacework
11 Pleasing to the ear
12 So-so mark
13 Emulates the birds and the bees
14 Mille ___ (Minnesota county)
15 "You're the ___ Care For" (1931 hit)
16 Parietal cell secretion
17 Block of Brie?
19 Not accidental
21 Paprika-seasoned stew
23 Meditation class chorus
24 Bull session participants?
29 Really come down
30 Pay one's share, with "up"
32 Gives and takes
33 Vinifera variety
34 It has 25 states
35 1 and 66: Abbr.
36 Barbers' challenges
37 General Motors division
38 Ancient symbols of resurrection
39 Hand a line to, say
40 How to sign a contract
41 "Our Gang" dog
43 "Moby-Dick" captain
44 Baptism of fire
47 Eye doctor
48 Have coming
49 Toned
50 ___-temps (meanwhile, in Metz)
51 King nicknamed "Longshanks"
57 Name in old politics
58 Extra innings
59 Craters of the Moon locale
60 Big problem for a pilot
62 By
64 Quite silly
65 Carried a torch (for)
66 Play to the rafters
67 Pitcher Martinez
69 Copy cats?
71 Epitomic
72 Headache intensifier
73 Football's ___ Bowl
75 Brightens
76 Its capital is Hagatña
79 Results of getting needled?
80 Looming choice
81 Bypass
82 One whose days are numbered?
89 Beowulf, notably
90 Stalactite site
91 Church council
92 Add just before the deadline
93 "Wayne's World" co-star
94 1983 Indy 500 winner
95 With 28-Across, some protests
96 "___ first . . ."
97 Annual opener
98 Pitcher
99 Foil relative
101 Joint with a cap
102 Singer Matthews
103 Of the ear
104 Non-P.C. wrap
105 Some Fr. martyrs
107 ___ cit.
108 Nabokov novel
109 It may be cut

by Frances Hansen

ACROSS

1 Doesn't just close
6 Morse bit
9 "This is fun!"
13 Not run
17 It's broken at parties
19 They're often kept in
21 Spike
22 Laser alternative
23 Like some vaults
25 Service expert
26 Fairness in hiring, say
28 One-dimensional
30 River through Belgium
31 Distress call recipient: Abbr.
32 Whirl
33 Fancy neckwear
34 Genetic code carrier
35 Sarcastic
38 Like cedarwood or cigar smoke
40 Coptic titles
43 Some TV's
45 Cutting tool
47 County north of the river Shannon
48 It's outstanding
49 Geometric figure
50 Rapid growth area
52 Alternative to buy
54 Apr. addressee
55 Computer site
58 Smidgen
59 Extras
62 "Love ___" (Beatles song)
64 "It Walks by Night" author
65 Part of E.R.: Abbr.
66 French vineyard
67 Hush-hush grp.
69 Albanian currency
70 Award for "Rent"
71 Toxin fighters
72 Caps
74 Certain duty
76 Dozes
77 Stab
78 It may follow a dot
79 Fan's opposite
81 Some Broadway fare
83 Personally bring
85 Calls, as a game
88 Clipped
89 Obliged out of integrity
92 Actress Ward
93 Sacs
94 Kind of mass, in physics
95 Villa in Mexico
97 Treat like a dog?
98 Antiquity, in antiquity
99 Balkan native
103 Rapid transit inits.
104 P.O. employees have them
108 Anthony Kennedy's Supreme Court predecessor
110 Winter league activity
113 "Are you ___ out?"
114 Incidental matter
116 Clef designation
117 To be, in Brest
118 Cradlesong
119 Stored, as fodder
120 Competitor of Bloomingdale's
121 Katie's "Today" co-host
122 Composer Rorem
123 Waist-length jackets

DOWN

1 Hot
2 Brits' floor coverings
3 Twist locale
4 1905 Shaw play
5 Suffix with hip
6 Contempt
7 Exiled tyrant
8 Multitude
9 Erased
10 Like the fox hunting set
11 Grandson of Eve
12 "___ Beso" (Anka hit)
13 Family group
14 The Lizard constellation
15 Sea nymph
16 Retaining wall site
18 No longer on deck
20 Watch
24 Exchange employee
27 Scottish landowner
29 Foot in a line
33 Trite sayings
36 "Mm-hmm"
37 Gothic feature
38 Prefix with benzene
39 Singer Green and others
40 Hurting the most
41 Late ___
42 Usually it's not included
44 Back on the briny
45 $200 Monopoly props.
46 "Beg pardon . . ."
51 Medical group output
53 Selling point
55 Shakespearean title word
56 Least interesting
57 Symbols of free speech
60 Mine artery
61 Proceed without the words
63 Teacher of Samuel
64 Factory conduit
68 Lumberjacks
73 Place for a guard
75 Weirdo
78 Syndicate
80 "Go on . . ."
82 Emulate Dürer
83 ___ anglais (English horn)
84 Actor Brynner
86 How peaches may be served
87 A fly-by-night?
89 Longhairs
90 New York city on the Susquehanna
91 Like some television
96 Flings
99 Hägar the Horrible's dog
100 Pronouncement
101 Dawn-colored
102 Merchant vessel officer
105 Ban
106 1942 Pulitzer novelist Glasgow
107 Coasters
109 "___ Tu" (1974 hit)
110 Concept
111 Dodge
112 Ashtabula's lake
115 Company that programmed Deep Blue

by Rich Norris

ACROSS

1 Souvenir item
4 Where to see an El Greco
9 It picks up things with a dish
14 1974 animal movie with three sequels
19 1977 Special Citation Pulitzer winner
21 Rousseau work
22 Lend ___ (listen)
23 Youthful times
24 Boot camp boss
25 Temperature symbol
26 Communicate silently
27 Shrub with showy blossoms
29 Tick off
32 British foe, 1899–1902
34 Forward
35 Entice
36 Rugged ridge
37 Before, once
38 Club of song
41 Economy airfare
43 Ice
44 Alcott book "___ Boys"
46 Agitated
47 Sombreros and others
51 Many new numbers these days
54 Linking verb
55 More than a stretch
56 Kind of instinct
57 Fruit component
59 Charity
60 Writing no-no
66 Savoy region
69 Wharf
70 Two-legged support
74 Cattle call?
75 French Revolutionary played by Gérard Depardieu

76 They've joined the family
80 Jobs for dentists
82 "Don't let go!"
84 Jackie's hubby
85 Off
86 Gold digger's target
89 "___ I care!"
90 Museum worker's deg.
93 Love, to Luigi
94 Easy on the eyes
97 Earn
99 Some memorization
100 Acute
101 Popular puppet show
104 Tipper's needs?
105 Jim Croce's "___ Name"
106 Poetic Muse
107 One may be under a bed
112 Rocker John
113 Partition
114 Not go by foot
115 Salon employees
116 Palace figures
117 Mattress brand
118 Snake's warning

DOWN

1 Mortarboard feature
2 "Ally McBeal" woman
3 Marine plants with ribbonlike leaves
4 Researcher's goal, maybe
5 "Awesome!"
6 In the style of
7 Actress Susan
8 Sounds of shock
9 Finally turned (to)
10 One into collecting
11 Acute
12 Veep who's a "Jr."
13 Illicit cigarette
14 Get into hot water?

15 Touched up
16 Cad
17 Rocket-propelled departure, acronymically
18 Carpet source
20 Paradise
27 "The Bostonians" actor, 1984
28 Budapest-to-Belgrade dir.
30 Bushes are in it
31 Start of the año
32 Count, in music
33 Tough exams
39 Celebration of deliverance
40 Places for religious statues
42 Reel's partner
43 Mrs., abroad
44 Elbow
45 ". . . ___ mouse?"
47 Florida city, informally
48 Each
49 Hurry
50 Blue Bonnet, e.g.
52 Goals
53 201 on a slab
54 Babyish
57 Fed
58 Chicken order
59 Alphabet book phrase
61 Big e-tailing season
62 Charged items
63 Reminder
64 Canada's ___ Morne National Park
65 Stat for Sosa
66 Refrigerator name
67 Howlers
68 This is a stick-up
71 Participate in court proceedings?
72 Paddle
73 This earns points: Abbr.
75 Cub's place
76 Catch

77 Creeps
78 Dream land
79 Ginger cookies
81 Enzyme enabler
82 Cigar holders
83 Sitting through a bad piano recital, e.g.
86 Soldier, often
87 Rap's Dr. ___
88 Gobble up
90 "Peel ___ grape"
91 Most exquisite
92 Pianist Watts and others
95 They come and go
96 Emphatic agreement
98 Tatar leaders
101 Not solid-colored
102 94-Across's opposite
103 Morning eyeopener
107 Skid row woe
108 Neighbor of Oman: Abbr.
109 Relative of calypso
110 ___ Aviv
111 Dark horse

by Elizabeth C. Gorski

12 INTANGIBLES

ACROSS

1 One wearing the pants in the family?
5 Gulf war planes
10 Gets back (to)
15 Education grp.
18 Something you might get at work
19 "Grease" singer
20 Where "Aïda" premiered
21 It lasts and lasts
22 OPEC-sold intangible?
24 Lighter offense?
25 Call out
26 Plan for later yrs.
27 Café lightener
28 Clear dishes
30 Not smart
31 Mike & ___ (candy brand)
32 Bank posting
34 Wallet items
35 Quite a few auctioned-off intangibles?
39 Heading to the finish?
41 1942 surrender site
42 Gunpowder ingredient
43 Fragment from an intangible?
46 Soprano ___ Lehmann
47 Take longer than expected
48 Penalty imposer
51 Person who spends a lot of time dressing
54 Hall-of-Famers Kaline and Lopez
55 Officeholders
57 When not yet due
60 Axle securer
61 Actress Headly
63 Bus. letter directive
64 Radar anomaly
65 Aix-___-Bains, France
66 Bright, shining intangible?
68 Air conditioner abbr.
69 Prior to
70 Dietary figures, for short
72 Toddlers' rides
73 Notepaper feature
75 Bashed, as a door
77 Wave carrier
78 Ambulance occupant, for short
79 One of the Horae
80 Marker's marker
82 Winter expense
84 Oscar winner for Best Original Screenplay, 1996
86 Freighterborne intangible?
92 Certain sorority women
94 Like some oak leaves
95 Like part of the circulatory system
96 Minuscule intangible?
98 Premium channel
100 Sugar amts.
101 A pint, maybe
102 Blight
103 Confucian concept
104 Twelve ___ (Tara neighbor)
106 Org. with an Office of Water
107 Despot Amin
108 Summoned
110 Tightly wrapped intangible?
113 It's thrown in anger
114 Name in 2000 headlines
115 Established
116 Clean the hard-to-get-at areas, say
117 Kind of sauce
118 1492 voyager
119 Relays
120 Part of a paper towel roll

DOWN

1 Dynasty member
2 Faucet attachment
3 Standard
4 Olympics jump
5 Duck
6 Travels by air
7 1980's NBC sitcom
8 Part of a driver, e.g.
9 Wavy
10 Indianapolis's ___ Dome
11 Cameo stone
12 Pop by
13 Trailers
14 ___ of a gun
15 Eight-quart intangible?
16 Removed, in a way
17 Some
18 Sporty Ford Motor products
23 Applied
29 "South Park" boy
31 Inuit homes
33 Chef Lagasse
36 They're poked in the eyes
37 Robert after whom seven U.S. counties are named
38 Rap's Dr. ___
40 Extracted chemical
41 Fashion designer Johnson
44 Undisguised
45 Metroplex city
49 Certify
50 Item in a tent
51 Plow pullers
52 Reviewer Roger
53 Spoon-administered intangible?
55 Prefix with structure
56 Blue Cream Soda maker
58 Commonly
59 "Don't even bother"
62 Put down
63 Evolutionary intermediate
67 1940's–50's actor Dennis
70 Advance again
71 Telegraph sound
73 Shampoo directive
74 Like a FedEx package
76 Meat shunner, informally
77 Hound's trail
81 Do wrong by
82 Place of growing concern
83 Call upon
84 Shore concealer
85 It's mostly talk nowadays
87 Border
88 Digital information carrier
89 Elective surgery
90 Gather
91 Lamb's output
93 Dweller on the Gulf of Aden
97 Dickens villain
98 Beach impostor
99 Part of a count
105 Delicate
107 Stipulations
108 Dash
109 It has a twist
111 Prioress
112 Unwanted "gift"

by Patrick Berry

ACROSS

1 Proper name in Masses
5 David's biblical predecessor
9 Tennis stroke
13 Zenith
17 Big Daddy portrayer, in "Cat on a Hot Tin Roof"
18 It's involved in arm-twisting
19 On delay
21 Mother of Hera
22 On the way to the bus stop to __ . . .
24 . . . Mrs. Herr decided she'd __ albums
26 Going nowhere
27 Realm of Morpheus
29 Ancient medium
30 Bound
33 New Hampshire is famous for them
34 Instigated
35 At lunch with friends she __ of meat back and ordered seafood
40 Enthralled
41 Rival of Bjorn
42 Sheathe
43 Afore
44 Spot remover?
48 Confessional list
49 Bond classic
50 Just as she started to __ to her lips . . .
53 . . . the waitress tried to __
57 Actress Myrna
58 Ear-related
59 Marked down
60 Ore of lead
62 Newspaper department
63 A drink was spilled all over her wallet and she had to __ clean
68 Effigy
72 Drawers
73 Some Italian designs
78 Woody Allen title role
79 Full of: Suffix
80 Next, she __ in the car and wanted to get it home
84 The waitress took forever with the checks and then __ change
87 Kind of bean
88 Chase of old game shows
89 Feat
90 Unhandled
91 Wish, with "to"
94 Occupy
95 Yemeni port
96 When she came back to top off the drinks, the waitress __ cup
99 Order of the British Empire and others
103 Chooses
104 Knock off
105 Orbital far point
106 Gourmet's sense
108 Cyclical thing
113 By then Mrs. Herr was ready to __ for incompetence
115 She wanted to __ for suggesting the place!
118 Prayed, in Paris
119 Smiths
120 He and she
121 With competence
122 Without
123 Has
124 Trader's abbr.
125 Quarter-pint

DOWN

1 Guitarist Hendrix
2 Flush (with)
3 Biological bristle
4 Not a teetotaler
5 South Carolina county or its seat
6 Menu phrase
7 Verse starter?
8 Actress Diane
9 Spot remover
10 Filmdom's Ian and Celeste
11 They fly by night
12 Low-tech missile
13 Like Niagara Falls
14 Steadying wedge
15 Singer Travis
16 Lightened
19 They're made during tantrums
20 Baster, basically
23 Decree
25 "Curses!"
28 Villa __ (town near Atlanta)
31 Echopractic ones
32 Feather, zoologically
34 "The Human Comedy" novelist
35 Big tech stock
36 Young Gonzalez
37 Complements on diamonds
38 "The Gondoliers" flower girl
39 E.P.A. concern: Abbr.
40 Allow for business growth, say
44 Swing around
45 He's a deer
46 Bradley, the G.I.'s General
47 Capital near Lilleström
49 Vier preceder
51 Actor McCowen
52 Arose
54 Claim
55 Farming prefix
56 Valleys
61 Have trouble with assessors?
64 Those cited
65 Apart at the seams
66 River of Frankfurt
67 Still getting around
68 Shirt label
69 Ancient Iranian
70 Lotion ingredient
71 Surround
74 Overlook
75 Ariz. neighbor
76 Linen tape for trimmings
77 Days-old
81 Name part: Abbr.
82 Looks straight in the eye, say
83 Flip
85 Maryland Air Force base
86 Old home decorations
92 Fretted instruments
93 Attention-getter
95 Violinist Leopold
97 Tailbone
98 Mayberry minor
99 Padlocks lock them
100 Theater offering
101 Kind of situation
102 Sigmoid moldings
103 Sturdy, in a way
106 Stem
107 This one, in Spain
109 Rocky projection
110 Prefix with polar
111 Gussy (up)
112 Form of nitrite
114 "Well, lookee here!"
116 Man with a law
117 Cold front?

by Cathy Millhauser

ACROSS

1 Rigging attachment
5 Man on first?
9 Riffraff
13 Walk fancily
19 Folk forename
20 Sweats
22 So to so, say
23 Use a fisherman to put the kibosh on?
26 Circle
27 Game point, in tennis
28 Argus-eyed
29 Authenticated "Death of a Salesman" manuscript?
35 You may be lost without it
38 Center of a ball?
39 Focus of a July 2000 crash investigation
40 Disparaging word
41 John Wooden Center site
43 Taken
47 Game portion
50 ___ corda (musical direction)
51 Obi-Wan Kenobi actor's thoughts about Gregory Hines?
56 Composer of La Scala's premiere opera
58 Where Peggy Fleming won gold
59 French Revolution figure
61 Homemade pistol
62 Kind of story
63 Gymnast's pointed part
64 Aries or Taurus
65 Choice marble
67 ___ age (long time)
68 Headline about Aniston and Pitt's breakup?
72 Bahraini V.I.P.
75 Kind of story
76 Opera singer Bostridge
77 Lago feeder
78 ___ pro nobis
81 Certain freight train
83 Extract forcefully
85 Voluntarily, perhaps
87 Oration station
89 Early spring sights?
91 Pastels and such
92 Hold back
94 Be in an altared state?
95 Splashy 1963 film title role, for short
96 Chinwags
98 Baseball card abbr.
100 New York University's ___ School of the Arts
104 Long period
105 Maple Leafs team photo?
112 South American capital
113 Immensely
114 Cavities
118 Warren Spahn?
123 Stilt's cousin
124 Score after a tie-breaking safety
125 Bad thing to be under
126 Choir section
127 Split personalities?
128 Shortchanges
129 Oats, possibly

DOWN

1 Like some nouns: Abbr.
2 ___ Arena (Kings' home)
3 Token taker
4 Family figure
5 How long one might stay
6 Prosper
7 Uris protagonist
8 AMEX, e.g.: Abbr.
9 A park may provide it
10 Ship assignment
11 Father of the Titans
12 Ward workers, for short
13 Pedestal base
14 Hurt
15 Kay and Kenneth
16 South-of-the-border sign-off
17 Old-time welcome
18 Suffix with law
21 Pursue
24 It may be in the palm of one's hand
25 Holiday hirees
30 "ER" actress Christine
31 Union city?
32 Suffix with boor or Moor
33 5K, maybe
34 Track team?
35 "Mr. ___ Steps Out" (Leo Gorcey comedy)
36 Legend maker
37 Employed busily
42 First name in advice
44 Deprive of courage
45 Begin chastising
46 Lent part?
48 ___-Boy recliner
49 Extinguish, as some lights
52 What an unappealing offer might get
53 Deep black
54 They may fly in the winter
55 Blessed bread holder
57 Financial page listings, briefly
60 Concern of some smokers
64 Army attack helicopter
66 Inferior
68 Dump, so to speak
69 It'll do for the present
70 Peace Palace's place, with "The"
71 "Later"
72 Runts
73 "Yay!"
74 Ted Williams Tunnel locale
78 Embryo sac encloser
79 People may lose their seats in this
80 Lighting of a torch
82 Oxcart's track
84 "Gross!"
85 Beat
86 Epitome of simplicity
88 "Jeepers Creepers" lyricist
90 Anti-fur org.
93 Many an exec
97 Plaster, in a way
99 Stuck
101 Cart
102 Fools
103 Hippy movement?
106 Orangish yellow
107 Stews
108 When many office workers return to work
109 Welfare grants
110 Some candidates: Abbr.
111 Poker ploy
115 Panhandler, perhaps
116 Number one starter?
117 Lentil, e.g.
118 Learned perfectly
119 It may be added to impress
120 Like a gas gauge just before a fill-up?
121 Filmdom's Ryan
122 Wrigley Field feature

by Joe DiPietro

15 PARTNERS

ACROSS

1 Headliner
5 Where a stranger may be taken in
12 Wall Street activity
19 Attire
21 Authorize
22 Picture receivers
23 Football's ___ Bowl
24 Partner of 60-Across
25 Classic answer to "Where's your homework?"
26 People with a poll position?
28 Doughy
29 Put on
30 Clockmaker ___ Terry
31 From Okla. City to Tulsa
32 Irritable
34 Where the monkey-puzzle tree grows
36 Once, once
37 Part of a wedding reception
38 Wrathful one in a "Star Trek" sequel
39 Dash
41 Where a hockey team has the advantage
44 Bearded, in a way
46 Hanukkah centerpiece
50 "The Tempest" king
51 Partner of 76-Across
52 Songbird
53 Where Solomon's navy was built
54 Go by bus
55 Partner of 88-Across
56 Makes waves?
57 To be, in old Rome
58 Dug, in a way
60 Partner of 24-Across
61 Partner of 108-Across
62 Wild West transport
63 Make true
65 Take on
68 Call for help
69 1972 Olympics site
71 Actress Gershon
75 Partner of 29-Down
76 Partner of 51-Across
77 Connectors appropriate to this puzzle
78 Deserved
80 More than admire
82 Introduction
83 Filch
84 Like some church statements
85 "Cabaret" director
86 Song parts
87 Flock tender, for short
88 Partner of 55-Across
89 Earthlike shape
90 Partner of 115-Across
93 End early
95 Not as aloof
97 Masterpiece
100 John ___ Lennon
101 Family
102 Declaration of Independence signee
104 Rush
106 Precook
108 Partner of 61-Across
110 On-line group
111 Wild
112 Dyemaking chemical
113 Just not done
114 They go around in the kitchen
115 Partner of 90-Across
116 Bit of greenery

DOWN

1 Partner of 79-Down
2 It may connect a limb to a branch
3 Ease
4 Frost
5 Nickname in adult publishing
6 Like an hour-long play, perhaps
7 Hide
8 Like many adages
9 Jackie Wilson's "Am ___ Man"
10 Came to grips with?
11 Suffix with sonnet
12 Partner of 98-Down
13 Saying "aah," perhaps
14 Piles
15 Put down, to Puff Daddy
16 Ensepulcher
17 Catches but good
18 Partner of 101-Down
20 Partner of 41-Down
27 Beach area
29 Partner of 75-Across
33 Lao-___
35 Kept
36 Was a bad player, perhaps
37 Ex-lax?
38 Injured sneakily
40 Harness
41 Partner of 20-Down
42 Shouts to toreadors
43 Up-to-date dressers
44 Superlatively Saharan
45 Partner of 85-Down
46 Kind of unit
47 Hard to find, to Hadrian
48 Kind of unit
49 Alts.
51 Protract
52 Flaubert style
55 One who envies the sitter?
59 Pioneer in probability
62 Withdraw
64 Rundown areas
65 Frost
66 Message starter
67 Kansas and Kentucky
69 Sedgy stretch
70 Juan's ones
71 Tough job
72 Don Juan's mother
73 St. Petersburg's river
74 Thirst quenchers
75 HBO alternative
79 Partner of 1-Down
81 Necklace pendant
82 Put off
85 Partner of 45-Down
86 School yr. part
88 Didn't just place
89 "The Third Man" author
90 Easy catch
91 Cockamamie
92 Rio Grande do ___ (Natal's state)
94 Gets bare on top
95 Handle
96 Part of the ear
97 Loon's cousin
98 Partner of 12-Down
99 Biblical words repeated after "O Absalom"
101 Partner of 18-Down
103 Two-time Indy winner Luyendyk
105 Flyboy's org.
107 ___ masqué
108 Shoot the breeze?
109 Attorney's object

by Michael S. Maurer

ACROSS

1 Track specialist
6 Steel braces with right-angle bends
11 Not reacting
16 Where a sock may go?
19 It may be pitted
20 One way to run
21 Marisa of "Slums of Beverly Hills"
22 Japanese band?
23 Inside look at a Theban king?
25 Brilliance
26 Secant's reciprocal: Abbr.
27 What some scouts seek
28 Busboy's job, sometimes?
31 Wastes
33 Like some picture frames
34 Flings
35 Tower in the water
38 Kernel's cover
41 Wharton offerings: Abbr.
43 "Yippee!," e.g.
46 "Take ___ at this!"
47 Fencing match inspection?
52 What a really outlandish claim may be?
55 Song of "Salome"
56 Kid's cry
57 Young hogs
58 Palazzo Madama locale
60 Prepare to wash, perhaps
61 Master of Bach suites
65 Precious strings
66 Spread
67 What a timid actor might do as a pirate?

71 Some people weave on them
72 Secular clergy members
73 Married Madrileña
74 Bar figures: Abbr.
75 Aquafresh alternative
76 Beat
80 A carrier has one: Abbr.
81 Cuba libre ingredient
82 Amazed exclamations from bullfight spectators?
88 Ventilation duct?
91 Monteverdi title character
92 Where piasters are currency
93 Promptness prompter
94 Loiters
97 "That's great news!"
98 Encapsulated observation
101 More than a nip
102 Mystery writer Marsh
105 Home games for the San Francisco Giants?
110 Cast
113 Novelist Radcliffe
114 Willow rod
115 Take orders from Lloyd?
118 Chinese philosopher Mo-___
119 Baby hooter
120 "This is ___ new to me!"
121 See 86-Down
122 Canal site
123 "Isabella" poet
124 Where to see an advert
125 "Steppenwolf" author

DOWN

1 Jane Smiley best seller
2 "Why should ___ you?"
3 "___ Rose" (song from "The Music Man")
4 They may be necessary
5 Drive away
6 The recent past
7 Type of racing bikes
8 A psychic may sense it
9 Some TV's and VCR's
10 Lifting devices hung from helicopters
11 Echo
12 Not putting on any weight
13 "Little" girl in "David Copperfield"
14 Get as a result
15 World's highest large lake
16 Athletic types
17 Not just up
18 Slender traces
24 Actress Merkel and others
29 Dam builders: Abbr.
30 Bills, e.g.
32 Starter starter?
35 Rare bills
36 "Nothin' doin'"
37 Don't skip
39 Like some trauma patients
40 Marine off.
41 Connecticut city
42 Hippie gathering of a sort
44 Future presenters, in the past
45 Spots for bees

48 March event, in more ways than one
49 "The Hot Zone" topic
50 Hall-of-Fame announcer Harry
51 Steely Dan's "___ Lied"
53 Peak in Greek myth
54 Famous dying words
59 Some burial vessels
60 Ostentatious
62 Running full speed
63 "Hogan's Heroes" corporal
64 "Quién ___?" ("Who knows?")
65 Radical 1960's grp.
66 Tears
67 Singer LaBelle
68 Bury
69 Ned Land's rescuer
70 Pitcher ___ Nen
71 1814 Byron poem
75 "The Third of May" painter
77 John Major, e.g.
78 "Imperfect Sympathies" essayist
79 Time to attack
81 It has precedents
83 Large-oared craft on a ship
84 .0000001 joule
85 Military branches: Abbr.
86 With 121-Across, they're bright on Broadway
87 Often-poked pitchman
89 Carry on
90 Foils
95 River isle
96 Bull: Prefix
98 Weaken

by Karen Hodge

99 "Who's the Boss?" co-star
100 Former Screen Actors Guild president
101 February forecast, perhaps
103 The lucky ones?
104 Nostalgia stimulus
106 ". . . mercy on such ___": Kipling
107 Reader's Digest co-founder Wallace
108 Fit
109 Give a hoot
111 Food for snakes
112 Studies
116 Fashion inits.
117 Course setting: Abbr.

ACROSS

1 Opponent of 120-Across
5 Mac
8 Den ___ (Dutch city, to the Dutch)
12 Little dipper
17 Roughly
19 Qualified
21 Tony : theater :: ___ : fashion design
23 Change a letter in 1-Across to spell . . .
26 Engage in histrionics
27 Place
28 Wife of Bath's offering
29 Away from the bow
30 Bill's co-adventurer, in the movies
31 Ninnies
33 Napoleon, for one
35 Imposture
37 Succumbs to gravity
38 Thicket
39 Eschew spontaneity
43 Dressage factors
45 Commandment pronoun
46 Change a letter in 23-Across to spell . . .
48 Those seeking junior partners?
50 Choral rendition
51 Affect
52 News office
53 Cast a line
56 The "W" of W. H. Auden
57 Rejoin rudely
58 Prefix with magnetic
60 Poet Mandelstam
62 Anteceding
63 Change a letter in 46-Across to spell . . .
66 "___ durn tootin'!"
69 "Swan Lake" piece?
70 Extreme shortage
71 Cellar, in real estate ads
75 Genesis locale

77 Secure, as a passenger
80 Nova follower
82 It's out of the mouths of babes
83 Trojan Horse, e.g.
84 Form of abstract sculpture
85 Change a letter in 63-Across to spell . . .
89 Fresno newspaper
91 Silver oak leaf wearer: Abbr.
92 Comic strip "___ & Janis"
93 Bulb
94 Place for a swing
95 "Mighty ___ a Rose"
96 Place where Gauguin painted
98 Drew Carey, e.g.
100 "When ___ door . . . ?"
102 Bit of "Big Brother" equipment
105 One of the singing Winans family
106 "Clan of the Cave Bear" author
107 His work inspired Broadway's "Nine"
110 Change a letter in 85-Across to spell . . .
114 Selena's musical style
115 Ante, in a sense
116 Birth-related
117 Connoisseur
118 Narrow margin
119 Out of reach
120 Change a letter in 110-Across to spell . . .

DOWN

1 He went for baroque
2 Sub
3 Port authorities
4 Summertime percentages
5 Canopy supports, perhaps

6 Last in seq.
7 Body work?
8 Camouflages
9 "___ ben Adhem"
10 H.S. math
11 "Hogan's Heroes" villains
12 Roast
13 Vinegar base
14 Minn. neighbor
15 Readily conscriptable
16 "Milord" chanteuse
18 Sylvester, to Tweety
20 Dieters' woes
22 Ambulance V.I.P.
24 Book before Deut.
25 Roundup aid
32 Noise from a fan
33 W.W. I soldier
34 Place where a 33-Down fought
36 La donna
38 Role for Liz
40 Starbucks order
41 Floral fragrance
42 Who should believe a liar
43 Ties up the phone
44 HdosO
46 Not running
47 Natives call it Misr
49 "For shame!"
50 Nautilus captain
53 Pix that perplex
54 Tarzan creator's monogram
55 Walk pigeon-style
56 Most judicious
59 QB's cry
61 Honshu honorific
63 Engine problem
64 Scruff
65 ASCAP counterpart
66 One-third of a phrase meaning "etc."
67 Clinker
68 Vicomte in "The Phantom of the Opera"
71 Bay's competition, in song
72 Treats unfairly
73 Venus de ___
74 Old Chinese money

76 Iron man?
78 "Three Coins . . ." fountain
79 Mysterious character
81 Lead a square dance
84 Take care of
86 Level of command
87 Out of sorts?
88 Settled scores
89 "Here comes the judge!" utterer
90 Swelled head
94 Like saltwater taffy
97 "To give her poor dog ___"
98 Unconventional
99 Unfamiliar
101 Something to bend or lend
102 1/20 ton: Abbr.
103 Sound of a frog?
104 Goya subject
106 Dilettantes' passions
108 Telecommunications setup, for short
109 Empty
111 Hebrew letter
112 Musician Brian
113 Proteus's domain, with "the"

by Henry Hook

ACROSS

1 Eat in a hurry
5 Comet rival
11 Low spot
15 "See you"
19 Jabir al-Ahmad al-Sabah, e.g.
20 Egg container
21 Touching activity
22 Author Hunter a k a Ed McBain
23 "Give me a mudpack," e.g.
26 Director of the "Dr. Mabuse" films
27 Collectibles, so to speak
28 Fume
29 Peace offering
31 Succeeds
32 Bad blood
34 Row of pawns, e.g.
35 Broker's action
38 ___ of Japan
39 "My suitcase is better than yours," e.g.
41 A Swiss army knife has lots of them
43 Subdued
45 Wands
46 They fill holes
48 "Any bullets in this thing?," e.g.
56 Land of the eland
59 Have an effect
60 Firing squad?: Abbr.
61 Rogue
62 Cut back
63 Best-selling car in America, 1997–99
65 "Olympic track events are thrilling," e.g.
70 Visibly astonished
72 Borrower's handouts
73 Game with a ball that no player ever touches
76 Gothic author Radcliffe

77 Paul of "Casablanca"
80 Says "please" and then some
81 "You might want to check the carburetor," e.g.
85 Roll top?
86 Fleeting feeling
87 How to get something from nothing, perhaps
90 Practiced
91 "I'll give you $100 for that buffet table," e.g.
97 Theater sound
99 Place for a plug
100 Little one
101 Says no
102 Carrier that bought Piedmont in the 1980's
104 Most strapping
106 Indicator of current trends?
107 Swamps
111 St. Patrick's home
112 "I'm making a quilt," e.g.
115 "Tess of the D'Urbervilles" cad
116 It may make a big haul
117 Optometrist's solution
118 Gathering
119 Stand in the flames
120 Dillies
121 Looney Tunes regular
122 Striped stone

DOWN

1 Tapestry thread
2 Baseball's Vizquel
3 Head hunters' targets
4 Order member
5 Difficult pills to swallow
6 Indulge, perhaps
7 Strikes out

8 Hieroglyph images
9 Spoil
10 First-aid item
11 Film director Vittorio
12 Play wrap-up
13 Papal name
14 Watercolorist ___ Liu
15 Put something on
16 Successor to the Studebaker
17 Bicycle type
18 Unwanted feeling
24 One way to sell something
25 A bird may have one
30 Toy factory equipment
32 Perceptiveness, in a manner of speaking
33 It's rarely a ratings hit
35 Swells (up)
36 He was spared by divine intervention in Genesis
37 U.S. citizen-to-be
39 The facts of life?
40 Like virtually all schools nowadays
42 Make airtight
44 Tire shop work
47 Starrett family savior
49 Vein
50 Wheel from Holland
51 Place for a Yale lock?
52 Ruining, as a deal
53 Platinum-selling 10,000 Maniacs album of the 80's
54 Athlete who wrote "My Game"
55 Thumbs down
57 Bristle
58 Italy's main broadcasting network

63 Plant with heart-shaped leaves
64 Ring of color
66 Horror film effects
67 They may be given from behind a curtain
68 ___ de plume
69 Male sheep, in Shropshire
70 Org. that aids the stranded
71 Stocky antelope
74 Transformer former
75 Compound in ale
77 Event in a forest
78 Spurred
79 Meter inserts
82 Evident wealth
83 Smooths
84 Racer blade?
88 Having only the upper part showing, as a heraldic beast
89 Sea air
91 Best Actor title role of 1968
92 Superior in lubricity
93 Overhaul
94 Rial spenders
95 Name on a dictionary
96 Least inhibited
98 Surprise party command
100 Underhanded
102 Release
103 Macho sort
105 Recipe abbr.
107 Cuba's ___ of Youth
108 "90210" extra
109 Comparer's problem, maybe
110 River whose name means "hateful"
113 Wahine accessory
114 Shooter

by Patrick Berry

ACROSS

1 A little lower
5 Like some respect
8 Secondary bank
14 One whose social life is going to pieces?
19 Utopia seeker
21 Bad-mouth
22 Voice one's view
23 Sadist
24 Embodiment
25 Empire
26 "Calling America" band
27 "Autumn in New York" co-star
28 Great money-saving achievement?
30 High beams
32 To be more accurate
33 ___ citato
34 Joan of art
35 Victim of erosion
36 J.F.K. posting: Abbr.
37 Phaser setting
39 Robert Conrad courtroom drama
41 Result of a moon-landing accident?
48 Toys with runners
50 Sea into which the Amu Darya flows
51 Biblical verb
52 Black brew
53 Even
54 Bacon bit
56 Hungarian wine
57 Pulitzer-winning novel of 1925
58 Make tiny knots
59 From Yerevan: Abbr.
60 Prefix with type
61 Religious figure in a hot-rod race?
69 Go along
70 ___ apart
71 Detroit-based org.
72 Considerable
73 Having eyes, in verse
74 Drivel
76 Medieval
79 Like a 911 call: Abbr.
80 Tease
81 Final Four game
82 Stonehenge priest
84 Disappearing restrooms?
87 "The Sound of Music" name
89 Groucho, in "A Night at the Opera"
90 Take off
91 Certain attachment
92 Good sign?
94 Disdain
97 Clear
100 Nonpaying gig
103 Veterinarian's promise?
105 Italy's Val d'___
106 Hindu title
107 Simple souls
108 Kind of duty
109 Lot
111 Hold firmly
112 Temporary wheels
113 Stomach
114 Calendario marking
115 Point up
116 Port Huron Statement grp.
117 River of Flanders

DOWN

1 Mill product
2 "A Passage to India" heroine ___ Quested
3 Drumstick for Fido?
4 Considerably
5 Noted French encyclopedist
6 Not abstainers
7 To be, in Bordeaux
8 Of the arm
9 Unmask
10 Opposite of après
11 Gangster called "The Enforcer"
12 Teaching assignment
13 Sub
14 One who knows how to swing
15 At full gallop
16 College student's declaration
17 Provide
18 Legal defendant: Abbr.
20 It has a head and hops
29 Western setting
31 Prong
32 Now
35 Infection suppressants
36 Not healthy-looking
37 Something blue
38 Ring around the collar?
40 Speeders make it
41 Mann of many words
42 Come to
43 "Try ___ see"
44 Nordic wonder
45 Grind away
46 1980 Tony winner
47 Land in Ezekiel
49 Parlor piece
55 Show signs of overuse
56 In a tough spot
57 Cast forth
59 Lace tips
61 Illinois birthplace of William Jennings Bryan
62 Color-changing lizard
63 Like some vbs.
64 Actress romanced in real life by Rudolph Valentino
65 First name in daytime TV
66 "For bonny sweet ___ is all my joy": Ophelia
67 Subject of an annual festival in Holland, Mich.
68 Beldam
73 Organ stop
74 Guardian Angels wear
75 Single-named supermodel
76 In drydock?
77 Year in Claudius's reign
78 Shingle letters
81 Brandy cocktails
83 Stage part
85 "Wrap" artist
86 Hoodoo
88 Disinfectant compounds
91 Manuscript units
93 Electron collector
94 Massacred
95 Novelist Barker
96 Volunteer
97 Ornamental loop
98 "Everybody is ___" (1970 hit)
99 Wrap (around)
100 Litter
101 Past perturbed
102 Floorer
103 About
104 Rembrandt contemporary
105 Ins. sellers
110 Prohibition promoter

by Richard Silvestri

ACROSS

1 Nasty campaign?
6 Insect trap of sorts
11 Cabinet display, perhaps
17 Singles
21 Not just decorative
22 Strength
23 In a New York minute
24 "___ here"
25 . . . food?
28 Lodge
29 "___ say!"
30 Algeria's second-biggest city
31 Nonclerical
32 More than devotees
34 Year Trajan was born
36 . . . song?
40 New York City stadium name
41 Bliss
43 Important spelling feature of "iridescent"
44 Actor Armand
46 Pitcher Shawn
47 Archeological find
49 Response: Abbr.
50 Give the eye
53 Jam
56 Kindly
58 "No ___!"
59 Pizzeria order
63 . . . animals?
66 Org. with a big PAC
67 Maintained
68 Supermodel Campbell
70 Move like a scared rabbit
72 Teeny
73 Sky-chart scales
74 Inter ___
77 "Nosiree!"
78 Belligerent Olympian
79 . . . boat?
81 . . . sci-fi flick?
83 Certain resale item, informally
86 Gun
88 Stab
89 Quadruple gold medalist, 1936
90 Kind of car
92 C.E.O.'s
95 Events for which to get decked out
96 Decked out
97 Tenn. neighbor
98 . . . actor?
102 Alternatives to Merlots
104 Bruise
106 Put away
107 American Indian pony
108 Solvent
110 Court action
111 Game usually played in a ring
113 Produce
118 Home of Gallo Winery
120 Wearer of 71-Down
121 Exact
123 Color quality
124 . . . TV character?
128 Deck
129 Place for police
131 French city heavily hit in 1944
132 South Dakota, to Pierre
133 Something taken into account?: Abbr.
134 Locale for pins
135 . . . James Bond movie?
141 Follows a recipe direction
142 Like many a phone caller
143 "___ Paris"
144 Val d'___, French ski resort
145 Mosquito, e.g.
146 Stinker
147 Forty-___
148 Old

DOWN

1 Flambé
2 Emphatic letters
3 Gangland communication
4 Cockpit dial: Abbr.
5 Fiddle-de-___
6 Brawl
7 Upright
8 Critical point
9 Hiver's opposite
10 Cancel, in a way
11 Report of proceedings
12 City where the first Woolworth's opened, 1879
13 "Arabian Nights" creature
14 Sign
15 Lots
16 E-mailer's option
17 Emulated a Boy Scout
18 . . . book?
19 Overdramatize
20 Stitches
26 Scraps
27 Doesn't maintain even consistency
33 Niels Bohr, e.g.
35 Suffix with social
37 Single
38 Like horses
39 Neighbor of Bhutan
42 Hold
45 Smart ___
47 Uncompromising law
48 Pollster's quest
49 Word in a tied score
51 Division of a subdivision
52 Toot
54 Something to believe in
55 Heater
56 Louvre Pyramid designer
57 Mat material
59 One-fourth of a 60's group
60 "Well, did you ___?"
61 . . . candy?
62 Used a lever on
63 Snow creation
64 Lennon/McCartney's "___ Loser"
65 A, as in Augsburg
69 Put ___ in one's ear
71 Clan's pride
73 N. Y. C. airport
74 "May I have your attention?"
75 Photographer's cover
76 Possibilities
80 Election news
81 Some think they're terrible
82 Scene of fierce W.W. I fighting
84 O'Neill's "A Touch of the ___"
85 Cutlass, e.g.
87 Tennessee athlete
89 John Boyd ___, 1949 Peace Nobelist
91 Check
92 Novelist Janowitz
93 Minnesota's St. ___ College
94 Beau ___
95 Sci-fi escape vehicle
96 ___ Dhabi
99 Very, to Verdi
100 Woolf's "___ of One's Own"
101 W's brother
103 Replies at sea
105 Most lamebrained
107 Time of smooth sailing
109 Summer heat-beaters
111 Checked out
112 Checks
114 Saigon celebration
115 Makes it
116 Ways to make a big splash
117 A Massachusetts symbol
119 The Alamo, for one
120 Coffee order
121 Cousin of a moccasin
122 Turned on by
123 Traffic
125 Common bacterium
126 LuPone stage role
127 "The Tao of ___" (2000 film)
129 Express approval
130 Biblical land
136 Student's cry
137 Night "The Monkees" aired: Abbr.
138 Role in Rabaud's "Mârouf"
139 Swindle, slangily
140 Hockey's Tikkanen

by Nancy Nicholson Joline

21 ONE FOR THE BOOKS

ACROSS

1 Airline info
7 It may be caught in winter
13 Ice cream shop employee
20 Ron of CNBC
21 Rocker Dee Dee, Tommy, Joey or Johnny
22 With a creamy cheese sauce
23 Redbook (1848)
26 Home (in on)
27 Princess tester
28 Final bit
29 They may be B.C. or A.D.
30 Owl hangouts
32 Present prefix
33 Runner Devers and others
37 Yearbook (1949)
41 1953 Emmy-winning actress
44 Wrong
45 Prefix with cortical
46 Brown of Talk magazine
47 Beetles may be found in them
50 Never gone
54 Tap idly with the fingers
55 Guidebook (1994)
57 Nest noises
58 Rice and Robbins
59 Org. with inspectors
60 Singer Zadora
61 Place for splints
62 Meandering curve
63 Bible book (1977)
67 Area between center and right, say
70 Bean ___
71 French collagist
72 CD-___
73 Ex-Cosmos great
74 Souvenir stand item
77 Comic book (1997)
81 When some people eat lunch
82 Erich ___, author of "Emil and the Detectives"
83 "Mr. Apollinax" writer
84 "The West Wing" actor
85 Not a thing
86 Fathers and sons
88 Songs sung by candlelight
89 Law book (1866)
96 Thirst (for)
97 Bibliophile's suffix
98 Bach composition
99 Setting for many jokes
102 Visibly peeved
104 Eyesore
105 New money
106 Review book (1982)
113 Curtainlike fish snarer
114 Charge, British-style
115 Chilling words
116 Marine food fish
117 Fills in
118 Big name in antivirus software

DOWN

1 Posh
2 "___ Majesty's Secret Service"
3 False friends
4 ___ Bell
5 Rock producer Brian
6 Hong Kong harbor sight
7 Cutters
8 ___ Solo of "Star Wars"
9 London label
10 Setting for "The Practice"
11 Feral
12 Program until 1966
13 Commonsensical
14 Don't let go of
15 0-for-5 performance for Mark McGwire, e.g.
16 You can dig it
17 Foot, to Fabius
18 What N.Y./Phila. baseball games are usually played in
19 Children's character in the Hundred Acre Wood
24 ___ mortals
25 Straight
30 Cry in a crowded hall
31 Angler's gear
34 Kind of proposition, in logic
35 Noted wine valley
36 Early time
37 Some tides
38 Sufficient, old-style
39 Lady lobster
40 Super Bowl XXXIV champs
41 5 1/2-point
42 "Ghostbusters" co-star
43 Small amounts
48 Struggle
49 Politician's declaration
51 Ball bearing?
52 Vigor
53 It lands at Lod
54 Slicing request
56 Sorceress
57 Chews on
61 ___-Hawley Tariff Act of 1930
63 "O.K."
64 They may be arranged in banks
65 Greek group, for short
66 #4 on ice
67 Wish granter
68 Star in Perseus
69 Pains, so to speak
70 Field of stars?
73 Kitchen light
74 Locker room supply
75 Child's bedtime treat
76 Actor Mandel
77 Barely covered
78 Classic drink
79 Code subject
80 Tubular food
82 Cousins
85 Child watchers
87 Quiets
90 Sappho's poet friend
91 Undergarment
92 Something to sing in
93 Swimming
94 Small thing
95 Word source
99 Well-muscled
100 Response to "Am not"
101 1953 A.L. M.V.P.
103 F.B.I. workers: Abbr.
105 Word prefixed by who, what or when
106 1,000 fins
107 French goose
108 Suffix with pay
109 16 oz.
110 Indecisive end
111 Dungeons & Dragons game co.
112 Acapulco gold

by Randolph Ross

ACROSS

1 Part of a combo
5 Person carried on others' shoulders
10 Vessels seen in "Saving Private Ryan": Abbr.
14 Dent in the coastline
19 Caesar's cry
20 Prefix with centric
21 Sieben follower
22 They stand for things
23 Time pieces
24 True
25 Cloning Dolly, e.g.?
27 Jacques Cousteau's life, in a nutshell?
30 Catches on
31 Address in Calcutta
32 Caddie, often
33 Cut down
34 Wacko
36 Examines closely
38 Skip town
44 Pam of "Jackie Brown"
47 What Broadway backers may have?
49 Judah's mother
50 Outshine
53 "O curse of marriage . . ." speaker
54 Feminine suffix
55 British can
56 Essen's river
59 Discouraging words
60 Items in a recycling bin
62 Like some items at customs
66 TV character, to some adolescent boys?
72 Superb
73 Give up
74 King of Kings
78 Guy Lombardo's "___ Lonely Trail"
79 Peerless
80 Speak like Sylvester
81 Big ape
84 Without heat
87 It ends a threat
88 Canceled credit card?
91 "Contrary to popular belief . . ."
93 Bugs
94 Fanatic
95 Lambs: Lat.
97 Barbecue bar
99 Dizzy
101 Some chanters
106 Timesaver
111 How OPEC communicates?
113 "E pluribus unum," e.g.?
115 Sirs' counterparts
116 Strong draft
117 Actress Aimée
118 Mmes., in Málaga
119 ___ ease
120 Siouan tribe
121 They might be loaded
122 Where to see a Sonora sunrise
123 Discourse detour
124 Verb with thou

DOWN

1 Gripes
2 Airy rooms
3 Secret stock
4 Cold fish
5 "The House Without a Key" hero
6 Maintained
7 "Look Back in Anger" wife
8 Strength
9 Forks over the dough
10 Galloway gal
11 U.
12 Saint known as the Little Flower of Jesus
13 Prepare (oneself)
14 Part of IBM: Abbr.
15 "Me neither!"
16 King in G. & S.'s "The Gondoliers"
17 Suffix with defer
18 Sounds from a scolder
26 Least tan
28 Skillful
29 Bluenose
33 Agcy. concerned with false advertising
35 Pizza ingredient
37 Like a bobcat vis-à-vis a pussycat
39 "Pipe down!"
40 City of northern France
41 Janis's partner, in the comics
42 Star player for the Cosmos
43 Those, to Tomás
44 Salami choice
45 Fats Domino's music, for short
46 "___ the train a-comin'" (Johnny Cash song opener)
47 Prize in a popular game show, for short
48 Old land bordering Luxembourg
49 On sale
51 Like some of the Rockies
52 Flipped out
57 Diminutive suffix
58 Taxi forerunner
61 Op. ___
62 What some games are won by
63 W.W. II zone
64 Prodded
65 Comfy spot
67 The Platters' "___ Mine"
68 Like corduroy
69 Song on the Beatles' "White Album"
70 Flip
71 Oversell
74 Church nook
75 "Very funny!"
76 Loads
77 Hard knocks
79 Ham container?
82 ___-Locka, Fla.
83 Picture of Elvis on velvet, e.g.
85 English author Lofts
86 Scholar's sphere
89 Some basses
90 Crunchy sandwich
92 Turns down
95 Acid neutralizer
96 Blow up
98 Prize money
100 Calls
102 Cry of terror
103 "Keen!"
104 They may be involved in busts
105 Shooting game
106 One who crosses the line?
107 Tennis star Mandlikova
108 Spanish bears
109 Actress Madlyn
110 Some hwys.
111 Zaire's Mobutu ___ Seko
112 Bone: Prefix
114 Didn't bring up the rear?

by Nelson Hardy

ACROSS

1 Crushing blow
10 Cook, for one: Abbr.
14 Shoot for, with "to"
20 Size up again?
21 Suburb south of Paris
22 They may be in trunks
23 Blocks
24 Daytime Emmy winners
26 Stable staple
27 Columnist Thomas
28 More frosted
29 Jai alai basket
30 ___ Gailey, of "Miracle on 34th Street"
32 Car dealer's offering
35 Needy people?
37 Play analyzer
39 "___ cost you"
40 Most cloying
44 Zany
47 A heap
50 Architectural feature
51 Some bullets
53 Pool party?
55 Draft org.?
56 Stable staple
57 River from Superior to Huron
58 Curtis and others
60 Sites for some analyses
61 One of the Cyclades
62 More than miffs
63 Belief
64 Best Song of 1961
68 Everything, to a lyricist
71 Morning glories
72 Traffic directors
73 He beat Arthur at the 1972 U.S. Open
74 "To Autumn," e.g.

75 Include
76 Lively, in scores
79 Early 50's game fad
84 Chemical suffix
85 Oyster's place
87 Wyoming's Grand ___
88 Hardly exciting
89 Oil producers
92 Out of this world
94 Clinic supplies
95 All, for one
97 Recipe direction
99 Viña ___ Mar, Chile
100 Catch
102 Disestablish
104 Kind of aerobics
107 Valuable viola
110 À la Thurber
112 ___ de trois
114 "King Kong" studio
115 Cry from Ralph Kramden
117 It may be tucked in
120 For one
121 Cognate
122 Clementine, e.g.
123 Called for
124 "Et voilà!"
125 Sky streaker

DOWN

1 Auto option
2 Prevent
3 Anne Frank's hiding place
4 Even
5 Paris picnic place
6 Like some suspects
7 Core groups?
8 Computer monitor, for short
9 Peggy Lee's "___ a Tramp"
10 Mozart opera title starter
11 Appetite arouser
12 Kilt patterns
13 Prepared a manuscript
14 Desert menace

15 Phantom
16 Neurological problem
17 Some savings
18 Software installation requirement, often
19 It, in Italy
25 Evolutionist's interest
28 Tie in
31 Bing Crosby's record label
33 One of the coasts: Abbr.
34 Move in mire
36 Delivery in the field
38 Spenserian beings
41 Allen and others
42 Luther Billis of "South Pacific," e.g.
43 Assignations
44 Chain units: Abbr.
45 Know-how
46 "Bustin' Loose" star
48 Sketch
49 Bergen spoke for him
52 Onetime lottery org.
54 Poor rating
59 Hook shape
60 Muumuu go-with
63 Drifted
64 Cancer, astrologically
65 Band aide
66 Make up
67 Sign of a winner
68 Brand of hair highlighter
69 Like a romantic evening, maybe
70 "Justine" star
71 Dairy Queen offerings
74 Leaves time?: Abbr.
76 Book ends?
77 English seaside resort
78 Big Mac ingredient

80 Buenos ___
81 R & B music showcase
82 "The Rum ___ Tugger" (song from "Cats")
83 Silly one
85 Children's author ___ Rabe
86 Hosp. tests
90 Was more than miffed
91 Threaten, like a dog
93 Hegelian article
96 Threesome
98 "High Sierra" star
101 1961 Heston role
103 Slow movement
105 Squeezing (out)
106 Guiding principle
107 ___ all-time high
108 Gloomy Gus
109 Force ___ (draw)
111 "Gossip" co-star Headey
113 Galley order
116 Showed signs of being in love
117 John, Paul and George: Abbr.
118 "Told ya!"
119 ___-state

by Elizabeth C. Gorski

WHO WANTS TO BE A QUIZ SHOW CONTESTANT?

NOTE: Each answer at 26-, 39-, 63-, 84- and 101-Across is a quiz question for which there is one correct response among the four choices in the clue. The circled letter in the answer is the correct response.

ACROSS
1 Alley
5 Fashionable 70's wear
10 Duke of ___, historic Spanish general
14 Bit of cleverness
17 Solemn responses
19 Captivate
20 Kind of cloth
21 Suffix with brilliant
22 Singer-actress Janis
23 Mario Puzo best seller
24 Medical advice, often
25 IV measurements
26 A. God of war B. Goddess of the earth C. God of love D. Ruler of the gods
30 Most of Mauritania
31 Flu source
32 Wear and tear
33 Head, slangily
34 Designer Wang
36 Story of France
38 Big voting bloc
39 A. "Les Troyens" B. "Pelléas et Melisande" C. "La Mer" D. "Faust"
46 Pay stub?
47 1962 film set in Jamaica
48 Consents
49 Tao founder
50 Early Eastern mercenary
53 Boeing rival
55 Talk, talk, talk
56 Snowy ___
57 Zip
58 Olympics
60 Two-time link
63 A. Egg and matzo meal B. Tomatoes and cheese C. Corn or barley D. Chickpeas or beans
68 Dump
69 Dish eaten with rice
70 Britney Spears, to some

71 Part of 1,000
72 "Whew!"
73 Calls off the romance
75 Translucent quartz
76 Heartbeat quickener
80 Gen. Lee's grp.
81 Snowmobile parts
83 Judge in 1995 news
84 A. Karl Malden B. Robert Mitchum C. George C. Scott D. Burt Lancaster
89 Make it up to
90 Big East team
91 Where Bill met Hillary
92 Movie pooch
93 See 5-Down
94 Anaïs ___ "The Novel of the Future"
97 Friction
101 A. "Mommie Dearest" B. "Lonesome Dove" C. "Angela's Ashes" D. "Times to Remember"
106 Pot top
107 Mrs. Chaplin
108 Like an early-evening sky
109 "___ Crooked Trail" (1958 western)
110 Preceding, in verse
111 Singer with wings
112 Not thinking well
113 Spell
114 From, in France
115 "Sure, I'm game"
116 Staggering
117 Within: Prefix

DOWN
1 Gemstone
2 Oven maker
3 [I'd like some oats over here . . . !]
4 Chisel
5 With 93-Across, words of delight
6 Actresses Dana and Judith

7 Besmirches
8 Last question in this puzzle
9 "Rich Man, Poor Man" novelist
10 1953 A.L. M.V.P.
11 Composer Frederick
12 Customs request
13 Busy bodies
14 Disease-causing bacteria
15 Piano teacher's request, maybe
16 Mosaic piece
18 Hit the roof
19 1950's soldier, in brief
27 Like some seals
28 Awards for Asimov and Clarke
29 Put in a new medium
35 Start and end of a magician's cry
37 Emulates Regis?
38 Card game with a pool
39 "Haven't heard a word"
40 Land
41 One of Dada's daddies?
42 Indivisible
43 Very much
44 Subject of a Nash poem
45 Swung, nautically
51 ___ set
52 Problem ending?
54 Meadow sound
55 Resembling preserves
58 Certain photo
59 Faction
60 Ban locale?
61 Slice for a pizza?
62 Popular dot-com stock
64 ___ Bay, Philippines
65 Fall event
66 TV announcer Hall
67 Egg ___ yung
73 Perceive
74 Fastidious

76 County near Liverpool
77 Cause of some disturbances
78 Stern with a bow
79 For instance
80 Barely speak
82 Shudder, e.g.
84 Fished with a net
85 The Wright brothers, e.g.
86 Fatuous
87 Revamps
88 Tunneler
93 Noted Impressionist
95 "It's the truth"
96 Even so
98 Medicinal aid: Var.
99 Evil one
100 Muse for a lyricist
102 Holler
103 Unwanted guest
104 "___ done deal"
105 Gulped

by David J. Kahn

ACROSS

1 Michener best seller
7 Fed. loan agency
10 Nolan Ryan, for one
15 Where to do some bodywork?
18 Gets the red out?
19 National League division
21 Limonite's pigment
22 Legend on the ice
23 Temporarily
24 Certain partner: Abbr.
25 They come on the 25th
26 It may be tidy
27 Ending with Juan
28 "The Carpet-Bag," in "Moby-Dick"
30 With 63-Down, a New Mexico county
31 Confectioner's goof?
35 Introduced
37 Merle Haggard, self-admittedly
38 Troubadour's tune
39 One of Thor Heyerdahl's boats
41 Snap brim, e.g.
42 Washington dingbat?
47 They're cross-shaped
48 Lixivium
49 London's Old ___
50 60's campus news
51 Forceful group?
52 Men in the hood?
54 Part of P.S.T.: Abbr.
55 Mexican sandal
59 Texas state tree
62 Street that hosts a music festival
64 Slash, for one
65 Meal for a moth
66 "Magnum, P.I." setting
67 Occasion to use the good china
69 Kisser
70 Victorian
71 Major introduction?
72 Serial novel's start

73 It gets into hot water
74 Stunt
76 X into MXX
77 Kind of propeller
79 Load line locale
80 N.F.L. coach with 347 career victories
82 Castle site?
83 Keep in a cellar, maybe
86 ___ colada
87 Dress decoration?
90 With 118-Across, part of a child's schooling
92 Tech stock choice
93 You, to Yves
94 Inventor Sikorsky
95 Trips
97 Samoan simpleton?
102 Physics Nobelist Penzias
103 One with unusually fine hands?
105 Goon
106 Lighter producer
107 Outmoded copier
108 Trans ___ (Asian range)
109 Like some nuts
113 Hertfordshire river
114 Calyx segment
115 Jiffs
116 Dominican's dwelling
117 Southwest extension
118 See 90-Across
119 Book before Esth.
120 Line feeder, of a sort

DOWN

1 Fido's greeting
2 ___ Minor (northern constellation)
3 Spring time: Abbr.
4 Florida island
5 Doshisha University locale
6 It spans the 33-Down
7 Fossil fuel found in coastal veins

8 Aromatherapeutic additives
9 Take ___ at
10 Five-star
11 Autumn arrival
12 Churchill's "___ Finest Hour"
13 It may bring on a sigh
14 Hosp. sites
15 Mediocre steamed dish?
16 Branch managers?
17 Philip II dispatched it
20 Letter drop, e.g.
29 Circular tube
30 20th-century tree painting?
31 Play in an alley
32 Not spectacular
33 Blue preceder or follower
34 Crow, e.g.
36 Reek
40 Author Rand
43 It's known for its bell ringers
44 Sports stat
45 Window alternative
46 One of the rare earths
51 Like some face powders
52 Terrorist's taboo?
53 See 84-Down
55 Uses one's 60-Down
56 Hives, medically
57 A party to a party?
58 Novelist Morante
59 Swift contemporary
60 Side flaps
61 Flashy dance?
63 See 30-Across
64 Cultural Revolution leader
67 Like some controls
68 Kepi-sporting soldier
73 Fujimori's land
75 They may be laid out
76 Easy dupes
78 Spain's Guadalquivir, e.g.

80 Stand in
81 500
83 Jason's charge
84 With 53-Down, smarts
85 Speculator's target
86 Teetotaler's order
87 See see as sea, say
88 Like a coxcomb
89 Vienna premiere of 1805
90 Pacer's place
91 Less certain
96 Snowbird's destination, perhaps
98 Recognition responses
99 Physician to Marcus Aurelius
100 Shows shock
101 Bridget Riley's genre
104 Lott's predecessor
107 Chinese menu letters
110 Besides
111 Unit of energy
112 Turn red, perhaps

by Dana Motley

ACROSS

1 Czech capital, to the Czechs
6 Take 5, clue 3
10 Private schools: Abbr.
15 Stop, in Paris
20 Mathematician with a formula named after him
21 ___ Kea
22 Harold of "Ghostbusters"
23 Distrustful
24 Take 4, clue 1
25 Hebrew fathers
26 Take 5, clue 5
27 Orgs.
28 TAKE 1
31 Risks
32 Marriage and others
33 Connery successor
34 Mother, colloquially, in Britain
35 Take 3, clue 1
39 How some pkgs. are sent
40 Lots
42 Decay constants, in physics
46 Illegal bank practices
48 Take 1, clue 1
49 Musical quality
50 TAKE 2
55 Those, in Tegucigalpa
56 Neighbor of Liech.
57 Quaint verses
58 Ancient Italic people
60 A-Team member
61 Auditor, e.g.: Abbr.
64 Hit the nose
66 Insurable Item
67 Chip dip
69 Folk's Guthrie
71 François or Henri
72 Vietnam War Gen. Creighton
74 Sled piece
77 Pleasureful retreat

79 TAKE 3
83 Underground
84 Discrimination against the elderly
86 Hulled grain
87 Prepare for war
89 60's Mets shortstop Chacon
90 ___ this earth
92 Burden
93 Versailles, for one
96 Suffix with absorb
97 No. of beachgoers?
99 Former Ugandan strongman
101 Award-winning Disney Broadway musical
102 Family docs
104 Clark's girl
106 TAKE 4
112 In a tizzy
114 Charlie Brown's exclamation
115 Algonquian tribe
116 Aussie marsupials
117 Treacherous ones
120 Witching hour
121 Colorful salamander
122 "Don't give up!"
123 Singer Horne and others
124 Brave one
126 "Let 'em have it!"
128 TAKE 5
135 Kitschy 50's film monster
136 Take 3, clue 3
137 Supernatural
138 Track gold medalist Rudolph
139 Build, as a monument
140 ___ que (because): Fr.
141 Recovers from a flood
142 Take 4, clue 4
143 Certain entrance exams, for short
144 Casino lure
145 Take 5, clue 4
146 Like Eric the Red

DOWN

1 Adamant ant?
2 Bride of Boaz
3 Wings
4 Thyme, e.g.
5 Recitalist Rubinstein
6 Gossiped
7 Keeler and Dee
8 Med. sch. subject
9 All-nighter, maybe
10 Athenian magistrate
11 Partnership
12 ". . . ___ old soul"
13 Sawyer or Keaton
14 Concordes
15 Crimson Tide
16 Take 4, clue 2
17 Take 3, clue 2
18 Sea eagles
19 Cobb and others
21 Sugar for beer-making
29 Company that grants trademark use
30 Arab chieftain: Var.
34 Work force measure
35 Shelter in TV's "Survivor"
36 Relative of -esque
37 Paris street
38 Humorist Bombeck
40 Like windows
41 Modern image makers, for short
42 Bank department
43 Take 5, clue 2
44 Suffix with liquid
45 Dewey Decimal ___: Abbr.
47 Chits
48 Lose one's blush
49 ___-night doubleheader
51 Making a team
52 Supplants
53 South Africa's KwaZulu-___ province
54 Certain constrictor
59 Tenement locale
61 Vena ___

62 Unlikely Playboy Channel watcher
63 Take 2, clue 1
65 Murmur
66 Encourages
68 Snick-a-___ (combat with knives)
70 Hodgepodge
72 "Begone!"
73 Graduated
75 Leprechaun's land
76 Take 5, clue 1
78 ___ spumante
80 Wharton hero
81 Charged
82 Common ___
85 Victorian virtue
88 More powerful
91 March instruments
93 Elder and Younger English statesmen
94 Citrus drinks
95 Tiff
97 Picnic dish
98 Prince Charles's avocation
100 Towards the tail
101 Many miles off
103 Attention amount
105 Take 2, clue 2
107 "You ___ Beautiful"
108 Memorable dos
109 Wool coat wearer
110 Detroit-based grp.
111 Calif. zone
113 Mom and dad
117 Jacket fastener
118 Make a member
119 1998 N.L. champs
120 Bandleader Cugat
123 110-Down part
124 Andrea ___
125 "Laugh-In" man
126 Take 4, clue 3
127 The light bulb, to Edison
128 Brewer's base
129 Says "I do"
130 Roman "fiddler"
131 Pet name
132 Dona ___, 1978 Sonia Braga role
133 Tricksters
134 N.B.A.'s Archibald
135 Avg. size

by Charles M. Deber

ACROSS

1 Band aid
7 "I, Robot" author
13 Tasters' testers
20 Higher ground
21 Couch, in a way
22 Beach in a 1964 hit song
23 Nice people collect them
25 It may be flared
26 In the limelight
27 "Honor Thy Father" author
28 Business graphics
30 Out of chains
32 Change a bill, say
34 Dwelling in Durango
35 Like some Riesling wines
38 Great balls of fire
39 Kimono closer
41 Sultanate citizen
42 Beat to a pulp
45 Sound system component
50 Statistician's margin for error
52 Standing rule
53 Savoie sovereign
54 Lao-___
55 Pianist Schnabel
56 Drink with a kick
58 Blotto
60 The Switchblade Kid of cinema
61 Secures under cover, with "in"
62 Big Band music
64 ___ Walton League (conservation group)
66 Skedaddles
67 Wise guy
68 Clamorous
70 Hummable, perhaps
73 Facial foundation
75 Chest-thumping
76 High-tech co.
79 Draft choice
80 Not quite right
81 Rites of passage
84 Suggestive

86 "Absalom and Achitophel" poet
87 "The Pearl Fishers" composer
88 Service arm: Abbr.
89 One of the Titans, in myth
91 Woodstock band, 1969
93 Drop down?
96 Sink hole
97 Flimflam
99 Some approaches on the links
102 Sweets
104 ___ Lang, Superboy's girlfriend
108 Alternative fuel
109 Claim in a collectibles ad
112 Sign of a goof
113 Siberians' relatives
114 In a weakened state
115 Section of London
116 Not in any way
117 Drives back

DOWN

1 Hick
2 Word after "Ole"
3 Cream ingredient
4 Slow
5 B & B, e.g.
6 Paper worker
7 Mac maker
8 Did a smith's job
9 Place for a pupil
10 Tiger, for one
11 East of Essen
12 Evening bell
13 Long in the past?
14 Part of the Bible: Abbr.
15 Punishment unit
16 Last "course" of a spicy meal?
17 Earth, in sci-fi
18 Sends out
19 Chili topper
24 Gull
29 Hot
31 Comic strip dog
33 More than sore
35 Yielding

36 Modern farm birds
37 Whipped up
38 Toots in a restaurant
39 Common name for hydrous silica
40 Entrance
43 Entr' ___
44 Book-cracking
46 Treble clef singer
47 Issue suddenly
48 Roasts, e.g.
49 White wine apéritifs
51 Adder's threat
52 Valuable plastic
56 Actress Farrow
57 Landing
58 Game-stopping call
59 Characters in fables, usually
60 Scuff
62 Low spot of land
63 Faced a new day
65 [Gotcha!]
66 Dundee citizen
67 The lightning bolt on Harry Potter's forehead, e.g.
68 Similar
69 Computer command
71 #1 spot
72 Bad trait for a politician
74 Grace's end
75 Spark for the Giants' 1951 pennant win
76 Biblical site of the temple of Dagon
77 Story connector
78 "Cómo ___?"
81 Hot off the press
82 Letter-shaped construction piece
83 Bygone car option
85 Distant settlement
86 Mid-6th-century date
90 Southern Australia explorer
92 Obedient one
93 Fibber of note
94 Kim of Rudyard Kipling's "Kim"

95 Kudrow and Bonet
96 Meted (out)
97 Rumor squelchers
98 Originated
100 Cage co-star in "Leaving Las Vegas"
101 Phone, slangily
103 Pins' place
105 Glorified gofer
106 Present time
107 Added stipulations
110 U.N. working-conditions agcy.
111 Wrath

by Nancy Salomon and Harvey Estes

ACROSS

1 G
5 Select, with "for"
8 Ah follower
12 Atomic pile
19 Moroccolike leather
20 Dramatic court action
22 Vital engine conduit
23 Working in a mess
24 Vain mountaineer's motto?
26 Didn't come to terms
28 Rank in the 40-Down
29 Disney V.I.P., once
30 Inactivity
32 Auxiliary
34 Like mesh
35 People who love baths?
39 Part of Q.E.D.
41 "When in ___ tell the truth": Twain
42 Soldier material?
43 Some fraternity men
44 Poke holes in
48 Like a monster
50 Wiretap victim's wish?
54 Seethe
55 Belgian river
57 U-___
58 Actor Greene
59 Düsseldorf donkey
60 Put on
61 Part of some gym exercise equipment
63 The very best
64 Problem for the Shanghai police?
67 James Michener opus
71 "Something of Value" author Robert
72 Blink of an eye
73 Abe's Mary
77 Lush material
78 "___ Ha'i"
79 Defraud

80 Switch add-on
81 Graffiti?
85 Coils
87 Rembrandt's land: Abbr.
88 High rollers?
89 Like a good bond
90 Make reparations
91 Sign seen in Times Square
93 Pirate flag in the summer sun?
98 Alexander, to friends
101 Like
103 Stop listening
104 Praline ingredient
106 Suffix with honor
107 Spoiled brat's display
111 Policy of a strict naval blockade?
115 Superman's mother
116 Spanish valentine sentiment
117 Give up
118 Grandson of Eve
119 It's far out
120 Take note of
121 Turner in Atlanta
122 Suggestive

DOWN

1 Trampled
2 ___ soit qui mal y pense (classic motto)
3 Squirrels' haunts
4 Matter of growing interest
5 Fish hawk
6 Electrician's need
7 Become attracted by
8 Some savings accts.
9 Drillmaster's syllable
10 Kind of garage
11 Nocturnal animals of the upper Congo
12 Aussie hopper, for short

13 Revolutionary Michael Collins's country
14 Pink-eyed panther, say
15 Union site
16 1960's–70's All-Star Luis
17 Start
18 Hear again
21 Go-between
25 Decked
27 No-see-ums
31 Sony founder Morita
33 Identical
35 Big name in Web software
36 Symbols of industry
37 Pulitzer winner Alison
38 Call a halt to
40 Service for a 28-Across
43 Freudian topic
45 Civil wrong
46 Part of A.D.
47 Page
49 Victim of Hercules
50 Big brass
51 Billiards need
52 Retreat
53 Ballet bend
56 "___ lied!"
61 One may be taken to the cleaners
62 Besmirch
63 Plastic surgeons' work
64 Piggish remark
65 Zero
66 It may get in your hair
67 Novel ID
68 Farm wagon item
69 Maine, e.g., in Metz
70 Manfred von ___ (The Red Baron)
73 Dry
74 Stars with a belt
75 Clergyman/poet John

76 Medicates
78 Light wood
79 Be relevant to
82 Dripping
83 Meal starter?
84 Playing to someone's vanity, maybe
86 War-torn capital of the 1980's–90's
92 Big Twelve school
93 Judd of "Taxi"
94 Long past
95 Like O'Neill's "Bound East for Cardiff"
96 Avoid a trial, say
97 Blotto
98 Hitachi competitor
99 Knock for ___
100 Lay low
102 Regrettable
105 Gentlewoman
108 Zola heroine
109 Leathery sunbather
110 "No sweat"
112 ". . . ___ thousand times . . ."
113 Deli choice
114 Early development

by Manny Nosowsky

29 BUSINESS CARDS

ACROSS

1 Stadium walkways
6 Actress Blanchett of "Elizabeth"
10 Something to talk about
15 Postponement
19 Suffix with sect
20 Woody's role in "Annie Hall"
21 Kansas City college
22 It may be hard to get out of
23 ___, Insurance Salesman
25 ___, Funeral Director
27 Remedy
28 Party wear, maybe
30 "Sabrina" star Julia
31 Royal Crown brand
32 Winter woes
33 Farmers' association
34 Five-time Derby winner
37 Western Pacific republic
38 Dirt expert
42 Big blow
43 ___, International Mediator
46 End of many e-mail addresses
47 A mean Amin
48 Noted Howard
49 Words before distance or discount
50 Dentist's request
52 Schism
54 ___, Travel Agent
58 Boozed (up)
59 Unending
61 Trade
62 Make over
63 Got the message
64 They come after quarters
65 Center of Los Angeles
66 Matriarch
68 Order in the court

69 Some pipes
72 Indian queens
73 ___, Children's Entertainer
75 It's tall when exaggerated
76 R.P.I. grads
77 "Gee whiz!"
78 Torch lighter at the 1996 Olympics
79 Excess
80 Big diamond
81 ___, Charity Organizer
86 Work well together
87 Long roads
90 Driving aids
91 Calls off
93 Summer colors
94 Jobs, to friends
95 Hearty cheers
96 1950's tennis star Pancho
99 Search party
100 How not to get caught
104 ___, Towel Manufacturer
106 ___, Literary Agent
108 Resembling, with "to"
109 Musical direction
110 It's breaking out
111 Item with a ladder
112 Dosage amts.
113 Fund
114 Source
115 French beans?

DOWN

1 Indian king
2 Get ___ for one's money
3 Alcoholic drink served over cracked ice
4 Coatings
5 Duke of Flatbush
6 Spiny things
7 Wings
8 Tubes

9 Socket
10 Wrapped, as for a football game
11 Tracks
12 Papal name first used in A.D. 140
13 Malicious
14 The very end
15 Seafood dish
16 Lawn mower brand
17 "I couldn't agree with you more!"
18 Play area
24 At all, in dialect
26 Life force, to Freud
29 Brio
32 Had a conscience
33 1951 Best Actress Emmy winner
34 "It's ___!"
35 Sector sides
36 ___, Suspense Writer
37 Branch
38 Intl. org. since 1948
39 ___, Shoe Salesman
40 1957 Detroit debut
41 ___ la Paix
44 British actress Holden
45 Simplifies
50 Up
51 Still there
53 Backstreet Boys fan, maybe
54 Garden needs
55 With it
56 Cap
57 Accord
58 Mystery or sci-fi
60 Puts on
62 Tyro
64 Pens, perhaps
66 Four-star
67 Russian alternative
69 Storm preceders
70 Fabulous time
71 Clockmaker Thomas and others
73 Shoots well

74 Oscar winner for "The Cider House Rules"
77 Giant hero
81 It might hold one back
82 Angel's desire
83 Match for Mars
84 Popular chocolate snack
85 Navy men
86 Light, white wine
88 180's
89 On guard
92 Bidding
94 ___ voce
95 Outbreak
96 Pre-desktop publishing photo
97 Frightful sounds
98 Understanding
99 Swimming site
100 "There ___ excuse!"
101 Settled
102 Turn over
103 A Spanish crowd?
105 Barry who sang "1-2-3"
107 Prefix with -cide

by Randolph Ross

30 FOLLOWING ORDERS

ACROSS

1 Rule-breaker
4 Certain residue
8 Sumer, nowadays
12 Broker's advice
18 Gist
20 Star impersonator?
22 Such that one might
23 Gag order?
24 1973 Rolling Stones #1 hit
25 Winston Cup org.
26 British exam taken at the end of secondary school
27 Postal order?
30 Mentions
31 Word-word link
32 Registering, as a dial
33 Exclusive
34 Atlanta-based cable channel
35 Ward of "The Fugitive"
36 They're found in veins
38 Writer ___ Louise Huxtable
40 Religious order?
48 Noblemen
49 Imperfection
50 "Keystone Kops" producer
51 Pecking order?
54 Washington and Shore
56 Detachable container
57 Got off
58 Indian Ocean swimmer
61 Reef lurkers
63 Bank
67 One year in a trunk
68 Becomes intertwined
70 Cookie with a crunch
71 Sly look
72 Fly, e.g.

73 Threatening words
75 Expensive trim
76 Stroked item
78 Small military vessel
80 Restraining order?
82 Gravedigger
86 Red-brown
87 New England catch
89 Batting order?
94 Eternally, in poetry
95 Courtroom entry
96 Kingdom on old Asian maps
97 Word to a doctor
99 Stout, freshwater fish
102 Money in the music business?
105 "Foucault's Pendulum" author
106 Odd-numbered page
108 Shipping order?
111 Fake ID holders
112 Collected
113 In conclusion: Fr.
114 Rush order?
116 God depicted holding a crook
117 Rephrase
118 Part of a tennis court
119 ___ Fitzgerald
120 Periods
121 Chinese money
122 Warner Bros. collectible

DOWN

1 It's striking
2 Batch of solicitations, maybe
3 Lab tube
4 Bona ___
5 Darling
6 Basketball's ___ Alcindor
7 They may be uncovered on a street

8 Tolstoy's ___ Ilyich
9 Sunders
10 Hidden motive
11 Direct order?
12 "___ She Lovely"
13 Whose ark?
14 Explorer ___ Núñez de Balboa
15 Heat up
16 Eyeballed
17 Split
19 Campbell of "Party of Five"
21 Lincoln's Secretary of State
28 Bazaar merchant, maybe
29 Short pieces
31 Believe
35 Tiniest bit
37 Gets (through)
39 Food for a doodlebug
41 Audience research focus
42 Wool cap
43 1970's–80's TV family name
44 Nonworking order?
45 Golden yrs. cache
46 ___-Cat
47 Constellation near Cassiopeia
51 Patriarch of the Flying Wallendas
52 Tennis's Nastase
53 Kind of curve
54 New World order?
55 Pas ___ (dance solo)
59 Western Amerind
60 Recover from a run
62 Whirled records?
64 Part of the U.S./Canada border
65 Kay of "Physical Evidence"
66 Team need
69 Daughter of Mnemosyne

72 Before the opening, say
74 Either Zimbalist
77 Youngest March sister
79 Accept
81 Sack
82 1950's G.O.P. name
83 Uncalled-for
84 Like some decorations
85 Held the top spot
87 Stays with
88 ___ Phraya (Asian river)
90 Jidda's locale
91 Tiny fraction of a min.
92 Terse
93 G.I. John?
98 Overnight spot
100 Single-named singer
101 Suffer defeat, slangily
103 Gather
104 Minneapolis suburb
106 Gain succulence
107 Carbon compound
108 Since
109 Twiggy digs
110 Runs out
111 Arizona city
115 Cross shape

by Patrick Berry

ACROSS
1 [I am shocked!]
5 Nogales nosh
11 More than impair
18 Completed
19 Popular salad ingredient
21 They help catch criminals
22 A fact-finding civil court judge __
24 Completed
25 Settles on, in a way
26 Hockey Hall-of-Famer Francis
28 Appeared
29 Active starter?
30 An improvising jazz musician __
35 Beeswax
37 Compass heading
38 With 44-Across, a veteran
39 Spots
42 Gala
44 See 38-Across
45 Corner
49 Directive
51 A helpful bridal shop clerk __
55 It may be forfeited
56 Silicon Valley giant
59 Writer Rand
60 Delayed
61 Piz Bernina group
62 Small amount
63 Traffic signal, at times
65 "Valley of the Dolls" girl
66 A hard-working coal miner __
71 Doone of fiction
73 Word with steak or search
74 Bruce nicknamed "The Little Dragon"
75 Noted sprinter
78 Ring of color
80 French article
81 __ prayer
83 Was behind
84 A bottom line-oriented executive __
87 Split part
89 Rum's partner
90 Last word of "Angela's Ashes"
91 Not so nice
94 __ Kippur
95 Turned on
96 Dickensian complaint
98 Convictions
100 A thorough insurance adjuster __
106 Like many Iranis
110 Witch
111 Ancient gathering place
112 Like some stables of myth
113 Supposes to be
116 A diligent police detective __
120 Exactly 3 hours for a marathon, e.g.
121 1997 film hit
122 Web destination
123 Bands of athletes?
124 End of an O'Neill title
125 Horse race

DOWN
1 Messenger
2 Spanish tourist town
3 Modern high school class, informally
4 Slangy forecaster's word
5 Smidgens
6 The Altar constellation
7 Big bloom
8 Turkish pooh-bah
9 Winter Olympian
10 Gold and silver, e.g.
11 Jailbird
12 Track part
13 With you
14 Wing: Prefix
15 Decorative loop
16 Where security is discussed
17 Old laborers
20 "It's __ of the times"
21 Stand for the deceased
23 Bad postures
27 Kind of partner
30 Like a heap
31 Expert finish
32 Ghost
33 Boat with a high bow
34 Not be careful with a bucket
36 In arrears
39 "Fernando" singers
40 "It's a __!"
41 "The Tempest" event
43 Zilch
44 Wide-ranging display
45 Big fund-raiser
46 Takes off, cowboy-style
47 Month after Ab
48 Sports award
50 Where Hamlet cogitated
52 One greeted on a ranch
53 Harp's cousin
54 Start of a boast
57 Actions at auctions
58 Chocolate treats
63 Nasty biter
64 Bounced checks, hangnails, etc.
67 Rumor
68 Aphrodite's lover
69 Appleton locale: Abbr.
70 Navy worker
71 Secular
72 "Yes __?"
76 City on the Truckee
77 Product encased in red wax
79 Kind of kitchen
81 Whistle-blowing spot: Abbr.
82 1-Down and others: Abbr.
85 Plops down
86 Timid
88 Double-dealing
92 It may be hit by a driver
93 The elected
95 Worse than tricks
96 Order to a dog
97 On high
99 Most discerning
100 Wedding band, perhaps
101 Word in the Boy Scout Law
102 One of a kind?
103 Put __ to
104 Like some coins
105 Finlandia House architect
107 Show again
108 "__ say . . ."
109 Atlas feature
112 "Moses" novelist, 1951
114 Fiver
115 Mantra sounds
117 Flee
118 Together
119 1999 Pulitzer Prize-winning play

by David J. Kahn

"C" CHANGE

ACROSS

1 Game equipment
7 Part of the Northland peninsula
13 Puzzled
20 Open, in a way
21 Indiana University campus site
22 In a disastrous way
23 Health-conscious fish?
25 Harmonize (with)
26 Bow
27 Spain's last King Ferdinand
28 [Oh, well]
30 Pier group work
31 Former European coin
35 Roof problem
37 Attack on a fort, maybe
38 Etcher's window work?
41 Clinton Cabinet member William
43 Kind of market
44 Trickster
45 Staple of Southern cuisine
46 Madly in love
50 Take for a while
51 Inspiration
52 Bank security
53 Lump of clay, say
54 See 79-Across
55 Information repository
58 Comment from a scolded person
60 100 dinars
61 Unhappy spectator
62 Ring around the collar?
63 Canada's ___ Bay
64 V-formation group
67 Op. ___
68 Told to shape up
71 Poker Flat chronicler
72 "Gulliver's Travels" feature
74 Keats was one
75 Rat-___
76 See 77-Down
78 Tree with tanning bark
79 With 54-Across, furnace emission
82 Eastern royal
83 Fixes, in a way
84 Fish hook
86 Half of an 80's TV duo
88 Smooth (out)
89 "A Loss of Roses" playwright
90 ___ tree
91 Most like Chianti, say
93 Relish
95 Hole in hosiery?
97 Do car wheels
100 Circle overhead
102 It's south of ancient Shiloh
103 Lord in love with Lady Clare, in Tennyson
105 Plug
107 Ring around the collar?
108 Dead on target
112 Backbreaking
114 Friendly sentry?
118 Outlaw
119 Traps, as an Arctic ship
120 Business practice
121 Breaks away
122 Cuddle up
123 Wee

DOWN

1 Lousy
2 Sit ___
3 Cubemaster Rubik
4 Like a defense contractor's contract
5 Kind of beetle
6 Eastern European
7 Activity for sunglass wearers
8 Earned
9 Part of a hosp. record
10 Kind of life
11 Replies to a newsgroup
12 Scandinavian land, to natives
13 64-Across's locale: Abbr.
14 Unbelievable
15 Loose
16 Activity for a crooked politician?
17 Any Platters platter
18 Armrest?
19 "Riders to the Sea" writer
24 Part of the Old Testament
29 Poor links play, as they might say in England?
32 Building inspector's topic
33 Troy, in poetry
34 Legs, slangily
36 It has a line through it
38 Is repentant
39 D-Day beach
40 Really severe economizing?
42 Be undecided
43 Apalachee Bay locale: Abbr.
45 Russian saint
47 Important guest group
48 Flip out
49 More fit
51 Butter at breakfast?
56 "Le Coq ___"
57 Maxwell competitor
59 Ally McBeal, e.g.: Abbr.
61 Mechanical device for baseball practice?
62 Spot for a cursor, maybe
63 Kitchen appliance
64 Emmy-winning Lewis
65 Persian Gulf land
66 Heavens: Prefix
69 "That's ___ . . ."
70 Lash
73 Hillock
76 Camera diaphragm
77 With 76-Across, a game ender
78 Make ___ (mug)
79 Hopper
80 Imperfect speech
81 Up to this point
85 Like two peas in ___
87 Blood vessel securer
91 Open up
92 Perception
94 Get off
95 Informant
96 Tiger Hall-of-Famer Al
97 Ishmael's people
98 "20,000 Leagues Under the Sea" actor, 1954
99 Of Nehru's land
101 Gain computer access
104 View from an oasis
106 Ball-bearing items
109 Reservoir filler
110 Garden decorations
111 On pins and needles
113 Vietnam War opposer: Abbr.
115 N.Y.C. clock setting
116 Up to, informally
117 Bestow on, to Burns

by Manny Nosowsky

LET FREEDOM RING

ACROSS

1 Distiller's grain
5 Thus far
11 Scratch
14 Friars Club emcees
18 "Commander," in Arabic
19 Loose dresses
20 Starbuck's skipper
22 Legal memo phrase
23 Arafat and Rabin, for two
25 Offspring of 11-Down
27 "Dr. Zhivago" locale
28 Early afternoon time
30 Overturn
31 Least trained
33 Roman war goddess
34 Marker
35 High roller's pocketful
36 G. & S.'s Lord High Everything __
37 Done for
40 It's a knockout
42 Singer Patti
43 Richard Wagner's second wife
44 Cybersearch result
45 They're full of dates
46 Quads' sites
50 Big force in politics
53 Part of A.P.R.: Abbr.
55 Gallic honeys
56 Islet
58 Baby Ruth ingredient
60 Ben Franklin proposal: Abbr.
63 Bathtub murder victim
64 Green Party V.I.P.
66 They help maintain balance
68 Sign
71 Beer-drinking consequence, maybe
73 Woolgatherer's state
74 Pugnacious
76 "How __?" (question to a diner)
78 Champion with a two-handed backhand
79 "Get it?"
80 Honey
82 Xi preceders
84 Crisp breads
85 "Don't __!"
86 "__ Gold" (Fonda film)
88 Comtes, comtesses, etc.
90 Opening with dexterity
93 __-Bo (exercise system)
94 It's for the birds
96 Exigency
97 Like scofflaws
99 Canadian peninsula
100 Crowd
104 Blue Eagle org.
105 Where change is made
106 Girasol, e.g.
108 Visit through primal therapy
110 Lithos
112 Relief pictures?
115 Carp
116 "I Puritani," for one
119 London flea market site
121 George and George W., e.g.
122 Fido's dinner, maybe
123 Melodic
124 Der __ (Adenauer)
125 Peter's "A Shot in the Dark" co-star
126 Ball girls?
127 Vacillate
128 __ up to (approached)

DOWN

1 Organic farmer's need
2 Unprincipled
3 Protection for the maligned
4 Town in County Kerry
5 Pit stuff
6 Prefix with resin
7 Naturalist Fossey
8 Prewar
9 Pass on the sauce
10 Big Bertha's birthplace
11 Principal in a well-publicized breakup
12 "Eureka!"
13 Toothed wheel
14 Takes the cake
15 Kind of protest
16 Cat in "Cats"
17 Withdraws
21 Major's successor
24 Initials at sea
26 Disposed
29 Dundee denial
32 W.B.A. stats
34 Mitterrand's successor
38 "Wait __!"
39 Galileo, for one
41 Marvel Comics hero
42 Warrant
43 They need a good whipping
46 Name on a can
47 Charlotte __, Virgin Islands
48 Fata morgana
49 "Shalom!"
51 Film material
52 Pressing needs?
53 Man in la famille
54 How a pun may be phrased
57 Pound sound
59 Maid's introduction?
60 Grounds for divorce, in some states
61 Brats' looks
62 African scourge
65 Be a water witch
67 City near Seattle
69 Effluvium
70 Modern forensic tool
72 Passive principle
75 Kind of officer
77 Former Barbary State
81 Gen. Robt. __
83 It's available in bars
85 Back
87 __ Hill (Oyster Bay, N.Y., landmark)
89 Joel Chandler Harris title
90 Poe miss
91 "Carnival" composer/ lyricist
92 Allen Ginsberg, e.g.
93 "Peter Pan" role
95 TV colleague for Mary
97 Dempsey foe
98 Vet
100 Early TV clown
101 Rue de __
102 Handle props?
103 Put down one's hand
105 Low
107 Half the "Monday, Monday" band
109 Author of "Il nome della rosa"
111 Smart-alecky
113 Platte River tribe
114 1998 N.L. M.V.P.
117 66, e.g.: Abbr.
118 Biblical rebuker
120 Roar

by Nancy Nicholson Joline

ACROSS

1 Swiss Mrs., maybe
5 Comparable to a wet hen
10 Bodybuilder's pride
14 Whip
18 O.K. Corral fighter
19 Get a rise out of?
21 Town on the Vire
22 Nestlé pet food brand
23 1983 movie cause of heartburn?
25 With 119-Across, country lunch customer of song?
27 Ruhr industrial hub
28 Baldwin, Guinness, etc.
30 Clinch
31 Sweet barbarian?
35 Bee's target on a flower
38 First name in architecture
39 Fleece
43 System starter
44 "Ta-ta"
46 MTV hosts
48 Whaler, for one
50 Fast-food snack?
56 River connected by canal to the Volga
57 Movie dog
58 Vegetable fats
59 Weirdos
61 Greek penultimates
65 Wayside stop
66 Hindu melody pattern
67 ___-com
68 Be a klutzy chef?
75 Globetrotters founder Saperstein
76 Past
77 Past
78 Peak of myth
79 Do a kabob job
81 "Dilbert" creator Adams
83 Iona College player
87 Jot
88 Won't fit, as a sash?
93 Place for Cicero
95 Double header?
96 Early Irish assembly site
97 Certain win, for short
98 Explorer Bering was one
99 Gave the slip
102 Satirize
104 Risk getting clawed?
110 Girlish
114 Strainer
115 Additional
119 See 25-Across
121 Midwest native American on TV?
124 "You Bet Your Life" sponsor De ___
125 Game-ending declaration
126 TV's ___ Lee
127 Giant chemicals corporation
128 Kind of leopard or goose
129 Offshore
130 Predilection
131 Hourglass part

DOWN

1 Luau, e.g.
2 Stands roars
3 God seen on "Xena: Warrior Princess"
4 Cheery
5 H.S. subject
6 Dry, in Versailles
7 Taj ___
8 St. Teresa's home
9 Cut
10 L.A. sked abbr.
11 People: Prefix
12 Drug-free
13 Swedish mezzo Anne ___ von Otter
14 Robert Burns was one
15 "Blondie" boy
16 Gush
17 Conflicted
20 Recess
24 Solid
26 One of the King Sisters of 40's music
29 Electronic control systems
32 Andrews Sisters, e.g.
33 Month after Nisan
34 Chain hotel, for short
35 Layer's lair
36 Unoriginal reply
37 Crotchety one
40 Actress Wood of "Diamonds Are Forever"
41 Mrs. Marcos
42 Conditioned reflex researcher
45 Pope Urban II, originally
47 Culottelike garment
48 Papyrus and such
49 Vile
51 Weapon in the game Clue
52 Film director Petri
53 City near Mt. Rose ski area
54 Get ahold of
55 Gem State
60 They may be checked
62 Presently
63 Trespass on
64 Take care of
68 Islamic militant group
69 Let up
70 "Romeo and Juliet" setting
71 Let out
72 Borodin title prince
73 "Forget it, Little Red Hen!"
74 Spread unchecked
80 Somalian model-turned-actress
81 Priers
82 Part of amatol
84 Like Woody Herman's sax
85 Town ENE of 53-Down
86 Where the Rhone and the Saône meet
89 George Ade's "The Sultan of ___"
90 The Oscars, e.g.
91 Graceful galloper
92 Cane material
94 It may be made of buffalo skins
100 Cane, e.g.
101 It may be passed
103 Beast that Apollo slew
105 Forster subject
106 Miss Marple finds them
107 Novelist ___ Tennant
108 1996 Madonna role
109 PC troubleshooters, for short
110 Overlook
111 Presently
112 The Eagles' "Take ___ the Limit"
113 Indian Ocean vessel
116 Burrow
117 Like "Star Wars"
118 Place to go for a spin
120 "___ minute"
122 Islet
123 "That's news to me!"

by Cathy Millhauser

ACROSS

1 Place to change
7 Film festival site
13 Powerful cliques
19 Cottonwood trees
20 Cousin of a meadowlark
21 Feminine
22 Some bomb squad members
23 Lunar craft
24 Moved with a davit
25 Start of a quote
28 Home to many Swiss banks
29 "___ Little Tenderness"
30 Nautical ropes
31 Istanbul currency
33 Leader of a flock
36 Itch cause, perhaps
40 Tore
44 Quote, part 2
48 "L'chaim," literally
50 1943 conference site
51 They're taken in punishment
52 Historian Durant
53 Elroy's pooch
54 Member of a sting operation?
58 Gentlemanly reply
60 Accelerator bit
61 Visits from Carry Nation
62 Atlanta-to-Miami dir.
63 With 65-Across, Irish writer and author of the quote
65 See 63-Across
67 Legal ending
70 Gap
72 Venue for the Blues Brothers, for short
73 Music shop fixtures
76 Checkers masters
80 Patricia of "Betrayal"
82 They sit near the violas
83 Two-handed lunches
84 One who's not out of bounds?

86 Nervous ___
87 Quote, part 3
92 One, in Köln
93 Jeanne d'Arc et al.: Abbr.
94 Cockeyed
95 Saddlery needs
97 Aligned
98 Stiff bristle
100 Allegro ___ (very fast)
105 End of the quote
111 Like some elephants
113 Environs
114 Runoff spot
115 In progress
116 Like meringue
117 Sites for fights
118 Book of Changes
119 Least hale
120 Sire, e.g.

DOWN

1 West Indies language
2 Wahine's welcome
3 Cakes with kicks
4 "Don't make ___!"
5 ___ motel (tryst site)
6 Part of N.A.A.C.P.: Abbr.
7 Pigments
8 Sheikdom of song
9 Stealth warrior
10 Network terminal
11 T.V.A. product
12 Muralist José María ___
13 End users?
14 Wacky
15 Ramadan observance
16 Captivated by
17 Partner of steak
18 Lead role on TV's "Providence"
21 ". . . it's ___ know"
26 Not esto or eso
27 Put ___ (ask a hard question)
32 Project conclusion?
33 LuPone role
34 Oklahoma county seat
35 Scuttle
36 Makes fuzzy

37 Prosodic foot
38 Play a key role?
39 Caesar's existence
40 Doesn't fold
41 Pumice features
42 Name in a Beethoven opus
43 Vietnam's Ngo Dinh ___
45 Gain entry
46 Beat, as the heart
47 Entreated
49 Marco Isl.'s locale
53 British Petroleum acquisition
55 Something to cash in: Abbr.
56 Tilter's need
57 Emulated Ananias
59 Comet competitor
64 Biddy
65 Big name in book publishing
66 Venerable one
67 Gastroenteritis cause
68 Knitter's buy
69 Test track features
70 Winter blankets?
71 Council city of 1409
72 Ten Commandments word
74 Beluga yield
75 Skilled
76 Michael Moore's "Downsize ___!"
77 Gun, slangily
78 Colleague of Dashiell
79 Horde
81 Matriarchal figure
85 Really big shoe?
86 Vezina Trophy org.
88 Serving up whoppers
89 Floodgate
90 Whooshed
91 Smack
96 Most of Libya
97 Grand name
98 Place for hospitality
99 They're pointless
101 Break off
102 Île de la Cité locale
103 The U.N.'s Kofi ___

104 Clarification preceder
105 Attached to
106 "___ known then . . ."
107 Prefix with valence
108 Actor Martin of "Hill Street Blues"
109 Carrier to Ben-Gurion
110 Kind of door
111 Violinist Kavafian
112 Rare polit. designation

by Elizabeth C. Gorski

36 OH, NO!

ACROSS

1 His last film was "The Night They Raided Minsky's," 1968
5 Work ___
10 Gold bug?
15 Utter a few choice words
19 Part of a C.S.A. signature
20 Rear
21 As ___ resort
22 Squabbling
23 Comedian who has only one-liners?
25 Neighbor of Fiji
26 "Bye!"
27 Do-gooder's quality
28 Instructions for a bottle cap?
31 Dynamited, maybe
32 Neur. readout
34 Office squawker
35 Walkman batteries
37 Beguilement
39 Cut out
43 Where many allowances come from?
50 Like rail vis-à-vis air
51 Diminutive suffix
52 Gauche
53 South Africa's ___ Paul Kruger
55 "ER" actor
56 Rent
58 "That's a ___!"
59 Sandbags, often
63 Shepherd's locale
64 Premature
66 Silver-tongued TV newsman?
68 Duchamp's "Mona Lisa," e.g.
69 Gold braid
70 Together, in music
71 Very cold draft?
75 Washington display
79 Clear
80 Takes
81 Basketful
82 Who's minding the baby, maybe
83 60's TV boy

85 It has many benefits: Abbr.
86 New Zealand minority
88 Remote target
89 Ranch wear
92 Exoneration for a group of actors?
96 Rampaging
98 "Uh-uh"
99 Row producer
100 Not this again!
103 Alternative to a Maxwell
106 Adventurer's stock
110 Like Erato when writing poetry?
114 Garrison Keillor specialty
116 Feodor I, e.g.
117 1920's–30's film star Conrad
118 What many pitched baseballs do?
120 ___ many words
121 "Half ___ is better . . ."
122 In a tough position
123 ___ v. United States (classic Supreme Court obscenity case)
124 Weak poker hand
125 Coppers
126 Gobs
127 Not a good sound for a balloonist

DOWN

1 Bygone Renault
2 "Be-Bop-___" (Gene Vincent hit)
3 Budget alternative
4 Unimaginative sequel, say
5 ". . . ___ saw Elba"
6 Café cup
7 Casino request
8 British verb ending
9 Dick Francis book "Dead ___"
10 Theatergoer's choice
11 Johnny Mercer's "___ My Sugar in Salt Lake City"

12 "La vita nuova" poet
13 Home of the Norse gods
14 Positions
15 Living end
16 Golden Spike locale
17 In ___ (as found)
18 "Immediately"
24 Like the laws of kosher food
29 Well product?
30 Dreamboat
33 See
36 Stranded on a mountain, say
38 Sporty truck, for short
40 First name in modern dance
41 Certain fishermen
42 The willies
43 Japanese fish delicacy
44 ___ Bator
45 Crane site
46 Daisy chains
47 Scuffle
48 Free restaurant serving
49 Exclusive
54 Infamous traitor
57 Mask
59 Scams but good
60 Touched ground
61 Baked beans, e.g.
62 Threaded metal fastener
65 London streets, in a manner of speaking
66 Hors d'oeuvre topper
67 "___ the lookout!"
69 Big name in book clubs
71 "The Lord of the Rings" hero
72 Flower
73 Patsy's "Absolutely Fabulous" pal
74 Heavy blow
75 Origin
76 Four-star
77 Holder of ancient riches

78 "It Must Be Him" singer, 1967
81 ___-guided
84 "Take your pick"
86 Plan (out)
87 Nix
90 Satisfy
91 New York's ___ Lakes
93 Swallows up
94 Engages in baby talk
95 Heads
97 Antique shop deal
101 Part of a train
102 "Let ___ Cake"
104 Stand for a portrait
105 Word go
107 Chihuahua canines
108 ___-Unis
109 Actor Green and others
110 Canal cleaner
111 Annapolis sch.
112 Former capital of Romania
113 Stretcher carriers, briefly
115 Sked figures
119 Playwright Levin

by Nelson Hardy

ACROSS

1 Charge
5 Auricular
9 Feature
14 Environmental hazard, for short
17 "___ grip!"
18 Kind of coil
20 Lickety-split
21 Certain something
22 "My word!"
23 Champion on the ice
26 Perky name?
28 Stone landmark
29 Second edition
30 Many a college teaching assistant
33 ___ Méditerranée
34 Parts of a krona
35 Düsseldorf dessert
36 July 4, e.g.: Abbr.
39 Quatrain scheme
41 A
42 Like the sound "ng"
45 Leave
48 Daisy Fuentes or Carson Daly
51 Many a sailor's downfall
52 The Tatler essayist
53 ___ voce
54 One who's up a creek?
55 Affectation
57 British banking name
59 Vibe
60 Pre-calc
63 Crushed
66 Impending
67 Whetstones
69 Response to a doubter
70 G.I. journalist
72 Stemmed
74 Delineated
76 Pursue intently
80 Like improved baby shampoo
81 Las Vegas landmark
83 Whitney Houston's record label
84 Sprays
86 Senate response
87 Perón and namesakes
88 Little dog, for short
89 ___ Aviv
90 Orch. section
91 Nasdaq news, in brief
92 Theater hit of 1878
101 Hesitating
103 Wife of Abram
104 Fit to be tied
106 Red Cross offering
109 Antiquated alpine apparatus
110 Just
111 Pitch
112 "The Far Side" exclamations
113 1965 jazz album
114 Kind of flour
115 Presidential nickname
116 Obsolescent conjunction
117 Bakery offerings

DOWN

1 Work week whoop
2 "The Tortoise and the Hare" writer
3 Draw on a board
4 Cold war warriors
5 Cheri of "S.N.L."
6 140 pounds, in Britain
7 "This ___ test"
8 You've heard it before
9 Sarajevo skiing gold medalist
10 Earth, for the most part
11 Actor Kilmer
12 Legendary skydiver
13 Went sniggling
14 Releases, as a fish
15 Herr's her
16 Today it's managed
19 Not much
21 Org.
24 French corp.
25 Sprawl
27 Drum site
31 Some Algonquians
32 Up to, informally
37 Potemkin Steps city
38 Pitcher Al for the Blue Jays and Mets
39 50's political inits.
40 N.Y.C. subway letters
41 ___ barrel
42 Makes official
43 Site of the 1973 Riggs/King "Battle of the Sexes"
44 Some Christmas decorations
45 46-Down, to Aphrodite
46 See 45-Down
47 Prominent media member
49 Biblical high priest
50 1984 Redford role Roy ___
51 Hospitalize
54 When doubled, a number
56 Not so naïve
58 1998 World Series star Ricky
60 Mall mainstay
61 The Joker player on 60's TV
62 With absolutely no spark
64 Headed up
65 Miniature
68 Tar
71 Oaf
73 Hatter affair
75 Teeth: Prefix
77 With approval
78 ___ lark
79 They intersect intersections: Abbr.
82 Annual report report
84 Laugh syllable
85 Central Park designer Frederick Law ___
89 1940 Karloff horror flick
90 Kind of column
91 Darin and Dee's "___ Man Answers"
93 Kindergarten game
94 Part of a work week: Abbr.
95 Comb
96 Old
97 Span. 15-Down
98 Aforementioned
99 Worry
100 French equivalent
101 Cpls., e.g.
102 Wine, for starters
105 Big times
107 Free (of)
108 Chemical suffix

by Martin Schneider

ACROSS

1 La Guardia posting: Abbr.
4 Pool ploy
9 Mosque officials
14 Logan's home
18 Wings
19 Bering Sea hunter
20 Shearer on the screen
21 Mrs. Charles
22 Musical version of "The Corn Is Green"?
25 Lament loudly
26 Like cardinals
27 Dump emanation
28 Port of Vietnam
30 Crown covering
31 Movie about a Mali malady?
34 Score unit
35 Snake, for one
37 Frasier's ex
38 Midlands river
40 Rebellious Turner
41 Pay
44 Pet name
47 Michael Jackson biopic?
50 Start a hole
52 Piece of work
55 Where Zeno taught
56 Latin lesson word
57 "Jennie Gerhardt" author
59 Crossword clue abbr.
60 Get into shape?
61 ×
63 Asylum seeker
64 Has the stage
66 Brace
68 Applies, with "on"
70 Arias
71 Between prime and good
73 High land
77 It gets hit on the head
79 Bunch of bills
80 Teriyaki alternative
82 Crosley or Nash
83 "Atomic Leda" painter
84 Yankee insignias
85 Remove marginalia
86 Bitter biblical epic?
90 Ultimate ending
91 Worked the land
92 Got together
93 The Jetsons' dog
97 Sister of Calliope
100 500 spot
101 Take (from)
102 Subtitle of "Elvis: The Army Years"?
106 Quick responses
108 Shoe reinforcement
109 Trigger control
110 Pennsylvania Dutch dish
112 Are, in Argentina
113 Part of the "Stare Trek" series?
117 Caber tosser
118 Sniggled
119 Piece of history
120 Priv. eyes
121 Blockbuster buy
122 Exchange at Wimbledon
123 W.W. II craft
124 Co. founded by Ross Perot

DOWN

1 Property transferor
2 Was behind schedule
3 Colonel's command
4 Martian marking
5 Deplaned
6 Artist Magritte
7 In the open
8 Peak in the Cascades
9 Precious bar
10 Havana's ___ Castle
11 Altar in the sky
12 Famous movie year
13 Beach annoyance
14 Straighten out
15 Documentary about cross-dressing?
16 Concert venue
17 Be undecided
18 Mountaineer's effort
23 "When Will ___ Loved"
24 Dot follower, perhaps
29 "Exodus" character
31 Attend
32 Custard dessert
33 Broadcast
35 McCourt matriarch
36 Traveling gunslinger
39 The folks over there
41 It may jackknife
42 Fall guy?
43 Short-straw drawer
45 Superimpose
46 Sea nymphs of myth
48 Visitor for a justice of the peace
49 Winery sight
50 "Oh, ___ Golden Slippers" (classic tune)
51 Jacob of journalism
52 Expelled tenant
53 Bacon orders
54 Film about a wedding on Everest?
58 Used-car deal
62 Quiet
65 Barely beats
67 Bailiwick
69 Spoiled
72 Introductory words, maybe
74 Whimper
75 Somewhat
76 High ball
78 La Scala star
81 On the other hand
87 "To ___ and a bone . . .": Kipling
88 Potent leader?
89 Crazy prank
91 Old TV series set in Coral Key Park
94 Took a header
95 Little streams
96 Haunt
98 Queen of Hades
99 Blotter letters
100 Shrug off
102 Cavaradossi's lover
103 Synthetic fiber
104 Down on one's luck
105 Morse minimum
106 Set up
107 Kind of wheels
108 Battery component
110 Normandy battle site
111 Pet plant
114 Tony winner Salonga
115 The lot
116 Cal. page

by Richard Silvestri

ACROSS
1 Fixes
5 Many a Sri Lankan
10 Herring family members
15 Visibly shaken
19 "By yesterday!"
20 ___ Kane of "All My Children"
21 Former Energy Secretary O'Leary
22 Alpine climber
23 Cooperstown nickname
24 Capital on the Willamette
25 Stripling
27 F.B.I.
30 Poor marks
31 Born abroad
32 Dangerous job
33 Not so new
36 Become less tense
38 Classified ad abbr.
41 Baseball manager Tony La ___
45 N.A.S.A.
49 Sharp feller
50 Cabeza, north of the Pyrenees
51 One way to enter
52 Causes an unearned run, perhaps
53 Pitch makers
57 Vietnamese neighbor
58 Vamp's accessory
60 Blood pressure raiser
61 Like oak leaves
62 Pie cuts, essentially
64 Salvager's gear
66 I.R.S.
72 Kvetches
73 Really enjoy
74 Term
75 Digital clock settings
76 Big belts
79 G.R.E. takers
80 Any of Yalta's Big Three
84 Groks
86 Daytime talk show name

88 Filmmaking family name
89 Prefix with sphere
90 E.P.A.
96 Some may mind this
97 Prefix with fuel
98 Pewter component
99 "___ Unplugged" (1999 album)
100 When it's low, it's good
102 One way to go
103 Flier to J.F.K.
104 U.S.A.F.
113 When printings begin
114 Debussy contemporary
115 Casino tool
117 Act the letch
118 Interviewer, perhaps
119 Kwanzaa principle
120 It's in the eye of the beholder
121 Reagan sentence starter
122 Mortimer Adler's "How to ___ Book"
123 Rose and Rozelle
124 Quits

DOWN
1 "Saturday Night Live" alum Mohr
2 From
3 Travelers in Matthew
4 Record holder
5 Bit of floorwork, maybe
6 Nejd desert dwellers
7 Leon Uris's "___ 18"
8 Clinched
9 Protect, as a document
10 Protect, as a seedling
11 "___ but known . . ."
12 Sea of ___ (Don River's receiver)
13 It may be kosher

14 Runners carry them
15 Paltry
16 First shepherd
17 Zoom, e.g.
18 Something to dial: Abbr.
26 Toyota offering
28 Doing
29 Japanese ___ (popular pet)
33 Like some judgments
34 Place for a checkered career?
35 Strong second?
36 It's hard to live on
37 Rancho units
38 "Dance in the Country" painter
39 Bit of raingear
40 Usher's request
42 Series
43 Buster, old-style
44 Declare
46 "The Dancing Couple" painter
47 Get one's fill
48 Where Regulus is
54 Tar Heel State campus
55 Siberian industrial center
56 Possible result of a sacrifice
57 Wide, to Cicero
59 In harmony
62 Add more ornaments to
63 As a preferred alternative
65 Publicizes, in a way
66 Some are mental
67 Vegetarian's demand
68 Bearded leader
69 "The Westing Game" author Ellen ___
70 Lose a lap?
71 Gain a lap?
77 Hosp. areas
78 Nurses
80 Source of sauce or milk
81 Penny-pinching
82 Dramatic beginning

83 Turndowns
85 Coffeecake topping
87 Yip or yelp
88 Approaches stealthily
91 ___ Gallery of Immortals (Greek pantheon)
92 "Generations of healthy, happy pets" sloganeer
93 Colder spots, often
94 Canute expelled him
95 A can of soda may have one
101 Fix
102 Flummoxed
103 Silk-stockings
104 Basic impulse
105 Hawk
106 Kiln output
107 Pool site, maybe
108 Nut, basically
109 All there
110 Toiling
111 Bring in
112 Cargo platform
113 John McCain, once
116 Sweden's capital?

by Matt Gaffney

ACROSS

1 Wanderer's words
6 What a writer might do
11 Outcropping
15 Create a solution?
19 Like part of the Arabian peninsula
20 Author Calvino
21 Somewhat, in music
22 Eyelet
23 Mockery, of a sort
24 Geological ridge
25 Insurable item
26 Writer ___ Stanley Gardner
27 Bit of a draft
28 Old-style revolutionary
30 Yarn spinner
32 Tweeted
34 Amuse with words
35 Caroler's syllable
36 That objeto
37 Feminine suffix
38 Like hair on the top of a bald person's head
40 Writes (for)
43 Recess at St. Peter's
45 See 14-Down
46 On drugs
47 Oust
49 Old station wagon, in slang
50 ___ War
53 Ice picker-upper
55 Waikiki wear
57 Not adhering to the subject
61 Buds
63 Ecstasy
67 Vietcong insurgent grp.
68 Give the slip
70 Protect from floods
73 Farm team
74 Fed. budget group
75 Some Amtrak cars
77 Heavy overcoat
79 Telltale sound after "I haven't had a drop to drink"
80 Not this or that, in Spain
82 Gazing hostilely

84 Orchard pest
85 "This ___ test"
86 Contracted cost
88 Teammates
90 See 48-Down
92 Bear hug
95 Black
97 "What ___?"
98 Animal with a black-tipped tail
101 Parts of a personality profile
103 Say "nothin'," say
107 Convenience outlet, often
109 Moons, e.g.
110 High hat
114 Tricky football plays
116 Homme d'___
118 Overseas price add-on
119 Dallas cager, briefly
120 It's dotted
121 Training places?: Abbr.
122 "Later!"
123 Brian of Roxy Music
124 "Later!"
125 Parapet
127 Exiled Roman poet
129 Bashes
131 Kind of boss
133 Country singer McCann
134 It has many slots
135 Clear the boards
136 White oak
137 Firewood carrier
138 Upper hand
139 See 83-Down
140 See 106-Down

DOWN

1 Crows
2 Strike caller
3 James Clavell best seller
4 Public house
5 See 1-Across
6 Prepare to sleep
7 Tie deciders: Abbr.
8 Deadeye Annie
9 1980 Economics Nobelist Lawrence

10 See 6-Across
11 Calculating sort
12 "The Sleeping Gypsy" painter
13 Start to malfunction
14 Get soused
15 "___ Believes in Me"
16 Ruin
17 Maltreated
18 Critical rocket maneuver
29 Actor Morales
31 Sales force
33 Matured
39 Aardvark features
41 Spanish silver dollar
42 Part of a sales force: Abbr.
44 Religious sch.
47 Acapulco article
48 Pull off a complete reversal
50 Parts of samba bands
51 Recently
52 Industry
54 Kind of glasses
56 Arrive, in a sense
58 Beatty of "Deliverance"
59 Pilot
60 See 57-Across
62 Three-time Cotton Bowl winners: Abbr.
64 Like a tough battle
65 Fosters
66 Crate
69 Start of many Italian surnames
71 Hold to a zero score
72 Symbol of Egyptian royalty
76 Angel's favorite letters
78 Vit. info
81 Cabalistic
83 Play direction
87 Sizes up?
89 Type sizes
91 [Make way!]
93 It usually comes in stripes

94 Laugh syllable
96 To now
98 They're hard to make out
99 Occasional paint surface
100 Newsmaking brother of 1903
102 Scoffing retort
104 6-0, in tennis
105 Bizet opera title character
106 Warning to motorists
108 See 107-Across
110 Certain camp
111 Drink
112 Scandal subject
113 Squared
115 Having hangovers?
117 Electronic game pioneer
126 Little fella
128 John ___
130 Pollutant
132 Play form using wooden masks

by Bill Zais and Nancy Salomon

41

PARDONABLE CRIMES

ACROSS

1 As is proper
6 Left
10 Cornwall town on Falmouth Harbor
15 Like some dinners
19 Scenic walk
20 Flash
21 German composer Carl Maria von ___
22 Something to pay?
23 Publicly disrupting a concerto?
26 Not deceived by
27 Doing counterfeit sculpture?
28 Augurs
29 Edge
32 Blood pigment
33 It's impolite
34 Handles the reception
35 Impossible score, in U.S. football
36 Car accessory
38 Informal term of address, in Britain
39 Council honcho
40 Cricket player
42 Valentine figure
45 Catches
48 Asian kingdom
49 Difficulties for wedding planners, maybe
50 Pianist's challenge
52 Actress Skye
53 Lifeboat lowerer
55 Cryer in movies
57 Aim
58 "Last Essays of ___," 1833
59 Thou of thous
60 Animated show on Nickelodeon
61 Utmost
62 Do business
63 Canceling a newsmagazine?
66 Young newts
70 Tocqueville's here
72 Beloved family member
73 A cuppa
74 Kind of drop

75 It's eaten with a cracker
78 Startled cry
79 Mountain in Exodus
81 Meat stew, for short
82 Scriptural elucidations
84 Place to sleep, in Britain
85 Places to sleep
87 Informal letter signoff
88 At no charge
91 Sly coverup
92 Rulers with thrones
94 Rule opposed by Gandhi
95 Appliance maker
97 ___ kwon do
98 Ally in Hollywood
100 Stench
102 Mathematician Turing
103 Company report abbr.
104 Dotty inventor?
105 Pilfering from a fertility lab?
108 Its motto is "Industry"
109 Robbing factory workers?
113 Seized vehicle
114 1948 Literature Nobelist
115 Comics dog
116 Not built-up
117 Sped
118 Indiana's state flower
119 Bit of thatch
120 "The Herne's Egg" playwright

DOWN

1 P.D. broadcast
2 Score that's "saved"
3 Lao-___
4 Table extender
5 1923 earthquake site
6 Flight formation flier
7 Less at ease
8 It's declining in Germany

9 Flavors
10 Like many TV movies
11 Bank amount
12 Sinker
13 Split
14 Internet address ending
15 Gunning down a night traveler?
16 Time of early youth
17 Refit
18 It may reflect well on you
24 Big wool source
25 They have many bends
28 It's heard from the herd
29 Pushed (for)
30 Financially compromised
31 Funnellike flower
34 Woman's shoe with a stiltlike sole
37 Jawbones
39 Municipal bldg.
41 Burglarizing a museum exhibition?
43 Assembled
44 City near Gibraltar, var.
46 Garbage ___
47 Where to set down roots?
49 Depravity
51 Suffix with differ
54 Bon ___
55 Nudge
56 Sailing
60 Bio. evidence
63 Like some lawn displays
64 Sign
65 Fannie or Ginnie follower
67 Lying
68 Attacks on horseback
69 Cut
71 Stick on a table
75 CBS, e.g., slangily
76 Feller
77 Gibbon, for one
79 Irrigation tool

80 Hamlet portrayer, 1996
83 Driver of a four-horse chariot, in myth
84 "Right Place, Wrong Time" singer, 1973
86 Citrus garden
89 Trample
90 Prosperous times, informally
91 Like many Rolls-Royces
93 Suffix on fruit names
96 Trinket stealer
98 Once-popular children's TV character
99 Hailey best seller
100 Page number
101 Hardship
105 Gondolier's need
106 Art class model
107 Swing about
109 Not square
110 "Patriot Games" grp.
111 Critic Hentoff
112 Bygone Manhattan sights

by Patrick D. Berry

42 SHAREWEAR

ACROSS

1 Beer pasteurization pioneer
6 French husband
10 You can swear by him
14 Lady of Portugal
18 An ice place to live
19 Spanish port
20 Pink-slipped
21 Periods divide them
22 Madras dress that's taken up by hitches?
24 Gown that's lost in a Florida town?
26 Uprose
27 "Airplane" co-star Robert
28 Tree in the Garden of the Hesperides
29 Female TV role played only by males
31 Overeater's worry
33 Not so taxing
35 Worldwide workers' grp.
36 Famed Bruin's nickname
38 Lexicographer Partridge
40 Hassle
42 Buttoned garment that's central to a 1970 movie?
45 ___ School (early 20th-century art group)
48 Son of Seth
50 [Pardon]
51 Wrap that's included with a landlord's sign?
53 Bird that's more than rare
54 Beloved, in "Rigoletto"
55 Detach, in a way
56 Arabic for "reading"
58 Take a chance
59 "Ed Sullivan Show" mouse ___ Gigio
61 Squeaked by
63 Cocked, as a hat

65 Borden brand
68 Quaint footwear
70 Big, as a concerto goes
71 Pursuit
72 Superlatively decided
73 Ulster, e.g.
74 Frankfurter link?
75 Brown shade
77 Large-scaled game fish
80 Brokerage offerings, for short
84 Money exchange fee
86 Underthing that's part of a bleeped phrase?
88 Pulitzer writer Sheehan
89 Spare
90 "Bewitched" witch
91 Old costume that enters a contest like bingo?
94 Animal's track
96 "Eye of ___, and toe of frog"
98 Raspberry
99 Kirk bench
100 Finishes
103 In harmony
105 Trig calculations
107 "En ___!"
109 Doesn't move
111 Adhesive
113 Waistband that's tucked in—pity, that!?
115 Thong that's covered with flaws, among other things?
118 Cane
119 "Sleepy Time Gal" songwriter Raymond
120 Befuddled
121 Strikes out
122 Perry Como's "___ Marie"
123 Hanger-on, maybe
124 Worked on a bed
125 Commencement

DOWN

1 Information unit
2 Rude review
3 Elides
4 Turns up
5 Avocations
6 They were once promoted with the slogan "Ivory tips protect your lips"
7 Ta-ta
8 Enigma
9 Final finish?
10 Cup at a diner
11 Kind of daisy
12 Vice ___
13 Japan's capital, formerly
14 Intensified
15 Protective cover that's found in an "Ave Maria" phrase?
16 Table salt, symbolically
17 Governor for whom a North Carolina city is named
19 Ariz. neighbor
23 Look at, in the Bible
25 Barbara of "Mission: Impossible"
27 Holdup
29 Popular fragrance
30 Honolulu's ___ Bowl
32 Old fashioned leggings are in—try for the impossible!?
34 Man with a nice laugh
37 Dirt
39 It might ring your neck
41 Alpine refrains
43 Plays it to the hilt
44 Hither's partner
46 Oafs
47 Dynamic prefix
49 ___ voce
52 Actress Van Doren
55 Raises
57 Former Japanese capital

60 Scraps
62 Homme ___ (statesman)
64 Water boy's task
65 Part of E.O.E.
66 Fencing actions
67 Article on a baby that's snatched up by a news anchor?
68 Early trade union
69 Ebro feeder
70 Geometry ending
72 Made, as cotton candy
73 French noble
76 Tinker's target?
78 Theologian's subj.
79 Thrust
81 Tries for a third trial
82 Pop singer Mann
83 A load
85 Iroquois Indian
87 Precincts
92 Magnetic induction unit
93 Big Florida destination
95 Thomas Gray works
97 Marinara ingredient
101 Lexicographer's concern
102 Gila Valley tribe
104 Doctor's cry
106 City near Salt Lake City
107 Kind of wrap
108 Husband of Gudrun
110 Mobile home?
112 "There ___ tide . . ."
114 In the know
115 Baby's wail
116 Jeans brand
117 Mil. craft

by Cathy Millhauser

ACROSS

1 Redemptions
8 Mitterrand's successor
14 1950's–60's Big Apple mayor
20 Classic ball game
21 Treasure State city
22 Make it
23 Wobbly band members?
25 1960's "Death Valley Days" host
26 Punta del ___, Uruguayan resort
27 911 respondent
28 Done for
29 Apollo loved her
30 Easy ___
32 American Revolutionary leader Deane
34 Visitors from afar
35 Follow
39 Subject of war propaganda
42 Hill, to an Arab
43 It covers ground rapidly
44 Wily style of diplomacy?
47 A little behind
50 Shell thrower
51 Harmony
52 Amazon dangers
54 Curse
56 Land with a queen in Kings
58 Extracts
59 Caesar's farewell
60 Plumbing problem abroad?
62 Member of a force: Abbr.
63 One in swaddles
66 Pentagon concern, for short
68 Rodgers and Hart's "What ___ Man?"
69 Mare's-nest
70 Questionnaire datum
71 Halloween mask?
76 Like New York's Radio City Music Hall, informally
79 Sighter of the Pacific Ocean, 1513
81 Capri, e.g.
82 Reruns, to summer TV
86 Place of legend
88 Position in 20-Across
91 Tarzan's pet
92 Mountain fortresses: Var.
93 Like an Englishman in the desert?
95 Bond rating
96 George W. Bush, as a collegian
98 Quantity
99 Paths of some streams
100 Pool necessity
101 Attention-getters
103 Sea salvage aid
105 Word with car or game
107 Mata Hari was one
110 Hound
111 Together, musically
115 Call for
116 Assault with crepes suzette?
119 Wynn of "Dr. Strangelove"
120 It's west of Sherman Oaks
121 Extraction
122 Attempts
123 Conveyed, in a way
124 Made a record of

DOWN

1 Rights org.
2 Long times in Lima
3 Spinoff group
4 Make artificially better, with "up"
5 Distant
6 Pins down
7 Quite a puzzle
8 Midwest city, familiarly
9 "Shucks"
10 Pelvic parts
11 Realizes
12 Fixed payment
13 Fairy tale locale
14 Some are critical
15 Part
16 Means of communication
17 Ivory or pink?
18 "Dynasty" star
19 Actor Auberjonois
24 Turns, so to speak
30 Modern name for the capital of ancient Galatia
31 Odd, spelled oddly
33 "___ Desire" (1953 Barbara Stanwyck film)
35 They're pressed for cash
36 Exult
37 Bore
38 Musical interval
40 Measurer of brightness
41 Millionaire's toy
43 ___-Ethiopian War, 1935–36
45 Like some surgery
46 "America, the Beautiful" pronoun
48 Constellation with Canopus
49 Some stockings
52 Settles
53 Alternatives to 747's
55 Subject of a composition
57 Relative of Camembert
60 Directions
61 Chaps
63 ___ ghanouj (eggplant dish)
64 Marble
65 What pregnancies produce?
67 Pupil's place
69 They're blue
71 Seattle athlete, for short
72 Actress Blanchett
73 Young zebra
74 Los ___, Calif.
75 ___ Cove ("Murder, She Wrote" locale)
77 Delineate
78 French journal
80 XXV Olympics site
83 Minus
84 Little ending
85 "___ who?"
87 "Gotcha"
89 Hoo-has
90 Power of old films
93 Wright brothers' craft, e.g.
94 Like a well-grounded argument
97 Didn't hesitate
100 Yuletide handouts
101 W.W. II guns
102 Subsequently
104 "Not ___!"
105 Main road
106 Initial
108 Kind of rock
109 Sound
111 Suit to ___
112 Not cheap
113 Press
114 Blue-___
117 Decked
118 USA alternative

by Nancy Nicholson Joline

"HEY, MISTER!"

ACROSS

1 Passage preventers
6 "Excuse me . . ."
10 Become less reserved
14 Bewitched
18 "Tzigane" composer
19 Stiff hairs
21 A whole lot of shaking going on
22 Aglio e ___ (pasta dressing)
23 Short loin products
25 "60 Minutes" regular
27 Not so hot
28 First of "The Chronicles of Clovis"
30 They help you make your goals
31 It goes around the world
34 M.B.A. hopeful's hurdle
35 Pianist Rubinstein
36 Roughed up
37 Superman's gift
39 ___ Cob, Conn.
42 Fell off
43 Kirkstall Abbey locale
44 Defeat by looks
46 Pointed ends
47 Signal to leave, perhaps
48 Not all there
49 "River ___ Return" (Mitchum/Monroe flick)
50 Skittish show?: Abbr.
51 Like old recordings
52 Describe
53 "60 Minutes" regular
54 Like some leaves
56 1972 Bill Withers hit
58 Spiro's predecessor

59 Decisive one
61 Public Citizen founder
62 Dressed down?
63 Dress down
64 Church figure
65 Sneak ___
66 Old peso fractions
67 Architect's offering
68 Southern sibling
69 Computer support, sometimes
72 Piled out
73 Six-Day War hero
75 Some need stitching
76 Use hip boots, perhaps
77 They were big in the past
79 "The ___ Bride" (Rimsky-Korsakov opera)
81 Latin father
82 Kenny G has two
83 F.D.R.'s birthplace
85 It may move you
86 Goodbyes
87 He homered 660 times
88 Needs a ring?
89 Vast
92 Vast
93 "We will ___ undersold!"
94 107-Across state
96 Chemical-free fare
101 Goodbye
102 Peut-___ (maybe, in Marseille)
103 Done for
104 "___ Sea" (Lemmon/Matthau comedy)
105 Hospital staffer
106 Farrah's ex
107 All there
108 People guilty of disorderly conduct?

DOWN

1 Monitor letters
2 You may see a reaction in one
3 Lacto-___ vegetarian
4 Non-Jews
5 Rained hard?
6 Up
7 Consideration
8 Pilot's announcement, briefly
9 Incense
10 For whom the bell tolls
11 Patricia Neal's Best Actress film
12 Zog I, for one
13 Vet's offering
14 "The Kiss" sculptor
15 Shakespeare title starter
16 Painter Mondrian
17 Kiddy litter?
20 Emerson collection
24 Went over the limit
26 Together
29 "Total Request Live" network
31 Signs
32 71-Down's predecessor
33 Numbskulls
34 Luzinski of baseball
35 ___ Magna (annual early-music festival)
37 Prefix with phobia
38 Glucose and fructose, e.g.
39 Gossip-filled gathering, typically
40 They have titles
41 Corral chorus
43 No socialite
45 Not too hard
47 Visit
48 Bar stock
51 Big name in applesauce
52 Enticed

53 Start of something big?
55 Theater area
56 Open
57 Wrap choice
58 Some are false
59 Rub
60 Catch, in a way
62 Hussies
67 Stacks for burning
68 Hide well
70 "Die Fledermaus" maid
71 32-Down's successor
73 Big name in personal planners
74 Gall
75 Grocery line?
76 Generous to a fault
78 Quaint contraction
79 Some have diners
80 Terminal tippees
81 Sand painting creators
84 Hearing aid?
85 Prefix with -morphous
86 Chevy truck model
88 Bakery offering
89 Ocean menace
90 2nd-century date
91 "Zounds!"
92 "The Grey Room" novelist Phillpotts
93 Former Senate Armed Services Committee chairman
95 Shooters' org.
97 It may be taken in spots
98 Siouan speaker
99 Wagering option, briefly
100 Spanish couple?

by Elizabeth C. Gorski

ACROSS

1 Trim
5 Story that may hold secrets
10 Dresses for cooking
15 Arrangement holder
19 "___ to that!"
20 TV executive Arledge
21 Appearance at home?
22 Endangered antelope
23 Outer layer
24 Things that are not appreciated
26 Space between the dotted lines
27 Hardly a cold snap
29 Notice
30 I.C.U. conduits
32 Produce a 130-Across
34 Actress Sorvino
35 From the East
36 Line of thinking
38 Quiet time
43 From an earlier time
46 Important test
48 Do the same as
49 Literary connection
50 Words of caution
54 ___ Day (Wednesday)
57 Portoferraio's island
58 "Death in Venice" author
59 Register
61 Like the Owl and Pussycat's boat
63 They're not me or you
66 Take a break
68 Govt. loan org.
69 Entices potential dieters
76 Go (for)
77 Upstate New York's ___ Lake
78 Calder Trophy awarder
79 Part of some facials
84 Complicated situations
86 Tennis's Nastase
87 Thunderbird enthusiast?
88 Unappetizing food
90 In succession
93 Flooded
95 They're fourth on the way up
97 Makeup artist's problem
98 Watered down
99 When many people get to work
104 Hebrews' first high priest
106 Say without thinking
107 Splitter who makes splinters?
109 Departed quickly
113 Can opener
116 Secure
118 Kind of smell
119 Actor Andrew
120 Popular activity for dogs
123 Built for speed
124 One and only
125 Big name at Notre Dame
126 Exquisitely wrought trinket
127 Car wash supply
128 A big person may come down with it
129 Round of four
130 Disturbing noise
131 Gut feeling?

DOWN

1 He left Oenone for Helen
2 Lady friend in Italy
3 Keep getting
4 Ultimate object
5 Musical run
6 See 70-Down
7 Despicable sort
8 How some legal proceedings are conducted
9 FleetCenter player
10 Italian tourist attraction
11 No. on a certain table
12 Result of a productive 21-Across
13 Coffee go-with
14 Wonder who?
15 Do work on the house
16 U.A.E. center
17 Since then, in song
18 Extinguished flames?
25 Some transfusions
28 Cartoon dog
31 News agency name
33 ___ cavity
35 Enjoyed to the max
37 Spotted
39 Ticket abbr.
40 Eye
41 Sticks figure
42 Ignoble
43 He played Castillo on "Miami Vice"
44 Reluctant
45 Singer with the Aliis
47 Musically connected
51 Understood
52 Chekhov and others
53 Peppery
55 It breathes
56 Blue Ribbon makers
60 Unwelcome one
62 Wound
64 Reply
65 Those seeking intelligence
67 Victims of an October 1998 sweep
70 6-Down's partner
71 Designer Picasso
72 Prince or princess
73 Not at full power
74 Complaint
75 Reason to use wipers
79 Kind of song
80 Nocturnal bird
81 "Back ___ hour" (shop sign)
82 Like some seats in a stadium
83 Diet
85 It may have a head
89 What's expected
91 Scolding
92 Destroy slowly
94 Suspension
96 Positions
100 They're not to be believed
101 Polished
102 Trading place: Abbr.
103 Conditions, in a way
105 Choice for travelers to New York
108 It's in the bag
110 Three quarters of the earth, basically
111 Macy's showcase?
112 "Mending Wall" poet
113 Attention getter
114 Concerned expression
115 Knockout
116 Spot of Italian wine
117 1990 World Series M.V.P. Jose
121 Coke's partner
122 Easter's beginning

by Joe DiPietro

ACROSS

1 Lead sharer
7 They're fare-minded
11 Farm call
15 Appointments approved by the Sen.
19 Like federal tax laws?
20 Therapeutic plant
21 Rolling rock?
22 Title role for Jodie Foster
23 "Don't mess with the Hurricanes!," e.g.?
25 Analogous
26 So
27 Capitol figure
28 Site for bells
29 Underhanded bum
30 Frigid
31 Select
33 "Howdy, ma'am," e.g.?
36 Area away from the battle
37 Tender spot?
38 Peanut product
39 Word of support
40 Dangerous answer to a sentry
41 "__ Plenty o' Nuttin'"
43 Clash of clans
46 Laertes' T's
48 Problem at exclusive schools?
55 Tanker troubles
56 Southern vacation spot
57 1920's tax evader
58 Talk up?
59 Cheats
62 Element used in electroplating
66 One from Wittenberg
67 Taking in calves?
71 Gene stuff
72 Makes a fuss
74 Fink on
75 Pinion's partner

76 They're out of this world
79 Revival technique
80 Peerless
82 Not take tailoring seriously?
87 Grouch
88 Pacific repast
89 Opening time, maybe
90 Actress __ Dawn Chong
91 Bagel topper
94 Home of "Friends"
96 Summons: Abbr.
97 Like some shows
101 Water-carrier's motto?
106 Outlet
107 Try it!
108 Started smoking
109 Give the cook a break, maybe
111 1967 N.H.L. Rookie of the Year
112 Words from a nonfolder
113 __ breve (2/2 time, in music)
114 Female improv?
116 Be a stool pigeon
117 Regan's father
118 Chancel wear
119 Slob's napkin
120 Hardly beauty queens
121 Like some D.A.'s
122 Silence of the staff
123 Furnish

DOWN

1 Tent tenant
2 Colorful percher
3 Reagan Supreme Court nominee
4 Lassie's lid
5 Sambuca flavoring
6 Concrete
7 Expensive spread
8 Get straight
9 "N.Y.P.D. Blue" creator
10 "Told ya!"

11 White-bread
12 Cleaned up after a fall
13 Flier's home
14 Winner of 1865
15 They're not pros
16 Forgiving
17 Prude
18 Vehicle drawn by draft animals
24 Purges, in a way
29 "The Crucible" setting
32 In a well-kept way
34 Player of the Four Aces
35 Audited
37 Push (around)
42 Gerard of "Soldier's Fortune"
44 Lines at a checkout?: Abbr.
45 1949 film classic
47 Under cover, perhaps
48 "The sweet small clumsy feet of __": E. E. Cummings
49 1957 #1 song
50 Camaro model
51 Farm call
52 Baseball's Garciaparra
53 Nautical pole
54 London area
55 Some writers work on it
59 Mathematical subgroup
60 "The Conspiracy Against Childhood" writer LeShan
61 Tally mark
63 Gulf war loser
64 Like raw diamonds
65 Approach, with "for"
67 Like a good mixer
68 Speaker of baseball
69 John or Paul but not George or Ringo

70 Gang land
73 Goya's naked lady
75 Least scarce
77 Chiefs' org.
78 Franc fraction
80 Part of C.P.U.
81 Tours turndown
82 Ivory tower, maybe
83 Having night vision?
84 Incurred
85 Big horn
86 Accord
90 Salad slice
92 "Wowie zowie!"
93 Creepy cases
95 Spicy, in a way
96 Getting the most "aws"
98 Traveled (along)
99 Hit the big time
100 Baby grub producer
102 Big bang producers
103 Booster rocket
104 0.946 liter
105 Poets' feet
106 Old hat
110 The Beatles' "Back in the __"
114 Area of Mars
115 Place to put one's feet up

by Nancy Salomon and Harvey Estes

47 STARTING COSTS

ACROSS

1 1983 film comedy with Bill Maher
6 Lovelies
11 Arguments
19 Now, in Nogales
20 Old drugstore name
21 Equivalent
22 Bona fide
23 Mother in "The Glass Menagerie"
24 Sawbucks
25 Subject of "The Haj"
26 Warehouse function, maybe
28 ___ T
29 Old-time actress Frances
30 With the situation thus
32 Popular fruit drink
33 Wine additive
34 Starting points
36 South Dakota
40 Female donkeys
41 "Haystacks" painter
42 However, briefly
43 They usually have yellow centers
44 Start of a count
45 Mine carrier
49 Edits
50 In toto
51 Tall, skinny guy
52 Turns
53 ___ Maples Trump
54 Washington's Sen. ___ Gorton
55 Bad start?
56 Things to chew on
57 Neighborhood convenience
59 ___-American
60 Computer add-on?
61 Items hit with hammers
62 Actor Keach
63 Plant pore
64 Maker of NBA Pro and NFL Blitz
66 Baby carrier
67 Showy
68 Pause for cold warriors
69 Bubbler
70 Migrating geese
71 Kind of chart
72 Displaying 5-Down
73 First in courage
74 They have panels
78 Least dull
79 Fruitless
80 Kayoed
81 Sports shoes, informally
82 Galoot
85 Zilch
86 It's not preferred
90 Valet employer
92 Drop off
94 Get ready to bite
95 "Lord, ___?"
96 Weaken
97 Payton of football
98 Faint dead away
99 Is unwilling to risk
100 Playing cards
101 "Crime and Punishment" heroine

DOWN

1 Florentine art treasure
2 Take after
3 This rises by degrees
4 Air on stage
5 Boor's trait
6 Bumps
7 Wood sorrel
8 Domain
9 Some legal scholars, for short
10 Blind feature
11 Certain missile
12 Like Beckett's "Endgame"
13 "The Big Heat" director
14 Apart from this
15 Challenge for a barber
16 "Who Do ___ Kill?" (1992 movie)
17 Skedaddle
18 Halvah ingredient
20 They think they're superior
27 "Indeed"
31 Mediums
33 Early jazz composition
35 Puts down, in a way
36 Men's fashion accessories
37 Just
38 On-line brokerage
39 "Come back, ___" (western line)
40 Shutter
41 Director Louis
44 They're measured by degrees
45 Not dry
46 Rest stop amenity
47 Chicken Little, for one
48 Post-firing task
49 Lift off
50 Best Picture nominee of 1996
51 Urban area
53 Matisse's world
54 Word on many a button
57 "Les Trois Mousquetaires" and others
58 Bit of rubble
59 Deals with guilt
61 Photo finish?
63 The Amistad and others
65 Unenthusiastic
66 Extra horsepower, in slang
67 Open
69 Popular corn chip
70 Swell
72 English tidbit
73 Calvin Coolidge's estate, with "The"
74 Aslope
75 Writer Fallaci
76 Dairy machine
77 Kind of vine
78 Problematic
81 Commemorative marker
83 Of no importance
84 Henry's tutee
86 Cleveland cagers
87 Son of Judah
88 Abbr. on a food label
89 Brand
91 Northerner's home
93 Before, of yore

by Manny Nosowsky

BEFORE AND AFTER

ACROSS

1 ___ Beds National Monument, Calif.
5 Difficult billiards shot
10 What "p" may stand for
15 Org. with eligibility rules
19 Sale sign
20 John of song
21 Drink
22 Pequod captain
23 SIDESTEP ___ WATERFALL
25 WATERFALL ___ BOOK CLUB
27 Shark shooter
28 Big name in stationery
30 Stock figures
31 Oats, e.g.
32 Putdown
33 Places for taps
34 Nourish
37 Achilles, e.g.
39 One with a fastball?
40 Pale
41 BOOK CLUB ___ ROOM SERVICE
43 Eliminate
46 ". . . like ___ not!"
47 Decant
48 Set
49 Subterfuge
50 Steer
51 ROOM SERVICE ___ TRICK KNEE
55 Reserve
56 Hedgerow tree
58 Gardner and others
59 Got an eyeful
60 O. Henry specialty
61 Earth Summit site
62 Place to get a burger
63 Nibble
65 Dispatch boat
67 It crosses the nave
70 Some German exports
71 TRICK KNEE ___ DRY CLEAN
73 Go out
74 Scads
75 Tough
77 Push
78 Gossipy Barrett
79 "On the double!"
80 DRY CLEAN ___ ORDER FORM
84 Polish name rarity?
85 Part of an accusation
87 Puts down
88 Plumbs the depths
89 Extremists
92 Sticks around a game parlor
93 Breathing space
94 As originally found
95 Cries of agreement
97 Handouts
101 ORDER FORM ___ LINE DANCE
103 LINE DANCE ___ TIME MACHINE
105 Tribe in Manitoba
106 Place for the highborn?
107 Go back to square one
108 Singer Tennille
109 Commuter plane trips
110 Center of French resistance in W.W. II
111 Gathered (in)
112 Woman's name suffix

DOWN

1 Certain dogs, for short
2 "Pronto!"
3 Number two
4 Show concern for
5 Two-to-one?
6 One way to read
7 Bowl over
8 Junior, e.g.
9 Makes beloved
10 Letter holder
11 Parrot
12 Like some colors
13 Park Avenue, for one
14 Intermission
15 Gab
16 Carolers
17 1973 Masters winner Tommy
18 Infernal regions
24 European liberal
26 Reliever's goal
29 "The ___ of English Poesie"
32 Market town
33 What to do
34 "The evidence of things not seen": Hebrews 11:1
35 Port city of ancient Rome
36 TIME MACHINE ___ SEAT BELT
37 Lament
38 Payola, e.g.
41 Long in the tooth
42 St. Louis's historic ___ Bridge
43 SEAT BELT ___ SIDESTEP
44 1975 Wimbledon champ
45 Kind of instrument
47 Get on the horn
49 "Lady Love" singer
51 They may get a licking
52 Spooky
53 To the point
54 Reserved
55 Queeg's command
57 Get in shape
59 Nick
62 System of shorthand
63 "The Godfather" actor
64 Not manual
65 Fusses
66 Lets off steam
67 Shorebirds
68 Missed, with "for"
69 Shades of blue
72 Torpedoes
75 Like the "ch" in Bach
76 Composer's pride
78 It's played against the house
81 Goes along
82 Word that's an example of itself
83 Bedroom fixture
84 River to the Rybinsk Reservoir
85 In groups
86 Package carrier
88 Cruised the Net
89 Nada
90 January in Guadalajara
91 "It's ___ in the right direction"
93 Boo-boo
95 Prefix with photo
96 Cardinal
97 Boater's worry
98 Pellets
99 In rapture
100 Classic railroad name
102 "Whaddaya know!"
104 "La la" preceder

by Greg Staples

ACROSS

1 Shook, maybe
6 Quarrel
11 Animal that has kittens
16 Litterae or poetica
19 Impersonations
20 Sky box locale
21 Fish may be kept in it
22 Lovey
23 Soave ___
24 Lethargy
25 1989 Al Pacino movie
27 Trumpeter Red
28 Gang types
29 Director Reiner
30 "Understood!"
31 Roguish
32 Grandchild of Japanese immigrants
33 Tony-winning Hagen
34 13th-century invader
35 People to hang out with
38 Former U.S. Open site
41 Stable sounds
42 Went to the top
44 Relieves
45 Like some pond life
47 Bygone New York newspaper
48 Brave
49 Sitting room?
51 "Uncle Tom's Cabin" girl
52 "Shoulda, woulda, coulda" thinker
54 Soccer star Hamm
57 Chat room abbr.
58 Goes (for)
61 Dark
63 Passbook entry: Abbr.

64 N.H.L. conference div.
65 It's good when they're extended
67 Broadcasting inits. since 1970
68 Number after cinque
69 Cause of some skids
70 Get rid of
71 Calendar abbr.
72 Quick scores?
73 "Dear" ones
74 Many a state name in D.C.
75 Dyes
77 Muffin ingredient
79 Sky boxes, perhaps
81 It's for the birds
82 Thin as ___
84 Keyboard key
86 Arrived
88 Wizard's home
90 Like some covers
93 Desires
94 Mythical bird
95 Hard roll?
98 "___ Had It" (1959 hit)
99 D.C. regulators
100 "___ Breckinridge"
101 Flutist's embellishment
102 Gluts
104 Numskulls
106 Rugged ridge
107 Trust fund babies, often
108 Titus, e.g.: Abbr.
109 Cuts corners?
110 Something to read word for word?
111 Began
112 River to the Irish Sea
113 Certain Oldsmobile
114 They can hold water
115 Practices

DOWN

1 Ohio River tributary
2 Artemis's twin
3 "Witness" co-star
4 ___ Stanley Gardner
5 Actress Cannon
6 Runway moves
7 Sings "Rock-a-Bye Baby"
8 Tow truck attachments
9 It's positive
10 Wagner's final work
11 Eclipse
12 Like stainproof fabric
13 They're fit for a princess
14 Organic compound
15 One who cries foul?
16 Last Supper guest
17 Lets on
18 Bull market necessities?
26 Be a go-between
32 Pacifier
34 Where, to a whaler?
36 Carrier at J.F.K.
37 Matadors' duds
39 Run-of-the-mill: Abbr.
40 Most overcome
42 Reds
43 Big name in brushwork
45 "Finally!"
46 Made "moonlight requisitions"
47 "ER" doctor played by Laura Innes
48 Where cows are sacred
50 Is a blabbermouth
52 Steamroll
53 Sam and Ben

54 There's no use in this
55 Does data work
56 Napping
59 Marketing device
60 Iberian Mrs.
62 Marathon mementos
66 Fall off
76 "___ cannot be!"
77 Something screwdrivers can help make
78 Small estuaries
79 Krazy ___
80 Negative reaction
82 1998 song by Rebecca Blake
83 Mold anew
84 Harsh critic
85 "Three Musicians" artist
86 They're boring
87 ". . . ___ quit!"
88 Skipped out, in a way
89 Common refrigerant
90 Bumble
91 Loath
92 Good news from lenders
96 Traffic light feature
97 Feudal lord
100 Kind of call
102 Bygone leader
103 Sleekly designed
105 Abbr. often appearing above percentages

by Elizabeth C. Gorski

50 TRAM TOUR

ACROSS

1 They're stuffed in delis
6 Train
11 Kids' game
19 Jiggers?
20 Uncertain
21 Like pigs' feet
22 Julia Roberts/Hugh Grant film
24 Best-selling 1969 album
25 Willa Cather heroine
26 John, Paul and George: Abbr.
27 Part of U.N.L.V.
28 Like 47-Down's bubbles
29 Kay Kyser's "___ Reveille"
30 He was Plato in "Rebel Without a Cause"
31 Emphatic type: Abbr.
33 Electrify
35 Sneaks one past
37 Radar gun wielder
39 Where Eliza Doolittle met Henry Higgins
45 Imagined
48 Dispositions
49 Have ___ at
50 Marmalade-loving bear
54 Rama VII's domain
55 Gastronomic capital of France
56 ___ artery
57 At another time
59 Split
61 Refreshment stands
63 Köln's river
65 ___ four
66 Organ with a drum in it
67 Theme of this puzzle
70 ___ Mochis, Mexico
73 Restaurant stack
74 Sinner's motivator?
75 "Fiddler on the Roof" setting
77 Eyeballed
80 Adventure
81 Sound
82 Felt bad about
83 Counterfeiters' nemeses
86 "Upstairs, Downstairs" setting
89 "Fables in Slang" author
90 Semi drivers?
93 Hardly hardworking
94 Coarsely abusive language
97 Censor's subject
98 Spot for a parade
102 Nev. neighbor
103 Tel ___-Jaffa
104 Not in the strike zone, maybe
106 Jeff Lynne's grp.
107 Exemplar of grace
110 Tire trapper
112 Change pocket
114 Capacitates
116 "___ Blues" (1924 Paul Whiteman hit)
119 British press, figuratively
121 Like some discussions
122 Party, e.g.
123 Needing kneading?
124 Certain bike
125 Friday's creator
126 Full

DOWN

1 It's hung and beaten
2 Unexpected, in a way
3 Jot
4 Re
5 They may need guards
6 Come too
7 Shakespearean ending
8 Tag line
9 Bird, once
10 One-named fashion designer
11 Sunscreen ingredient
12 Finance workers, for short
13 One up, e.g.
14 In-case connector
15 SALT II signer
16 Yours, in Tours
17 New Jersey's ___ University
18 Countercurrent
21 Polo clubs
23 Pellagra preventer
32 She married Mickey
33 Fellow students, e.g.
34 Breathed
36 They're kept behind bars
38 Hoisting devices?
40 "Mahalo ___ loa" ("Thank you very much," in Maui)
41 Go places
42 Harry Belafonte song phrase
43 Swelled heads
44 What one little piggy had
46 Like pigs' feet
47 Island entertainer
50 Peak discoverer
51 Inter ___
52 French Christian
53 Incessantly
55 Decision-making method
58 "The Nanny" butler
60 Fender benders, e.g.
62 Short composition
64 Star bursts
65 Chefs aim to please them
68 Mace source
69 Post-delivery handout
70 Mother of Helen
71 Of the 66-Across
72 ___-eyed
73 Kind of student
76 University of ___ (the Golden Hurricane)
77 Excite, slangily
78 Quattro or Cabriolet
79 Striptease
84 Track challenge
85 Reversed
87 High-cholesterol concoction
88 Former first family
90 Pulled off
91 John
92 Didn't tip
95 Department store section
96 Develop
99 Soften
100 Comic John
101 Made introductions, maybe
105 Power statistic
107 Place on the schedule
108 Film editing effect
109 Grace period?
110 Ill-bred
111 Reconditioned, e.g.
113 Kick
115 Spanish tar
117 Drillmaster's word
118 Murder ___
120 Bowie collaborator

by Nancy Nicholson Joline

ACROSS

1 Tempted a traffic cop
5 It may be dismissed
10 Conk
13 Musical treasure
18 "___ Simple Man" (#1 Ricky Van Shelton song)
19 Graceful girls
21 Drop the ball
22 Started a line?
23 Completely
25 Flipper's question
27 Come to
28 Like a gull
29 Dieter's concern
30 Pathetic poetry
32 Big part
34 Like some vows
37 Chafe at
38 ___ Wars (Caesarean campaigns)
40 Jay follower
41 Eastern way
43 Jay preceder
44 Kind of limit
45 "Let's Fall in Love" songwriter
47 Part of some film reviews
48 Coll. major
51 Not up
52 Not hot
53 Who might be to blame
54 On the safe side
58 Pro ___
59 She won five Emmys for her sitcom title role
60 Kind of idol
61 Like angel food cake
63 Wide-eyed
64 Where fans may be found
65 Displayed ostentatiously
66 Like Zeppo, among the Marx Brothers
69 Operator's accessory
70 Smashes from Sampras
71 Downright
72 Outlooks
74 Freebie
75 Directly confront
76 Composer Arensky
77 Depth charge targets
78 Refuse transporter
81 Véronique, e.g.: Abbr.
82 Read lines, in a way
83 Computer choice
84 Shipping way option
85 Decay
88 Billy Budd, for one
89 Inn stock
90 Dropping off the dry cleaning, e.g.
92 It may have a string attached
96 Makeshift
99 Doesn't just tear up
100 Hack's question
101 Guffawed
103 Stood
105 Barbershop figure
106 Stadium special
109 110-Down, e.g.
111 Use
112 Time before
113 "Planet of the Apes" savages
114 "Behold!"
115 Bookstore category
116 Drops on blades
117 Just know
118 Owner's acquisition

DOWN

1 Kitchen gizmo
2 Let out of the can?
3 Overdoes it onstage
4 Like some returned goods
5 Winter hrs. in Wichita
6 French silk center
7 A, in communications
8 Fruitery problem
9 Moved the earth
10 Executes, in a way
11 Sci-fi writer ___ Scott Card
12 Put out
13 Penetrating
14 Hurricane home
15 He left Maria for Jackie
16 Address book abbr.
17 Some cards and tags
20 Pocket
24 Kiosk eye-catcher
26 Mature
31 When Paris is burning
33 Resort near Waikiki
35 Quarreling
36 "Moonlight Gambler" singer
38 It's a gift
39 Exhibits fear, in a way
42 Court contest
46 Bridges in movies
47 Expensive band
48 Some are slippery
49 Straight, at the bar
50 Begin before the others
51 Cannon attachment
53 Undo
55 R. J. Reynolds brand
56 Like 73-Down
57 They're found in scores
58 "Wild" ones
59 Dress down
61 Like sinners, to preachers
62 Iron-fisted ones?
65 Easy out, perhaps
67 Part of a jukebox
68 ___ and Wear (English county)
71 Grp. that gets the shaft?
72 Sweeping
73 Pachacuti's people
77 Initiated
78 Risqué
79 Clear dish
80 Like some lots
83 Tank buildup
85 Third person ending of old
86 Root crop
87 Uncapped?
89 Slayer of Python, in myth
91 Motel inhabitant?
93 "No fighting, please"
94 This second
95 Didn't just snack
97 Go around the world
98 Sore spot
100 Makes independent, in a way
102 Pulled out a piece
104 Go over
106 "Doo" follower
107 Ab ___ (from the start)
108 Sit-down strikers of 1937: Abbr.
110 Memphis-to-Biloxi dir.

by Harvey Estes

ACROSS

1 Director's order
7 Bench item
11 Rough projections
16 They go to market
21 Dove's discovery, once
22 Start of a Jimmy Durante song
23 Black-and-white outfit
24 Popular invitees
25 President of the Lunar Society?
27 It might be tempting
28 Trattoria topping
29 It has a spot on it
30 "What's this!"
31 President of Misers of America?
34 Poet Teasdale
36 Like certain talk shows
38 Harass
39 "What did I tell you?"
40 Paris's rival
43 Big galoots
45 Mistake follower, at times
47 President of the Bakers' Union?
53 Beer belly
55 Shooting star, maybe
59 Wool derivative
60 Skip past
61 Majorette's motion
63 Hitchhike
64 Silver Springs neighbor
65 President of the Mapmakers' Group?
68 Journalist Whitelaw ___
69 "To your health!"
71 Model T alternatives
72 Coloring
73 Product placements

74 Montana tribe
75 Lets off some steam
77 Abominates
79 President of the One-Member Association?
83 Bottom of a chest
86 Disgusted
87 Alexander, e.g.
88 Sci-fi danger
91 Betelgeuse's setting
92 ". . . ___ short pier!"
93 Meets defiantly
95 It's in vein
96 President of Truck Part Manufacturers, Inc.?
101 Conductor Boulanger
102 Actress Swenson
103 Virgil creation
104 Modern ice cream flavor
105 More circumspect
107 Singer Redbone
108 Put the kibosh on
109 President of the Foundation for Religious Heroism?
112 Brut alternative
114 Z ___ zebra
115 Snockered
116 Bathroom installation
119 Cornerback Sanders
122 Notes
126 They're uneven
130 President of the Screen Actors Guild?
133 Self expression?
136 Turn into confetti
137 "Crime does not pay," e.g.
138 Female demon
139 President of Quitters International?
142 Gamut

143 "My stars!"
144 Qabus bin Said's land
145 Sudden pain
146 "The Rape of the Lock" concern
147 Cyclades Island
148 Payoffs
149 "You don't say!"

DOWN

1 Foreign dignitaries
2 Susan Lucci's character
3 Circus employee
4 Magazine article?
5 Lay flat
6 Delineate
7 Itinerary word
8 Bisected
9 It's all wound up
10 "Guitar Town" singer Steve
11 Restrain, in a way
12 ___ avis
13 They cause blowups
14 Two-inch putt, e.g.
15 Suppresses one's wanderlust
16 "White rump," In Shawnee
17 Novelist Waugh
18 Cautious person's concerns
19 First name in cosmetics
20 Winter warmer
26 Entice
32 Adam's first wife, in Jewish lore
33 Crunch maker
35 Historian Toynbee
37 Darlin'
41 Kan. borderer
42 Year in Edward the Confessor's reign
44 Card sentiment, sometimes
46 Less sophisticated
47 "La Traviata" mezzo

48 Fought the clock
49 "Henry & June" character
50 Grid parts
51 Issue
52 Pack item, for short
53 Slapstick projectiles
54 Eight-time Norris Trophy winner
56 Looks
57 It's handed down
58 Groups of spies
62 A question of possession
65 Stewart's role in "Harvey"
66 Company
67 Social swimmer
69 Smoking or non, e.g.: Abbr.
70 It's over your head
74 Hutch contents
75 Moth repellent
76 Big 10 sch.
77 Catch some Z's
78 Fraternity row characters
79 Frequent Rose Bowl team
80 Refuse
81 Shoots again
82 They sometimes flash "12:00"
83 Shell competitor
84 Tony-winner Worth
85 Coward, in Aussie slang
88 "The Age of Bronze" sculptor
89 It may be bid
90 Long
92 Jet black
93 Vier preceder
94 In the near future
95 Neville Brand western
97 Onion chopper, e.g.
98 Name in Ugandan history
99 "Good boy" of rhyme

by Trip Payne

100 Scrap
101 Narthex end
105 Kind of center
106 Discovery I computer
110 Cold front, e.g.
111 ___ choy
113 "My Cup Runneth Over" singer

114 Brute
116 Sting
117 "Toy Story" animation company
118 Dress type
120 Went nowhere
121 Old enough
123 Magic amulets

124 Enterprise rival
125 Fix a chart
127 Dreary sound
128 Dreary sound
129 Photographer's choice
131 Roleo needs
132 Open-air swimming pool

134 Naysayer
135 Cut
140 Dash measures
141 Day or way preceder

ACROSS

1 Keel attachment
5 Crowd features
10 "A Jug of Wine, a Loaf of Bread—and Thou" poet
14 Needed to say "Oops"
19 Member of the chorus
20 Coffee allure
21 Dear, in Italy
22 Unknowing
23 1974 Stylistics hit
27 Leave the union
28 Spin
29 Inasmuch (as)
30 Josh
31 Stylist Vidal
34 Heart locations
36 Flap
38 "The Drew Carey Show" setting
39 Part of a front-end alignment
41 Bar selections
43 Make, as a putt
45 Ask, as for aid
48 Cat scanners
49 "___ pal . . ."
50 Singled out as important
52 Slave's response
54 Attention grabbers
56 Words with hole or all
57 Sends
60 "Cleopatra" director
62 It's gender
64 Like an expired parking meter
65 Advice for a rejectee, maybe
66 Standard & ___
68 "La Vita Nuova" poet
69 Down
72 Up
75 Zodiac symbol
80 Dutch artist Jan

81 Batman and Superman, to villains
83 Not stand on ceremony?
84 Asian palm
85 Entanglement
86 Ancient region of France
88 ___ Maria
89 Search
91 Envoy
94 Year Dryden died
95 Mr. Pecksniff of "Martin Chuzzlewit"
97 Blabs, when doubled
99 On the job
100 Language suffix
101 Month before Adar
103 Last
106 Joker
108 Masters
110 Street with stores, usually
111 Dictatorial sort
114 1977 Foreigner hit
119 Crucifix spots
120 Kind of organ or dream
121 Unelected group
122 Catalog card abbr.
123 Mess up
124 Box with headgear
125 Take out or in
126 Physics unit

DOWN

1 Giants' retired number 24
2 Emollient
3 1960 Elvis Presley hit
4 Marisa of "My Cousin Vinny"
5 Faux
6 "You ___ here"
7 Dot follower
8 The Sage of Concord

9 They may be cracked
10 Cat with a banded tail
11 ___ du pays (homesickness)
12 Wall St. pros
13 Baked dish
14 A Cosby
15 Pennsylvania home of TV Guide
16 1979 Anita Ward hit
17 She raised Cain
18 Morning glory?
24 Stick (on)
25 Classified ad abbr.
26 Time without end
31 Divert
32 Kind of pump
33 Observatory observations
35 Decorous
36 Welcome warmly
37 Compound with two double bonds
38 Indian near the Platte
40 Fabric suffix
42 MS. inclusion
44 Man hiding a cape
46 Weekly cry
47 Heraldic border
51 Like some fishing
53 Passé
54 ___ law (physics formula)
55 Not passé
58 Former British Foreign Secretary Douglas
59 Workers in white, for short
60 Scout group
61 "Do I dare to ___ peach?"
63 Architect Mies van der ___
65 "Big Mouth" Martha
67 "Star-Spangled Banner" word

68 Baseball twin-killings: Abbr.
69 High spots
70 1958 Jerry Lee Lewis hit
71 Bravo competitor
72 Half a brayin'
73 City near the Caspian Sea
74 ___ Le Pew
76 Shut (up)
77 1956 Perry Como hit
78 These have many extras
79 Ken
80 Wine-making equipment
81 Figures ending many prices
82 "Socrate" composer
85 Topper
87 Reason for a third serve
89 Entangle
90 Plants with aromatic oils
92 Lucrative
93 It goes off-road: Abbr.
96 Followed obediently
98 Historic Fort ___
102 Certain opera singer
104 Good cheer
105 53-Down, to Juanita
106 1999 Pulitzer Prize-winning play
107 Chipped in
109 Deejay's worry
111 Peter, e.g.
112 Land on the Strait of Hormuz
113 Take-out sign
114 Rels.
115 Prefix with center
116 Standards issuer, briefly
117 I.R.A. increaser
118 A.A.A. suggestion

by Bill Zais

ACROSS

1 Warm over
7 Alexander ___, real-life prototype of Robinson Crusoe
14 Lay away
19 Verdi opera
20 Trample
21 Mount that last erupted in 1786
22 Baby bottle
23 "The Snake Pit" director Litvak
24 First name in TV talk
25 Smog?
27 Betty Crocker?
29 Knuckleballer ___ Wilhelm
30 13-Down source
31 Bad thing to blow
32 Contents of some sacs
35 Patient's woe
39 Freelancer's encl.
41 Alarm time, for some
44 Repair the spine of
45 Plague
46 Not merely paying attention
50 Stock exchange figures
52 Grizzly remains?
55 It's moved in limbo
56 1975 title role for Isabelle Adjani
57 Unlike a klutz
58 Support the Salvation Army
60 Nevil Shute's "___ Like Alice"
63 They have the best seats in the house
65 Approach bedtime
66 Horse?
71 Lobster festival?
73 "Tiny Alice" playwright
74 Feminist Eleanor
76 Constellation next to Scorpio

77 Prayer book
79 Supreme Court justices, e.g.
82 Grateful Dead leader
86 Printemps follower
87 Troubadour's trouble?
89 Some racers
90 Nick
92 Marais ___ Cygnes (Kansas river)
93 Drill directive
95 Like Serling stories
96 Archer of myth
98 Flooring it
100 E.R. pronouncement
101 1877 Manet painting
103 "Must be something ___"
106 Have ___ (freak out)
108 Aerobics exercise?
110 Spice rack?
117 Reduced
118 Off base, perhaps
120 Rub
121 Made purely academic
122 Shea Stadium players of 1965
123 Decorate differently
124 Moore's TV boss
125 "With Reagan: The Inside Story" memoirist
126 Compact

DOWN

1 First name in gossip
2 Needle holder
3 What a Hamburger may be called
4 Designer Peretti
5 Beth preceder
6 Lethargy
7 Shake up
8 Sea bird
9 Like some meat

10 "The Greatest American Hero" star
11 Liz said it often
12 Virginia colonist John
13 Slow ring
14 Some are animated
15 Port on the Strait of Gibraltar
16 On the move
17 Firewood measure
18 Repository of fame?
21 Texas sch.
26 Australia's ___ Rock
28 Johnson's "Hellzapoppin'" co-star
30 Crash site?
32 Tasmania's highest peak
33 Got in the game
34 Wheel turner
36 Title for some bishops
37 Skewbald
38 Setter's warning
40 Got rid of, in a way
42 What a family film is appropriate for
43 Track-and-field official?
45 Elect
47 Go down
48 Church plate
49 16th-century council site
51 Pythagorean P's
53 Aqueduct Racetrack, familiarly
54 Heel?
59 Its capital is Pamplona
61 Walked the earth
62 '69 Series winners
64 ___-Cat
66 Having a label
67 High class
68 "Rosmersholm" playwright

69 Counting-out rhyme starter
70 Went long
72 Cartesian adverb
75 Island of W.W. II fighting
78 Italian beach resort
80 Side by side?
81 Puddin'
83 Firewood measure
84 Personal prefix
85 Not docked
88 Equip anew
89 For this reason
91 Chemical salt in some inks
94 Like Anna's students
97 "The Executioner's Song" author
99 Racer, of a sort
101 The Ten Commandments, in large part
102 Illegal firing
104 Brick type
105 Strengthened, with "up"
107 Artist Max
108 Site of a 1929 exhibition by 107-Down
109 Adventure writer Buntline
110 Head for the Riviera?
111 Well
112 "Memphis" director Simoneau
113 Romain de Tirtoff, familiarly
114 Phrase starter
115 Work on People
116 ___ Martin Cognac
119 Make tracks

by Richard Hughes

ACROSS

1 Encourages
7 Bit of filming
11 Be in harmony
15 Islamic leader
19 Rio Grande city
20 Director Kazan
21 "Fee, fi, fo, fum" caller
22 Rider's handhold
23 So-called devil's darning needles [2000]
25 Beer-and-cider drink [2001]
27 General concern
28 Numerous
30 Like some modern communities
31 Fourth Spanish letter
33 Part of an old-fashioned pinup
34 Bedim
35 Based on the number six
36 Western [2002]
40 Diploma [2003]
42 Spiny sea creature
43 Profs.' helpers
44 Root problem?
45 Language group that includes Yucatec
46 Title for a young Madrileña: Abbr.
47 Like home plate
49 New Balance competitor
53 Oration station
54 Jungle gym [2004]
56 John Wayne's "True Grit" role [2005]
63 "Death of ___" (1793 David painting)
64 ___ Park (Chicago suburb)
65 Latin I word
66 Clay mineral
68 "Be ___ . . ."
69 Selfish person [2006]
73 Risky purchase [2007]
76 Uncanny: Var.
77 Penn name
78 Short street of converted stables
79 Hefty competitor
80 They cause lost bonuses
85 Raises
86 Poetic contraction
87 Label for many a photo
88 1960's TV war drama, with "The" [2008]
94 Robust winter appetizer [2009]
96 Charts again
97 Eat like ___
99 Form letters
100 Part of a musical gig
101 Like ballerinas
102 Like flour
103 Christmas, in the Vatican
106 Orange-and-black perennial [2010]
108 Foolish [2011]
112 ___ a good thing
113 Away from the wind
114 Big Twelve Conference city
115 Cantankerous
116 Tobacco-curing chamber
117 Elizabeth Taylor's third
118 Nap sacks
119 Dark suit

DOWN

1 Antiquity
2 Long-jawed fish
3 New York City park
4 Plant with bell-shaped flowers
5 Nitrogen's lack
6 A regular one has internal angles of 140 degrees
7 Of the science of data transmission
8 Pop singer Tatyana
9 Butcher shop offering
10 Drawing support
11 Biblical king who abolished idolatry
12 Tune out
13 It's removed from white rice
14 Hair-raising cry
15 Protect with a dike
16 It may come with a small umbrella
17 Hospital worker
18 Like the sound of oboes
24 To-do
26 Discharge
29 Some appliances
31 Bud
32 Bar mitzvah highlight
35 Seed
37 Nonsense syllable in a doo-wop song
38 Berlin article
39 "Midnight Cowboy" role
41 Composer Satie
46 Variety of chalcedony
47 Instead of
48 Cape ___
49 Can't hit the broad side of ___
50 Brazilian airline
51 Fit to be tied
52 Michaelmas daisy
53 ___ gratias
54 Unstable particle
55 No. 2 hit of 1978–79
56 Cuts the mustard?
57 Blast from the past
58 The end
59 Beau
60 Unable to decide
61 British governor of Massachusetts, 1775
62 Inits. in music licensing
66 Square
67 TV's "Judging ___"
69 Average name
70 Green lights
71 Outdated means of communication
72 Genuine warmth
74 Oscar org.
75 Noodge
79 Grandmother, old-style
80 ___ Avivian
81 Suppositions
82 Relieved
83 On-target
84 Michaelmas's mo.
85 Speed, e.g.
87 Nightclubs
88 Elizabeth I or II
89 Pals
90 Ability
91 Fulminated
92 Minded
93 Actress Tyler
95 Kaffiyeh wearer
96 Pi, e.g.
98 Post-op time
102 Missile holder
104 Modern Maturity org.
105 Director Wertmüller
107 Midback muscle, for short
109 Inflamed
110 Poetic preposition
111 Bad from the start?

by Peter Gordon

56 DOUBLE SCALE

ACROSS

1 Prized clam
7 Take back, in a way
12 Big trouble
20 Too firm, perhaps
21 Ristorante offering
22 Parenthetical figure
23 Come to
24 Valuable game tiles
26 Reason to look in a rear-view mirror
27 Poison conduit
28 1970 Medicine Nobelist Bernard
29 Fish in a tank
30 Comparison center
31 Auto that debuted in 1899
33 Wallop
35 Big name in computers
36 Mailer's request
42 Wildcatter's find
44 Jay preceder
45 Soccer announcer's cry
46 It parallels a radius
47 It is contracted
49 Some chocolates
51 Dissect, in a way
53 Gets a glimpse of
57 Surreptitious stock buyer
58 Pageant contender
60 Scratch post?
61 Super-duper
65 Harrow rival
66 Postpone
67 Celebrity
71 Puzzle contestant who eschews aid
73 Play kneesies, maybe
74 Room to swing ___
75 Shut (up)
76 Letter abbr.
77 Places with tapes
81 Dictate
84 Match-opening cry
85 Invitation word
87 Spartan serfs

88 Vane dir.
89 Memorial Day event, for short
90 Rara avis
91 Car co. purchased by Chrysler
94 Stratego piece
96 They were hot in Detroit in 1984
101 Road crew's supply
103 Ghana neighbor
105 Termite, e.g.
106 Dry ___
107 Work translated by Pope
109 Corner
111 Magwitch of "Great Expectations"
113 Lecherous
115 One with animal magnetism?
118 "Forget it!"
119 Touched up
120 Mythical swimmer
121 Carol opener
122 Feel dizzy
123 Survived
124 Beat

DOWN

1 Astronomical discovery of the 1960's
2 Foolish
3 Noted landfall
4 Raise
5 Split result, usually
6 ___-X
7 Headline News news
8 Hands-together time
9 Bullet
10 Linen vestment
11 Central part
12 "Couldn't help it!"
13 "Prometheus" muralist
14 Pro ___
15 Links annoyance
16 Blemished

17 Blew
18 Swimming sensation of 1926
19 Junkyard deal
25 It may be due
27 Cabbies' targets
32 Flips
34 Hawks' kin
37 Inured
38 Trophy
39 63-yard field goal kicker Jason
40 Cross characters
41 Annie Oakleys
43 Misinforms
48 Toast
49 Andorran's tongue
50 Lining
52 Legally prevent
53 Assign to, as blame
54 Corrupt
55 Dahl and others
56 Defensive position in fencing
57 Something to take a chance on
59 C.I.A. worry
62 Legal, so to speak
63 Show worry
64 Frontier trophy
68 Kind of transplant
69 Reversals
70 Bibliographical phrase
72 First bishop of Paris
78 Expert
79 Attention getter
80 Fries, maybe
82 Conductor of a sort
83 Stopper
86 Norse war god
87 Borscht belt locale
91 Muttered comments
92 Jazz star
93 Bromide
95 Over there
96 Level, e.g.
97 Prompt
98 ___ Lawrence, inventor of the cyclotron
99 Until now

100 Didn't merely cut
102 Goodbyes
104 Incriminating evidence, with "the"
108 Prohibition
110 Bed choice
111 Fighting
112 Give away
114 Sidewalk stand sales
116 Electronics giant
117 Central truth
118 Bag

by Joe DiPietro

ACROSS

1 Onetime N.F.L.'er
6 Illegal crop
10 Philosopher's study
14 Yield
19 "I Still See ___" ("Paint Your Wagon" tune)
20 Pointless event?
21 Soprano Moffo
22 Quartz variety
23 Fishwife?
25 Turning down a satirical magazine's subscription?
27 Astronaut's wear
28 Clowns' aids
30 "Eureka!"
31 Mr. Miniver in "Mrs. Miniver"
33 Storms, in a way
35 Mal de ___
36 In pieces
39 Rid of vermin
41 More wet behind the ears
45 Society page word
46 Expert bird doctors?
50 Pilot's place
51 "___ Made to Love Her"
53 "Daniel Deronda" author
54 Helga's husband, in the comics
56 Like some profs.
57 Trillion: Prefix
58 Became inedible
60 Where Bentleys may be parked
62 Kind of strap
63 Arrows' partners
65 Tacky?
67 Becomes evident
69 Comic Louis
70 Window cleaner's goof
72 Spleen
73 Ladies' men
77 "Here's to you!"

79 They're sometimes running
82 Tidbit for an echidna
83 Rationed (out)
86 "The ___ of the Courtiers" from "Rigoletto"
88 John, abroad
89 Roundup sounds
91 Nether world
93 Court employee
94 Yugoslav patriot
95 Cattle breed
97 Triple-barreled weapon?
100 Elevator ___
101 Western director Sergio
102 Token taker
103 Knickknack holder
105 Year in Martin I's papacy
107 Urchins
110 C.E.O.'s convenience
111 Throw
115 Japanese, e.g.
117 School mos.
120 Duke's closetful?
122 Result of Thanksgiving dinner?
125 Bail out
126 Eins + zwei
127 Barrie pooch
128 Lookout point
129 Starts of some pranks
130 Graf ___
131 TV Guide info
132 Marathon legend Waitz

DOWN

1 Gumshoe Archer
2 Shake it or break it
3 Purges
4 In itself
5 "Could It Be Magic" singer, 1975
6 With it

7 Actor Omar
8 Chances upon
9 Sword of Damocles
10 Serration
11 Hot
12 Prefix with valve
13 Johns
14 Frequent Degas subjects
15 Divided into cell-like areas, as a ceiling
16 "A fickle food upon a shifting plate": Dickinson
17 Flight board data, briefly
18 Wine selections
24 Places for canvases
26 Elemental ending
29 Watch readouts, briefly
32 ___ Park, N.J.
34 One who knows the drill
36 Hand and foot
37 Stairway post
38 Not putting clothes purchases in a bag?
40 Bygone autocrats
42 Obstetrics?
43 "If ___ Would Leave You"
44 Printed in an anthology
47 Amscrays
48 Hole makers
49 Special forces units
52 Sony competitor
55 Suicide squeeze result, maybe
59 Ideal
61 Miff
64 Neuter
66 A bit peaked
68 Venomous cobra
71 Total
73 President Nasser
74 "___ ear . . ."
75 "I'm impressed!"

76 Shredded sides
78 "Heart and Soul," to young pianists
79 A bit thick
80 Crimean native
81 In cartoons, a whistle may follow it
84 Blue-pencils
85 Name in the front of a book
87 Tony-winning conductor Lehman ___
90 Butch's pal
92 Rasta's messiah
96 Fraternity handshakes, maybe
98 Formal introduction?
99 It may say "Hello"
104 Minnesotan
106 Jean-___ Picard of "Star Trek: T.N.G."
108 Tools
109 QB's ploy
111 Blown away
112 Big Indian
113 Watchful one
114 Neptune and Pluto
116 It ranges from −1 to +1
118 Poop
119 "S.N.L." offering
121 Noted Zurich artist
123 Flit (about)
124 Shoe store spec

by Fred Piscop

ACROSS

1 "I Enjoy Being ___" (Rodgers and Hammerstein tune)
6 Ballpark figure follower
10 Year of Christopher Columbus's death
14 Discountenance
19 See 8-Down
20 The U.S. has a Great one
21 Home of ancient Persepolis
22 Third-largest asteroid
23 Jerry & Sharon's favorite building material?
25 Larry & Carrie's favorite bird?
27 Atlantic food fishes
28 Above ground?
30 Weep for
31 "Yikes!"
32 Habit
33 Twining plant stem
34 Disheveled
37 John & Nancy's favorite miscreant?
40 Member of the clergé
44 Van ___ administration
45 Ravel's "La ___"
46 How some films are viewed
48 Belfast grp.
49 List maintainers
51 Too precious
53 Young one
54 Reason for detention, maybe
56 Curt & Bill's favorite parts of dams?
59 Mouth that doesn't talk
61 Skyline parts

63 Big name in bonding
64 Miami and others
65 Conversation pieces
66 Loud mouths
67 One way to meet
68 Red Guard's movement
69 Express
70 Long-eared pet
71 Washington product
72 Gene & Eliot's favorite vacation area?
74 Mail carriers' paths: Abbr.
77 Person who makes calls
78 Rocker in a lullaby
80 Tavern sign abbr.
82 Fronton shout
83 Sci-fi villain
85 "Whoopee!"
87 Commingle
89 States under Stalin: Abbr.
90 Hank & Gale's favorite weather?
93 Far from shy
94 Make the grade?
96 Hearty hello
97 Kind of language
98 Ascetic of old
101 Given to gab
102 Hustled, e.g.
105 Karen & Jaclyn's favorite worker?
107 Grant & George Washington's favorite artisan?
110 Place in a Pullman
111 Converse competitor
112 Wagon part
113 1969 Beau Bridges film, when doubled
114 Paul Klee or Max Frisch, e.g.

115 Thumb one's nose at
116 Doesn't keep
117 Dr. Sattler of "Jurassic Park"

DOWN

1 Pres. appointee
2 Irving hero
3 Langston Hughes poem
4 Did more than edit
5 Shelley & Learned's favorite writing style?
6 Prefix in medicine
7 Essex contemporaries
8 With 19-Across, California city
9 Mrs. ___ cow
10 N.H.L. Hall-of-Famer Stan
11 Hardly serious writing
12 Place for a rooster
13 Like Paderewski's Minuet
14 Of interest to Audubon
15 Sully
16 Flushing Meadow stadium name
17 British carbine
18 Trophy won by 10-Down, 1967 and 1968
24 Rat
26 Plays footsie
29 "The West Wing" co-star
33 Louis-Dreyfus's "Seinfeld" role
34 Aaron's 2,297
35 It's all around you
36 Günter & Dennis's favorite drink?
37 Longtime Hungarian leader Kádár

38 Therewithal
39 White-collar crook
41 Alexander Graham & Timothy's favorite garment?
42 Weatherworn
43 Norse poems
45 Glens
47 Many-sided problems
50 Either Zimbalist
51 One may be roasting on an open fire
52 Huntsman Center team
55 Turn into a brat?
57 Pooh-pooh
58 Mer de ___ (Mont Blanc feature)
60 Bird that gets down
62 Net gain?
64 Girl in Eliot's "Romola"
65 Star and Sun, e.g.
66 Cost to cross
67 Not well-thought-out
68 French brandies
69 News clip
70 Twig broom
72 Yells "Heads up!" at
73 I-80 runs through it
75 Whiffenpoofs
76 Likely to turn on?
79 Charlotte ___ (sponge cake desserts)
81 Larry & Nicolas's favorite pet item?
84 Views
85 Regretful one of song
86 Fight to keep the faith
88 Kind of race
91 Hypothetical

by Charles M. Deber

92 Move down the runway
93 Anjou alternative
95 Signs of life
97 Sits tight
98 Withdraws
99 Great deal
100 It may cover an Indian
101 Room to move
102 One who isn't swift
103 Good opponent?
104 Slicer site
106 Like some scientists
108 Tic-tac-toe loser
109 104-Down request

ACROSS

1 Computer command
6 Santa ___
11 "___ girl!"
15 Salon cut
19 Metallic prefix
20 Fuel deliverer
21 Lows
22 Actress Hatcher
23 Affair update?
25 Captain Hook, in his dreams?
27 Italian town near Perugia
28 Secured, with "off"
30 It's often used in a pool
31 French wine-producing hillside
32 33-Down initials
34 Wise men
36 Conscription org.
37 Toronto-to-Ottawa dir.
38 Early
39 Iranian money
40 Bro, for one
42 Reply to a No. 1 son, e.g.?
47 Ground cover
51 Kind of butter
54 Soothing application
55 Daughter of Cronus
56 Smart
57 Corday's victim
58 Long Island town near Bay Shore
60 Like a home, often, before it's sold
62 City just east of Utah Lake
63 Symbol of strength
64 Downed
65 Modifier: Abbr.
66 Musial's manager, at times?
71 911 respondent
72 Oz creator and others
74 1948 Pulitzer-winning poet

75 Individually
77 Like some computer printers
81 Unexpected pleasure
82 Kansas motto word
83 Spills
84 Confucius's "Book of ___"
86 "___ Need" (1985 Jack Wagner hit)
87 Tangled
88 Looks out (for)
89 Paddy wagon?
92 Bang into
94 Word following an omission
95 Questioning syllables
96 Monthly income source: Abbr.
99 "Exodus" hero
102 Colada flavoring
105 Star Wars, initially
106 Bright students have them
107 Like some servants
109 Religious headpiece
112 Abate
114 Fiction writer's problem?
116 Governor's official cook?
118 Stuttgart title
119 Ireland, to the Irish
120 Yellowish-brown
121 Lucky ___
122 ". . . so long ___ both shall live?"
123 Answer defiantly
124 Minimum
125 Rapunzel feature

DOWN

1 Do away with
2 "On the Road Again" singer
3 Sibelius's "Valse ___"
4 Banks on the diamond
5 Fixes
6 No-frills bed

7 Make-up artists?
8 Choir part
9 Enlist anew
10 Elderberry wine additive, in a Kesselring play
11 Electric guitar adjunct
12 Reason to raise a hand
13 85-Down's rider
14 They want to know
15 Manche department's capital
16 Relieves
17 Locales
18 Hems in
24 First six tracks, say
26 Armpatch, e.g.
29 Browne's "cure of all diseases"
33 Down-in-the-mouth sort?
35 More artful
38 Sharpen
39 Not as proper
41 Breakfast cereal ad?
42 One hopping along the Cape Cod coast?
43 Haile Selassie disciple
44 Groundbreaking 90's sitcom
45 It's found in banks
46 Flannel feature
48 Essays
49 Powerful speakers
50 Barrett of Pink Floyd
51 Member of a Latin trio
52 Geometry line
53 Wolf or lion
59 Fold
61 ___ Lingus
66 Boom producer
67 Big pictures
68 Digger of "The Life of Riley"

69 Pitcher Bob of the 60's Pirates
70 Led on
73 Hardly a close win
76 Wages
77 Mil. medal
78 Mythical bird
79 Response to a court oath
80 Radio tube filler
82 "My Michael" author Oz
85 13-Down's horse
90 Kind of scanner
91 Copper?
93 Fabrics that shimmer
96 Gather into a bundle
97 Browns
98 Sights on ski slopes
99 Series opener
100 Gets to
101 Old artificial leg material
103 Glass-polishing powder
104 Household spray targets
105 Stock holders
106 It has many rays
108 Peut-___ (maybe): Fr.
110 Woeful words
111 First name in country
113 Subordinate title: Abbr.
115 ___ publica (commonwealth)
117 Scrap

WORDS HILLBILLY-STYLE

ACROSS

1 Whizzes
5 "Well done!"
9 It can give you a pointer
16 Some sports cars
19 Response to many a punch line
20 Domain
21 Fitness
22 Directional suffix
23 "Ah like to ___ with diffr'nt huntin' spots"
25 "Don't let the man stand outside, ___!"
26 Royale automaker
27 Most overcome
28 Rose and Fountain
29 Persistent critic
31 Forward
32 Is under the weather
34 Typo
36 Writing surface, in old Rome
38 Many Forbes readers have them
40 Sound units
41 Encyclopedia offering
44 "___ is gettin' a bit tight on mah finger"
46 Gulf port
48 Took some chips, maybe
51 Bleach
53 Goddess with the gift of life
57 Jeans man
58 Cancel
59 Brogue or twang
61 Darrow of "King Kong"
62 Ancient Asia Minor region
65 Distance around
67 Supporter of arms, for short
68 "___ tard of this bad weather"

71 "Let's hep preserve our natur'l ___"
73 Bill's partner
74 Takes a powder
75 Harass
76 Capital of Romania
77 Oahu attire
79 Classic suit
81 It's above the tonsil
85 Basic French verb
86 Left alone
89 "On the Road" writer
90 Many bucks
92 "___ pa? He feelin' better?"
94 Show that's launched many film careers: Abbr.
95 1994 Peace Nobelist
98 Ratón chaser
100 Member of a ladies' club
102 End of a race
104 Onetime World Cup star
105 Become flabby
110 Crescent-shaped
111 Title words before "Music" and "You Knocking"
114 "It doesn't matter"
116 "Disgusting!"
117 "___ drink Pepsi, but ah'll have a Coke few don't mind"
119 "The waitress will be heah soon. I ___"
120 The Divine, to da Vinci
121 Hubble telescope subjects
122 Recommend
123 Chemical endings
124 Mateo or Diego, e.g.
125 Gorge crosser
126 I-80 and U.S. 10, e.g.
127 Come clean, with "up"

DOWN

1 Newsgroup messages
2 Indian coin
3 Drink, so to speak
4 Archeological bit
5 Get specific
6 Perfume source
7 Horseman?
8 Fill the bill?
9 Gives up the fight
10 Life preserver?
11 Pittance
12 Ionized gas
13 Glasses may improve it
14 Rouses
15 Transmission site
16 "Ma momma's from Virginny, and ma daddy's from ___"
17 "The Power and the Glory" novelist
18 Pig patter
24 Good comedian
28 Relative of the banana
30 Like a break-in at a burglar's house
33 Tennis's Nastase
35 "The wolf"/"the door" connector
37 Like some reading lamps
38 Elementary particle
39 Caviar fish
41 Texts for eds.
42 Army member
43 "I'm gonna use mah new ___ to cut the grass"
45 Actress Lollobrigida
47 Departure
49 Water-to-wine site
50 Literally, "skill"
52 One of the Kramdens
54 "___ up, why dontcha grab me a beer?"
55 About
56 RR stops
60 Temper

63 "Waiting for Lefty" playwright
64 "Piece of cake"
66 Fussy film director
68 Capstone
69 Landslide
70 Give the slip
71 Title for Jesus, with "the"
72 City near Virginia City
75 One of the "Little Women"
78 Sawbones
80 Cubemaker Rubik
82 Runs down
83 Singer Janis
84 Seventh-century date
87 Proof part
88 Like some citizenships
91 Contest player
93 Late golf champion Payne
95 Bridge signals
96 She played Cher in "Clueless"
97 "Ken I have ___ 'stead of the sausage?"
99 Bad blood
101 Post-It
103 Word with ear or peace
104 Check word
106 Typographical flourish
107 Woolly
108 Shriners' headwear: Var.
109 Lock
112 Old-fashioned police cry
113 Airline to Ben Gurion
115 Extremely successful
118 U.K. award
119 It might bite

by Greg Staples

CHRISTMAS CACHE

ACROSS
1 Pilgrims to Mecca
7 More than a cause
14 Enjoyed a soak
20 Protozoan
21 Having a few buttons missing
22 Fighting
23 Start of a verse
26 Quake
27 Mauna ___
28 Fairy tale meanie
29 Pupil's place
30 Newsmaker of 2/20/62
32 Mystery writer Josephine
33 Kind of whale
37 Not even-tempered
38 "Out, dagnabbit!"
39 "Passion According to St. John" composer
43 Like new
44 Game in which the 13 spades are laid faceup
45 Buck's love
46 Tortosa's river
47 More of the verse
54 To boot
55 Cries of discovery
56 Prom needs
57 Johnson's vaudeville partner
58 Secretary of War, 1940–45
60 Hunk
62 Thorny
63 Loose
65 Old holder of writing fluid
67 Loud
70 Epoch in which mammals became dominant
72 New York tribe
76 Actor Reeves
77 Either of two O.T. books
78 Site of the forges of Vulcan
79 River inlet
80 More of the verse
85 Rain check?
86 Suffix with Christ
87 Nosegay
88 Gr. 1-6
89 "A one ___ two . . ."
90 Before, once
91 Yellow shade
93 Nita of "Blood and Sand," 1922
94 The works
95 Chili accompanier
96 Blackbird
98 Kind of dame
101 Table scrap
102 Helped in a heist
106 End of the verse
111 "Mysterious" locale
112 Strips
113 They're seen at court bashes
114 Aware of, slangily
115 Girl of barbershop quartets
116 It's flashy

DOWN
1 "Left!"
2 Writer Kingsley
3 "How ___ the little busy bee . . ."
4 King in II Kings
5 Footnote word
6 Yellowish-red
7 Driver who talks
8 Hightailed it
9 Burma's first P.M.
10 Moved easily
11 In Shakespeare, the star in "The star is fall'n"
12 Israeli leader with an eyepatch
13 Conductor ___-Pekka Salonen
14 Planned for, in a way
15 Wroth
16 Actual
17 Sartre's "___ Clos"
18 Extensions
19 Batiking need
24 Opposite of 1-Down
25 Department store department
30 Blood's partner
31 Nut
33 Jimmy of "N.Y.P.D. Blue"
34 Red or white wine
35 Ballade conclusion
36 Map abbr.
37 Dallas team, informally
38 Solidarity's birthplace
39 "Coronation of the Virgin" painter
40 Humiliate
41 Town ___
42 Like rhinos
44 James Bond woman in "Thunderball"
48 Patent medicine, e.g.
49 Gunwale pin
50 Everyone has one
51 ___-law
52 Razorbacks
53 Actual
59 The old folks
60 Ancient market
61 Designer's job
62 Pretty, to Burns
64 Sharpen again
66 How some arguments are conducted
67 Dog with a long, curled tail
68 Satirist Brendan
69 Nixon's first Defense Secretary
71 Tip
73 Part of a fire safety program
74 Felt bad
75 Game ragout
77 Prague's ___ University
78 Start of North Carolina's motto
81 Bows before
82 "Wheel of Fortune" choice
83 Mud, say
84 Indeed
91 Leatherneck
92 Tricky
93 Birdbrain
94 Concerning
95 Like many wartime messages
96 Medicine's ___ system
97 Red-spotted creatures
98 Halliwell, formerly of the Spice Girls
99 Baseball stats
100 Sheltered
102 Addie's husband in "As I Lay Dying"
103 "___ she blows!"
104 Architect Saarinen
105 Humdrum
106 Salaam
107 Writer LeShan
108 Infamous Amin
109 Cognizance
110 Wind dir.

by Frances Hansen

TURIN THE COUNTRY

ACROSS

1 Eagle org.
4 Chuck alternative
8 Whiplike?
13 Surly
18 Make fun of
19 Truck stop entree
20 "___ Was a Lady" (1932 song)
21 Go back to the drawing board
23 What an Italian wheeler-dealer wants?
26 Completely
27 Instruments used by the Beatles
28 Popeye's rival
29 Snappy comebacks
30 1954–77 alliance
31 Highest point in Italy?
34 Shoe specification
35 Passionate
37 Shakespearean prince
38 Dumfries denial
39 1974 title role for Dustin Hoffman
41 When Georges burns
42 Golden Horde member
44 "___ bien"
45 Midwest Indian
46 Barton and Bow
48 Filled Indian pastry
51 Do boring work
54 Outfit
57 Wedding wear
58 Like some terminals: Abbr.
59 One of the Simpsons
60 Off the street
61 Sorry sinner
63 Baton Rouge sch.
64 Kitchen gadget
65 1984 Jeff Bridges film
66 Sea off Sicily
69 It's charged

70 Peter Jennings or Shania Twain, by birth
72 Neanderthal man, for one
73 Exile site of 1814
75 Scratch the surface of
76 Atlas abbr.
77 With the mouth wide open
78 Parliament prize
79 E'erlasting
81 Dress down
82 Staff associate?
84 Dress fancily, with "out"
85 Distinguished
86 Diploma word
89 Billiard table cloth
91 "___ time"
92 Cutesy add-on
93 Fifties revival group
96 Some sports score notations
97 Italy's leading auto manufacturer?
101 Part of a joint
102 Presided over
104 On the double
105 Hit the road
106 At the tail
107 No particular place in Italy?
110 Make hard to read
111 Shearer of "The Red Shoes"
112 G.P.A. spoilers
113 Athletic supporter?
114 Struck out
115 Gray
116 Bygone era
117 Job listings, e.g.

DOWN

1 Number two wood
2 Full of wisdom
3 Provoke
4 Styx ferryman
5 Millinery
6 Olive kin
7 Yemen, in biblical times

8 Like Iran's government before the Ayatollah
9 Barbie's maker
10 "Later"
11 Carnival locale
12 Jack's inferior
13 One of the L.A. Rams' Fearsome Foursome
14 Lake cabins, often
15 As far as
16 Top and bottom of an Italian room?
17 Make stout
22 Hardly unconcerned: Var.
24 Stuff
25 AAA
29 A.A.A. suggestion
31 Closed in on
32 One in numismatics
33 Expose
36 Accommodations on an Italian ship?
40 British blueblood
43 Feather bed?
44 Greatest possible
46 Checked item
47 Bob's cousin
48 Daily occurrence
49 Tom, to the piper
50 Italian medical man?
52 Pounce upon
53 ___ Thursday
54 Big 12 team nickname
55 King of music
56 Italian Thanksgiving serving?
57 Lachrymal
61 K-12 grp.
62 Browning work?
65 Fugue feature
67 Fail to mention
68 Opening time, maybe
71 N.B.A. Hall-of-Famer Holman
72 Hound
74 The gamut
77 Thou

80 Parks of civil rights fame
81 Pin
83 Lower in quality
85 Escaped
86 Choral composition
87 Squeaky, maybe
88 Symbols of authority
89 Bowling game
90 Within reach
91 Like Bach's "Magnificat"
92 Warhol works
94 Army command
95 Spruce
98 Joined a conger line?
99 The Beatles inspired it
100 Full of cattails
103 Object of devotion
105 Cold draft
107 North Sea feeder
108 Name in Cambodian history
109 Old Olds

by Richard Silvestri

ACROSS

1 One of a study group?
7 Strengthen
13 Checked for heat
20 Potential tennis opponent?
21 Can't take
22 It may be represented by a tree
23 Chevy Chase and others
24 Like a 54-Across
25 Like standard music notation
26 Somme time
27 Start of an idle question
30 Lip
32 Can't take
33 Old lamp fill
34 "My Friend Flicka" author
37 Key material
39 Face of time?
43 Question, part 2
49 Gathering point
50 Beethoven's Opus 20, e.g.
51 Washed away
52 Finger board?
53 "King ___" (1950–65 comic strip)
54 Boot part
56 Athenian H
59 Prospector's dreams
60 Cold development
62 "Apollo 13" subject
64 Knighted dancer ___ Dolin
66 Pilothouse abbr.
67 With 69-Across, asker of the question
69 See 67-Across
71 Push-up aid?
74 Muff
75 Actor Andrews
77 Psychopharma-cologist's prescription
79 Donnybrook
82 Wasn't off one's rocker
84 Nodding one, sometimes
86 ___ mundi
87 Cloudiness
88 Propeller holder, perhaps
90 1954–76 national capital
92 Helps with a con job?
93 Question, part 3
96 Nordstrom rival
97 Work time
98 Like a 117-Across
99 Bow
100 They're heard when Brits take off
103 Sound from a pen
107 End of the question
116 Soccer ___
117 Encircling ring of light
118 Like AB negative, of all major blood types
119 It was defeated in 1588
121 Reedlike
122 Pilot
123 Unsubstantial
124 Service providers?
125 Time-___
126 Superlatively slick

DOWN

1 Loafer's lack
2 "West Side Story" girl
3 Memory units
4 King of France
5 From the top
6 Musician John
7 "King of Hearts" star
8 Up
9 Cheese place
10 Preoperative delivery, once
11 Start of a break-in
12 Helen's mother
13 Smooth
14 How baroque architecture is ornamented
15 Digging, so to speak
16 A-line line
17 Intoxicating Polynesian quaff
18 Major Hoople's outburst, in old comics
19 Take-out order?
28 They may be lent
29 Twelve
31 Infatuated with
35 Get a move on
36 Masters
37 ___ lamb
38 Dwell
39 Botherer
40 One way to serve coffee
41 Plot, perhaps
42 Big name in chips
43 Autocrats
44 Toast beginner
45 Archilochus work
46 It doesn't sting
47 Hero of medieval romances
48 They might get drunk in the summer
49 His "4" was retired
55 It's good to meet them
57 Red ___ (Japanese food fish)
58 Vantage point
61 North American dogwoods
63 Shade provider
65 Unliquidated?
68 "Tuning in the U.S.A." broadcaster: Abbr.
70 68-Down's medium
71 "You are correct!"
72 Talk a blue streak
73 It may precede other things
74 Some are lean
76 In ___ way
78 Head set?
79 Corp. recruits
80 Portoferraio's place
81 Vichyssoise ingredient
83 Schussboomer's transport
85 Took away (from)
89 Accident-assessing areas, briefly
91 Wonderment
93 Dispute subjects, perhaps
94 Beekeeper's exclamation?
95 "Now ___ you . . ."
97 Greeter
100 Spelling and Amos
101 Skip
102 Focus of some tests
104 Effigy
105 Meeting points
106 It's headquartered in Troy, Mich.
107 Stinger
108 Molokai show
109 Vultures were sacred to him
110 Carnival sight
111 Winged one in Wonderland
112 Latin I word
113 Collapsed
114 Highland toppers
115 Oblast on the Oka
120 What "5" can mean

by Elizabeth C. Gorski

ACROSS

1 Lets up
7 Rosé alternative
13 Rogue
18 Rossini setting, in España
20 Ancient galley
21 Funnies format feature
22 Start of a verse
24 Where matches are booked
25 Done, for Donne
26 Embedded, in a way
27 1969 Series winners
29 Arab League member
30 Conical-toothed tool
32 Verse, part 2
36 Bargain hunters look for them
39 Nero's title: Abbr.
40 Inveigled
41 Most reliable
45 Start of a recipe direction
48 Place to hibernate
49 Verse, part 3
53 Clayey deposit
56 1951 N.L. Rookie of the Year
57 Suffix with tyranno-
58 Big number, slangily
59 Cal. page header
61 Skydived
64 Verse, part 4
70 Like some sculptures
72 Shine, in commercial names
73 Titillates
74 Verse, part 5
79 Becomes less high, with "up"
80 Indeed
81 Sch. founded by Thomas Jefferson
82 Drone, e.g.
84 Capital of Moravia
85 King Mongkut's realm
88 Verse, part 6

93 Noted Turner
95 Stocking shade
96 Table with a map
97 Metal marble
101 Long-jawed fish
103 Actress Kelly of "Chaplin"
106 Verse, part 7
112 Collars
114 Vexed
115 Prefix with phobia
116 They may compete with boxers
119 Prompt
120 Ace, maybe
122 End of the verse
126 1996 Madonna musical
127 Cricket teams, e.g.
128 Rushed at
129 The Haggadah's read here
130 Bar food
131 Way out

DOWN

1 Nancy, the first woman in Parliament
2 Take off the top
3 Reluctant
4 Hall-of-Fame pitcher Keefe
5 Big South Conference college
6 Pivot around
7 Telephone part
8 A fleur
9 Sphygmomanometer's place
10 French cathedral city
11 Roast host
12 Grow grinders
13 Where one might take off on a vacation?
14 Early American colony
15 Feeble
16 Gun wielder, say
17 Did some shaving
19 Kind of D.A.
20 "America" pronoun
23 Old verb ending
28 Smooth, in a way

31 Medium for announcements
33 He played Yuri in "Doctor Zhivago"
34 Salon creation
35 Check
37 Director Jean-___ Godard
38 Málaga Mrs.
42 Capt.'s aide
43 Attempt
44 Bull's head?
46 Like some errors
47 SEATO part
49 Hula dancers
50 Daewoo competitor
51 Shorthand system inventor
52 Island north of Montecristo
54 Parents, e.g.
55 Lake of Four Forest Cantons
56 "Home to Harlem" novelist Claude
60 Bas-relief medium
62 W.W. II action locale
63 Morse code click
65 Grp. that sang "Do Ya"
66 Sentences
67 Abbr. in ages
68 Sticky stuff
69 Applied well, as sunscreen
71 Great Lakes fish
75 Level
76 Prego rival
77 Mort from Montreal
78 "Waiting for the Robert ___"
83 Fraction of a joule
86 Personal account
87 ___ fides (bad faith)
89 Sharp quality
90 Squad
91 Special person
92 Musician Brian
94 Brown of Talk magazine
97 Pinches
98 Flourish
99 It moves in a wink

100 Emulates Rembrandt
102 Spring cheepers
104 Unbranched flower cluster
105 Corrupt practices
107 Happy-go-lucky song part
108 Shack
109 Treat for Rover
110 Entreaty for Rover
111 Congers and kin
113 Origins
117 Gala
118 Portmanteau pollution mixture
121 Besmirch
123 "The Loco-Motion" singer Little ___
124 Was a bellwether
125 Are all wet

by Cathy Millhauser

ODD COUPLES

ACROSS

1 Telephone user
7 Obeyed "Down in front!"
10 Everybody
13 Clean the last bit
18 Not straight up
19 A "man that is not passion's slave," in Shakespeare
21 Home of Kansas Wesleyan University
22 Antic
23 Energize
24 Roswell visitors?
25 Cry from Homer Simpson
26 System of measuring cereal by weight?
28 When repeated, an island NW of Tahiti
29 Down
30 ___ while
31 Cracker Jack surprise
32 Big name in real estate
33 Where diners use dinars
34 Prison library's contents?
38 Baseball fig.
39 Stared off into space
41 Sticky stuff
42 Place for a pad
43 Reeve role
44 Family's coat of arms, say
47 In a group of
49 Not yet actualized
52 Ordinary worker
53 Mayan ruin site
57 Grayish
58 Columbus's birthplace
59 Ship salvager's aid
60 Actress Thurman
61 Forbidding
62 Unhip cabbie with passenger?
65 OS/2 company
66 Play bumper-cars
67 "There's ___ In My Soup" (Peter Sellers comedy)
68 Frighten
69 "My ___!"
70 Sit in the bleachers
72 Overhauled
73 Himalayan kingdom
75 Impressionist
76 More sullen
78 Reagan Cabinet member
79 Original Stoic
81 Swiss snowfield
82 Garment industry innovator
87 Line in a voting booth: Abbr.
88 Complain at restaurants?
92 Popular paperback publisher
93 Common desk items
94 Kind of tracks
95 Lobster eggs
96 ___ Xing (street sign)
97 Propeller-head
98 The Merry Men in Sherwood Forest?
103 Hospital V.I.P.'s
104 Took to the stump
105 Musical embellishment
106 Family men
109 They're called "transfers" in Britain
110 Condition sometimes treated by hypnosis
111 Pilgrim's goal
112 Perfect places
113 Ringed?
114 LAX monitor info
115 Most like Iago

DOWN

1 Fort Peck, for one
2 First name in dance
3 "The Naked and the Dead" star
4 Island in a Scottish bay?
5 Grp. with standards
6 Business solicitor
7 33-Across, once
8 Top-notch
9 Fictional teen sleuth Belden
10 Diagonally
11 English professor's deg.
12 Leopold's partner in crime
13 Southeast Asian natives
14 Actress Lena
15 Gun with a silencer?
16 Rattle
17 Bible reading
20 Name on a fridge
21 Clip joint?
26 200-milligram unit
27 Straddling
28 Auction action
29 Exhausted
35 Of the breastbone
36 John ___
37 Fenced-off area
40 Cartoon dog
42 Flesh and blood
45 Lycanthrope's catalyst
46 Waterskin
47 Wing-shaped
48 Bébé watcher
49 Hideouts
50 Music org.
51 Mostly-empty spice rack?
52 Pressed one's nose to the glass
54 Surg. study
55 Planetary shadow
56 Irish P.M. ___ de Valera
58 Doggedness
59 Took places
62 One way to explain a coincidence
63 Algae product
64 Pop singer from Nigeria
69 Emotional scene with actor Grant?
71 TV's "___ Sharkey"
72 Evasive answer
73 Greeted a shepherd
74 Part of H.M.S.
77 Miner's quarry
78 Duncan ___
79 Numbers on letters
80 Went back on stage
81 Laplander, maybe
83 Watch words?
84 Be situated above
85 Goes downhill
86 Objective
88 Potters' needs
89 Flip comment?
90 Chevalier
91 Cheapen
99 Hall-of-Famer Coveleski
100 Performer who fills the club
101 Tarpeian Rock's location
102 Pare, say
106 Preamble to the Constitution?
107 Stanley Cup org.
108 Primed

by Patrick D. Berry

ACROSS

1 See above
7 Refuse
12 Less cool
19 Three-time hockey M.V.P.
20 End product
22 Artist known for his street scenes of Paris
23 Actor getting bad press?
25 Destroy a person
26 Light opening?
27 Gymnast's perch
28 Barely beat
30 Actress who's cold?
34 Karate schools
38 Scriptures volume
41 Suffix added to large numbers
42 Son, sometimes
44 They may be picked out
45 Actress with punishing roles?
49 Sack
50 Tool points
51 Begin liking
52 Grampuses
53 "The __ the limit!"
54 Seconds
55 Article in Der Spiegel
56 Fan sound
57 Slip-up
58 [Boo-hoo!]
59 "Min and Bill" Oscar winner
64 Manilow song setting
65 State-of-the-art
66 Actor who plays terrorists?
69 Trans World Dome player
72 A pluviometer measures it
74 Come before
75 __ breve
76 Go around
78 Tiny particle: Abbr.

80 It comes in sticks
81 Hitter of 660 career home runs
82 Start of a selection process
83 Mrs. Dithers, in the comics
84 Pull out
87 Word processing command
88 Telephone __
89 Actress famous for boxing?
91 Read the U.P.C.
92 Dead accurate
94 Hideaway
95 Equals
96 Baby food
97 Actress in a dressing room?
102 One may be silent
104 St. Paul's architect
105 Grp. with holes in its organization
108 Sri Lanka's capital
111 Actress with the keys to a city?
116 Patron saint of shoemakers
117 Impeach
118 Gelcap alternative
119 Do-nothing's state
120 June of "The Dolly Sisters"
121 Says scornfully

DOWN

1 Fünf und drei
2 Miss Marple's discovery
3 Eastern royal
4 His #4 was retired
5 Big step up from the bleachers
6 Gave a darn?
7 It may be organized
8 Roaster, perhaps
9 "What would you like to know?"
10 Suffix with hand or fist
11 Strips blubber

12 Urbanite's vacation spot
13 Langston Hughes poem
14 More dignified
15 Ford failures
16 France's Belle-__
17 "Boola Boola" singer
18 Ex-Yankee Guidry
21 The Hambletonian, e.g.
24 Heyerdahl craft
29 Lady of Spain
30 Jackson and James
31 Its business is growing
32 Laughfest
33 Words after "yes"
35 Actor with a special way of talking?
36 Initials, maybe
37 Common thing
38 Bunco artist
39 Firebird
40 Actress who does the twist?
43 Julio, e.g.
45 It had the earliest parliament on the European continent
46 They're sometimes split
47 Textile trademark
48 Like some love affairs
53 Forest runner
57 Archaic attention-getters
60 Aquanaut's base
61 Dict. listing
62 "Saving Private Ryan" craft: Abbr.
63 Tampa-to-Orlando dir.
64 Some liqueurs
66 Punster
67 British surgeon Sir James
68 Chopin piece
70 Three-time placer in the 1978 Triple Crown

71 "Free" people
73 Station closing?
75 Comedian, e.g.
76 Framed
77 Actor Reeves
78 Feldspar variety
79 Fremont National Forest site
83 Midwest city, on scoreboards
84 Mark for life
85 Assam silkworm
86 Screwballer Hubbell
89 Sound system components
90 Unearthly
93 Peace of mind
95 Scribe
98 Gulf of Finland feeder
99 Registration datum
100 Dernier __
101 "Endymion" writer
103 Power stats
105 "Here Is Your War" author
106 One on the move
107 Stratagems
108 Early third-century date
109 First or second, e.g.: Abbr.
110 Capp diminutive
112 Color TV pioneer
113 Informal British address
114 Sussex suffix
115 Tad's dad

by Lloyd E. Pollet

ACROSS
1 Wild place?
5 Here, elsewhere
8 Zimbabwe's capital
14 Plow puller
18 Doozy
19 Narrow margin of victory
21 They may come from Qom
22 Big Indian
23 Dull routine
24 "Good Stykeeping" award?
27 Garlicky dish
29 Princess of Nintendo games
30 Three-time Wimbledon winner
31 Report from a Pamplona beer bash?
37 Relative of a mandolin
38 Some are wicked
39 Financial backer
42 Simps' syllables
46 Shoot for
47 Humped ox
51 Gem symbolizing the soul
53 Kind of jacket
54 Biblical particle?
56 Fumbles for words
57 Popular analgesic
59 "___ boy!"
60 Set free
61 Chew the rag
62 Burst into laughter
64 Franklin and Jefferson, for two
65 Understudies for a star of "The Piano"?
70 Nickers?
73 Bring back to life, in a way
74 Whup
77 Oppenheimer development
78 Elhi orgs.
82 Timex competitor
83 Kachina doll carver
84 Containers of gourmet ice cream?
86 Application blank info
87 Scottish ___
89 Souvenir buys
90 Coarse-grained
91 Fast time?
93 Symbol of authority
94 Pizzeria order
95 Not up
97 Feeling ill, simply put?
107 Divert
109 Silly
110 Regulars' requests
111 Uneasy feeling regarding have-nots?
117 Thumbs-down reactions
118 Complex division
119 The Sandwich Islands, today
120 Georgia Senator until 1997
121 Yellowfin, e.g.
122 The King of Egypt sings in it
123 91-Across ender
124 Véronique, e.g.: Abbr.
125 Cut down

DOWN
1 Defeat
2 Methuselah's father
3 Stiff hairs
4 Terrified ones
5 Be firm
6 Rimsky-Korsakov's "Le ___ d'Or"
7 Maker of the Amigo S.U.V.
8 Poet Doolittle
9 Thundering
10 The "so few" of 1940: Abbr.
11 It makes men mean
12 Shred
13 Second sight
14 Lucky strike
15 Like some roofs
16 Cracked open
17 Oast filler
20 Extra-wide
25 Unser Jr. and Sr.
26 McCarthy's quarry
28 Comedian Poundstone
32 Logician's abbr.
33 "Middlemarch" author
34 Priests
35 City named for an Indian tribe
36 Classified listings: Abbr.
39 Far from ruddy
40 March Madness org.
41 Stare, like a tourist
43 Oscar-winning actress Miyoshi
44 Sanctuary
45 Frère's sibling
46 Singer DiFranco
47 Pueblo builders
48 Diner sign
49 Jolly old chap
50 Instruments from 119-Across
52 Root beer brand
55 Express doubt about
58 Rock's Reed
62 Sauce style
63 Kind of dispenser
64 Clear, in a way
65 Apples, e.g.
66 Townie
67 Pol's concern
68 "Barnaby Jones" actor
69 Numeral in a Uris title
70 Slew
71 Anne Nichols hero
72 Stop listening, with "out"
74 Related
75 Eat like ___
76 "Great shot!"
78 Romeo's rival
79 Wrist-radio wearer
80 Befuddled
81 Onetime lottery org.
83 Recruits, in a way
85 Troy Aikman's alma mater
88 Encourages
92 Espied, to Tweety
94 Appear
96 "The ___ Identity" (Ludlum novel)
97 Actor Dennis
98 Former court org.
99 "Socrate" composer
100 Biblical land of riches
101 Never, in Nuremberg
102 Nascar broadcaster
103 Big bills
104 "Le Bestiaire" artist Dufy
105 "Uncle Vanya" woman
106 Blue-book filler
107 Light hue
108 Certain bond, for short
112 Any ship
113 Regulatory org. since 1958
114 Injection reactions, maybe
115 Maze runner
116 Where Windsor is: Abbr.

by Brendan Emmett Quigley

68 TWIN STATES

ACROSS
1 Scampi ingredients
7 Pent up
12 Wire-haired terrier of film
16 Soften up
20 More than budding
21 Down East town
22 Axis/Allies conflict: Abbr.
23 Take out
24 They never need to be renewed
27 Kind of situation
28 "You got that right!"
29 Opposing
31 Plundered, old-style
35 Jet
36 Confucian path
38 Bit of energy
39 Pharmaceutical giant
45 All __ Airways
50 Bicyclist's choices
51 Haemoglobin deficiency
52 Uncreative
53 Unrefined
54 Series continuation
57 Poet Sexton
59 Thou
60 Walter Reuther's org.
61 Suffix with cannon
62 Cable staple
65 They're coated with red wax
68 Inadvisable action
70 Spanish wave
71 One may be a favorite
72 Thick-plumed songbird
73 London landmark
77 Ladies of Versailles: Abbr.
79 Doesn't keep
80 "The Old Wives' Tale" playwright
81 One may be taken to the cleaners
83 Actress Graff
85 "Zuckerman Unbound" novelist
88 Relieves
90 1991 Midler/Allen comedy
95 Yamaguchi's rival at Albertville
96 Literary inits.
97 Korea's Roh __ Woo
99 Seat of McLennan County, Texas
100 Invest
101 Kelly classic
106 "Black utopia" of 1920
107 It may be recombinant
108 Sending to the canvas
109 One available for future reference?
110 Traveled in tandem?
112 Remove the dirt from?
114 Wife of King Mark of Cornwall
116 Flaw
118 They have a glow about them
119 More apothegmatic
120 Look like
124 Roadside jumpers: Abbr.
126 "La-la" lead-in
127 Ages
128 Hebrew for "delight"
129 "L'Isle joyeuse" composer
136 Tracy's pair
138 Beleaguering brother
139 Question from one who doesn't get it
146 Perfidies
147 Women's rights pioneer
148 R. J. Reynolds brand
149 Aiea apparel
150 Perturb
151 Turner and others
152 Like Henry VIII
153 Procure

DOWN
1 Compadre
2 Diamond letters
3 Furry fellow of 80's TV
4 Job experience?
5 "Don't look at me!"
6 "__ People" (Le Carré best seller)
7 Begins airing
8 Hammer in oil
9 Elapse
10 Chemical ending
11 L'Age __
12 Dr. Seuss's "Horton Hears __"
13 Go through channels?
14 Home of the brave?: Var.
15 Laon's department
16 Enterprise counselor Deanna
17 "Foul Play" star
18 Message on a tag-sale tag
19 Didn't stop
23 Occupying oneself with
25 "Melodies and Memories" autobiographer
26 Length and width
30 Bouquet __
31 Firefighter, at times
32 Where many Goyas hang
33 Add to the dossier
34 Scrabble draws
36 Bar need
37 Vigorously
40 Joseph Smith's denom.
41 One kept in the bag?
42 Menotti hero
43 When many people punch in
44 Indian of the Sacramento River valley
46 Lustrous velvet
47 Frequently exhibiting
48 Steal a march on
49 Atomic experiments
54 Game show lineup
55 Like an idol
56 Flat rate
58 Eponym of an old auto
63 "Really!"
64 See 143-Down
66 "Happy Days" fellow
67 Bankruptcy follow-up
69 Raised-eyebrow remarks
74 It was once divided
75 Where to have a cabin
76 Anita Brookner's "Hotel du __"
78 Goof
79 Staff differently
82 Houston-to-Dallas dir.
84 __ Valley, San Francisco
85 Take the chance
86 Of no use
87 More chic
89 Writer Shelby
91 Hereditary title
92 Teed off
93 Crescent moon
94 Attacks, in a way
96 Targets of criminal probes
98 Unpaid debt
102 Lions' prey
103 "Sunny" singer Bobby
104 Less emotional
105 St. Gregory's residence

by Frank Longo

111 Bearded revolutionary
112 Embargo
113 Small suckers
115 Kind of secret
117 Robbins and others
118 Riviera resort
121 Hoi polloi

122 Look good on
123 Nursery supply
125 Early adders
129 High-hatter?
130 It may be found in a cone
131 Iraqi V.I.P. Tariq ___
132 Ubangi feeder
133 Eskimo transport

134 Wallop
135 Fast Atl. crossers, once
136 Eye
137 Short end
140 Equi-
141 Pick up
142 It's heard before a snap

143 With 64-Down, 1964 Beatles tune
144 Rapa ___ (Easter Island)
145 Starter's need

MALE BONDING

ACROSS

1 Like some transit
6 Pessimist's lack
10 Unlikely class president
14 Times when headlights are turned on
19 Saudi neighbor
20 "Couldn't have said it better myself"
21 Tony's cousin
22 Winning
23 Mustang feature, maybe
25 Skylarking
27 Harvard hater?
28 Columnist Herb
29 Horse halters
31 They're found on palms
32 Home of Tivoli gardens
34 Revel
35 Brunch cocktail
36 Occasion to stand up
37 Star turn at La Scala
38 Bits and pieces
39 Mosquito breeding ground
43 Crow's home
47 45 __
50 Orchestra section
51 Pushed
53 Like some chances
54 Muse for D. H. Lawrence
57 One after another?
58 Travel guides
60 Star's rep: Abbr.
61 Louisiana, the __ State
63 Photo session
64 Jollity
66 It's known as "Insurance City"
70 Kind of offender
71 Narodnaya is the tallest of them
72 Came from behind

74 Part of Kramden's guffaw
75 Tony-winning dramatist Hugh
77 Ever so slight
79 Relatively rational
80 Royal educator
82 Mate bees with fleas?
83 Clemson mascot
85 White-bearded grazer
86 Cold buffet slice
88 Airline entree?
92 Choreographer/ dancer José
94 Targets of men who make passes
95 Shared airs
98 1982 Richard Pryor comedy
100 Scuba gear
102 Hit a hard drive that's caught, in baseball
104 Oranjestad native
105 Jumpy
106 Whence the Magi, with "the"
107 Oriental tie
108 Leveling
110 Tumble-down
113 Help a forgetful actor
114 Role model, maybe
115 Cut and paste
116 Observant one
117 Whirling
118 __ Noël
119 Ellipsis
120 Commercials

DOWN

1 Like a boxer before a bout
2 Necklace item
3 "Carlito's Way" actor
4 Press, so to speak
5 From a mold
6 N.H.L. goalie Dominik

7 Overcast sky, say
8 Nugget size
9 Climbs aboard
10 Hide-and-seek proclamation
11 Tropical wood
12 Holders of glasses
13 Cool, modern-style
14 Habitually humiliated person
15 Springs
16 British guns
17 "Charmed Lives" author Michael
18 1974 Sutherland/Gould spoof
24 Calculus
26 "Just for the thrill __"
30 Part of Q.E.D.
33 Nanas' daughters
34 Madrid museum
35 Ways
37 One way to start
38 Molten metal channel
40 "I can't __ satisfaction" (Rolling Stones lyric)
41 Hoaxes
42 Fiber that travels well
44 Bothering
45 Draftable, maybe
46 Ambulance staffers: Abbr.
47 D.D.E., for one
48 Readies the oven
49 Fictional Mrs.
52 Kind of wing
55 Spare change?
56 Like base 8
58 "Grab __!"
59 Welcome sight for a castaway
62 At the close of
63 One trying a hiccups cure
65 Where John Wooden coached

67 "Guys and Dolls" writer
68 Plays
69 Hardly Mr. Right
70 Hera's mother
73 Joanne of "Red River"
76 "Goody!"
77 Orchestra section
78 Roe
81 Relative of turquoise
83 Fooled around
84 Salad slice
87 Stronghold
89 Places for trophy displays
90 Beach shades
91 Get the point
93 Like some old records
96 Grew fond of
97 Certain apartment
98 "__ words were never spoken!"
99 "Amadeus" star
100 Drift
101 Go fish
102 Lives on
103 Stadium sections
104 Start of an incantation
105 ". . . under the whelming __": Milton
106 Give forth
109 Nada
111 Hornet's nest
112 One with a beat

by Nancy Salomon

ACROSS

1 Congressional matters
5 Risking dizziness
10 Winner's feeling
14 Salon supply
19 Like some speeds
20 Rich kid in "Nancy"
21 Schleps
22 See 33-Across
23 London Magazine writer
24 ___ Heights
25 This and that
26 "The Age of Anxiety" poet
27 Cable talk show trademark
31 Acid neutralizers
32 Smart stuff
33 With 22-Across, Federal law enforcement matter
34 ___ Royale, Mich.
35 See 2-Down
36 Shrewd
37 E.M.S. course
40 Clubs: Abbr.
43 Subjects for forgiveness
44 The Thinker, for all we know
45 Tongue locale
46 W.W. II military trademark
51 "Aladdin" prince
52 Aggregate
53 Astronomical figures
54 Beat, so to speak
55 Improve
57 "Our ___ Sunday" (radio soap)
58 Bit of a draft
59 China's ___ Piao
60 TV comedy trademark
67 Singer Acuff
68 Palacio feature
69 "I guessed it!"
70 Welsh emblem
73 Quick notes?
76 Pink-slips
78 Driven types
81 Phenom
82 Art world trademark
86 Plodding sort
87 Controls
88 Actual existence
89 Composer Bruckner
90 Noted cathedral town
91 Truck treatment
92 Prefix with sphere
93 Drake Stadium site
95 Kind of block
96 Cornstarch brand
97 "Good night, sweet ladies. Good night, good night" speaker
100 1940's film trademark
105 Running errands, say
106 Ring dance
107 Month after Adar
108 Band
110 Lodge member
111 Like most proverbs: Abbr.
112 Diaphanous linen
113 1997 Oscar-nominated title role
114 Last Supper attendee
115 Care for
116 Quite a bargain
117 Choice word

DOWN

1 You may stand in it
2 With 35-Across, a sign of spring
3 Hardship
4 Short result?
5 Historic Scottish county
6 Novice
7 Author Have-lock ___
8 Verve
9 Many years ago
10 Certain print
11 Eye-openers
12 Sponsorship
13 Pill passage
14 Hardly plentiful
15 Bluenose
16 Hitch, in a way
17 Part of A.B.A.: Abbr.
18 Driving needs
28 Mix it up on the mat
29 Stylish music
30 Breathless
35 Perjurer
36 "High Hopes" songwriter
37 Circuitry site
38 "The Dunciad" poet
39 Symbol of slimness
40 Man in a garden
41 Coastal catch
42 Appealing
43 Lips service?
44 Leaves off
45 Kind of column
47 Inflamed
48 For the boys
49 Check
50 Small belt
56 Glean
58 Sign by a ticket window
59 Columbia squad
61 "Return of the Jedi" girl
62 Some investments
63 ___ Minor
64 Amiens is its capital
65 Chinese dynasty before the birth of Christ
66 Push back, perhaps
71 Come back
72 Insightful
73 Salinger girl
74 Stake driver
75 Any NATO member
76 Top of a range?
77 "Judith" composer
78 Gymnastic finishes
79 Bygone sign on U.S. highways
80 Not so newsworthy
83 Long green
84 Free
85 Veggieburger, to a hamburger, e.g.
91 Play varsity ball
92 Businessman Hammer
93 Ex-New Jersey college, founded 1893
94 French fashion figure
95 No-goodnik
96 Moses' brother
97 Davis in Hollywood
98 Totally
99 Film "___ of God"
100 Extinguish
101 "O" in old radio lingo
102 Cheer
103 Single
104 Brawl
109 Comment before "I don't know"

by Lou and Fran Sabin

ACROSS

1 Out
7 Greeting from Pooh
12 Accumulation
17 Ventilating slat
18 Neighbor of Turkey
21 ___ Belt (constellation feature)
23 Good fight, in old Rome?
25 Teller of secrets, in a saying
26 Hockey's Mikita
27 Diplomatic trait
28 Smash really bad
30 They give sum help?
31 Costing a fish two fins?
34 Anesthetic, once
38 Hotel room fixtures, for short
39 He hides in kids' books
40 Taken ___
41 This, to Luis
43 Gumption
45 Classic prefix
48 "Oops!" to a paramecium?
51 Trunk with a chest
52 Author O'Brien
53 Digs of twigs
54 Regarding
55 The Flintstones' pet
56 Holiday music
57 Biblical food fight?
59 Know-it-all
62 "Tom Jones" script writer John ___
66 Fix firmly
68 Basic shelters
69 World's longest wooden roller coaster, located in Cincinnati
71 What a citizen like Galileo had?
73 Did lining
74 Feature of some winds
76 Express regret
77 Squire
81 Word on some Procter and Gamble lotions
82 He "spoke" for Bergen
84 Cutups at a record company?
86 Parked oneself
87 Fixes firmly
88 "The other white meat"
89 Certain thallophytes
90 Seed scar
92 Whack
93 Rescuers
95 Cadillac driven by Monica's interviewer?
101 Covered for court
102 Hightail it
103 One's own, for a starter
104 Unprofessional, slangily
108 Edgar and Hugo, e.g.
110 Unusual brass polish?
113 Social surroundings
114 Coastal town crier
115 Parenthetical lines
116 Twisty-horned antelope
117 Some stars
118 Ones sticking their necks out to entertain?

DOWN

1 Celebrants' wear
2 Grate stuff
3 Selene's counterpart
4 Hunter a k a Ed McBain
5 U.S. trading partner, formerly
6 A hydrogen atom has one
7 Get cracking, in a way
8 Mountain crest
9 K-O filler
10 Moolah
11 Whopper toppers
12 Cry with catches
13 Subject to court proceedings
14 1997 basketball film
15 Musicians' behavior, in the end?
16 New York hoopster
19 Speck
20 Pre-med course: Abbr.
22 Cinco follower
24 Celtics' Archibald
29 Olympics athlete Carl
31 Polynesian carving
32 British poet laureate Nahum
33 Prefix with second
34 Songwriter Sammy
35 Shawm descendant
36 Raven sounds
37 C.D., for one
41 Deserve
42 Slide specimen
43 Word ending many company names
44 Stem
46 When Plácido Domingo was born
47 Welcome sites
49 Tropical vine
50 Laura who plays Dr. Weaver on "ER"
51 Quartet on a Quattro
52 Verve
55 Saul's successor
56 Indian valuable
57 He was more than a neigh-sayer
58 Dried, maybe
60 Of a pelvic bone
61 Cathartic drug
62 Others at the Alhambra
63 N.F.L. coach Don
64 An obese Lugosi?
65 Mind
67 Animal handler
70 Lemur's hangout
72 Imitation
75 Voiced pauses
77 Java neighbor
78 "Tantum ___" (part of a Eucharist hymn)
79 Purim's month
80 Applications
82 Aspersion
83 Ices, perhaps
84 Know-nothing
85 "B.C." abode
87 Cheer
88 It's saved by E-mail
91 James Michener narrative
92 Thick-trunked tree
93 Skirt feature
94 Ho's hi's
95 Streetcar
96 Mandel of "St. Elsewhere"
97 Takes steps
98 Libertine
99 String quartet member
100 Teen faves
104 Entice
105 Abbr. on egg cartons
106 Spin tail?
107 Pianist Dame Myra
109 Nord's oppostie
111 Scolding syllable
112 Phenomenon such as ESP

by Cathy Millhauser

ACROSS
1 Morse code bits
5 Reveals
10 Legislation
14 Toughie
19 Israel's first U.N. representative
20 ___-Lodge
21 No quick trip around the block
22 ___ Kristen of "Ryan's Hope"
23 Increased pay rate, Bard-style?
25 Angry reaction
26 Your place or mine
27 Like some guesses
28 20th-century combat, Bard-style?
31 Move, in a way
32 The Mustangs of the N.C.A.A.
34 Ride, so to speak
35 Stew ingredient
36 "Uh-uh!"
38 Spring times
40 Legit
43 Empathic remark, Bard-style?
47 Inched
49 Charles who was dubbed "the Victorious"
50 Abbr. on a discount label
51 Auto purveyor, Bard-style?
57 Pulver's rank, in film: Abbr.
58 Pack away
59 Synchronous
60 Heiress, perhaps
61 Sales people
63 Kicked off
65 It may fill a lib. shelf
66 "Kramer vs. Kramer" director Robert
67 Hunks
69 Bamboozles
71 Card combo

73 Travel agt.'s suggestion
75 Moderator's milieu
76 Time to act
79 Person with a day
80 Rating giver
82 Eshkol once led it: Abbr.
84 Zoological mouths
85 Hierarchy, Bard-style?
87 First word?
88 Knock the socks off
89 Marner's creator
90 Takes advantage of, Bard-style?
94 Harness ring
97 Scuffle memento
99 Rocker Nugent
100 Black and tan ingredient
101 Like Chippendale furniture
104 Hunter's quarry
106 Book of the Apocrypha
110 Easy schedule, Bard-style?
114 Perfectly matching
116 Capt.'s inferior
117 Two-liter bottle contents
118 Miserly, Bard-style?
120 1973 Rolling Stones hit
121 "Be that ___ may . . ."
122 Customers: Abbr.
123 N.Y.P.D. employee
124 Spring purchase
125 France's Coty
126 Titter
127 Informal shirts

DOWN
1 Ward off
2 Stand for
3 Overplay
4 Carnival treat
5 Tuckered out
6 Stuntmen's woes
7 Folding challenge

8 Military E-1 or E-2, e.g.
9 Convertible, perhaps
10 Of a heart part
11 Public announcers
12 Edison contemporary
13 Manipulates, as data
14 Loading site
15 Minnesota's St. ___ College
16 Six-winged being
17 Access
18 Try again
24 Singer Merchant
29 Animals with calves
30 Opposite of bid
33 ___ tree
37 Qualified for the job
39 Age
41 Warmed up the crowd
42 Like some glass
43 "Your turn"
44 Durable wood
45 Like many Harlemites
46 Soviet co-op
47 Kind of block
48 Contemptible newspaper
52 Density symbol, in mechanics
53 Attached, in a way
54 Forsakes
55 Prefix with system
56 Half a cartoon duo
59 Summon up
62 Fore-and-aft sail
64 Balzac's Père ___
66 Puts in a blue funk
68 Pie chart section, perhaps
70 Playwright Pirandello
71 Medicinal amt.
72 ___ de vie
74 Antiquity, once
75 Having no master

77 Slangy suffix
78 [bo-o-o-ring!]
80 Vietnam's ___ Dinh Diem
81 Combat zone
83 Stone name
86 Dynamite component, for short
91 "Sprechen ___ Deutsch?"
92 Dab
93 Skelton catchphrase
94 Indian drums
95 "Seinfeld" role
96 Goren gaffe
97 "No ___!"
98 Sharpened
102 Prize for Page or Cage
103 Embraced
105 All-American name
107 Held up
108 Busy
109 Sidewalk Santas, e.g.
111 Pound, in Piccadilly
112 Versatile vehicles
113 "Now!"
115 In ___ (actually)
119 Break the ___

by Fred Piscop

ACROSS

1 Plantation workers
7 Where Renata Scotto debuted
14 Like some eggs
21 Heartthrob's fan
22 Call up, as reservists
24 Having missed the boat?
25 "Goose Feathers of Monte Cristo" by Alexandre Dumas
27 Cook's collection
28 Finger __
29 Many a millennia
30 Company
32 Traffic director
33 Wallet fill
34 Accounting acronym
35 "Exodus" hero
36 Chocolate treat
38 J.F.K. regulators
41 More than zero
42 Soybean paste
43 "Liberate My Sons" by Arthur Miller
46 Two-time Smythe Trophy winner
47 Never, in Nürnberg
48 Blanket
50 Bikini, e.g.
51 Urban bell site
52 Unruffled
54 Filmdom's Mr. Chips
56 Grimace
57 Remain unmoved
58 __ Gatos, Calif.
59 Hydrolysis atom
60 Iroquois foes
62 Old potentate
63 Horrible one
66 Printers' problems
68 Stay glued to
71 Busby Berkeley's real last name
72 Actress Archer
73 Steve Martin's "All __"
74 In working order
75 Carnival city
76 Papal hat

77 Whoop-de-__
78 Munchkin
79 Loop loopers
80 Veteran
82 Milky Way maker
83 Classic cars
84 "From where __..."
85 Mudslinger
86 Having the upper hand
88 Bohemian
89 Newspaper page
90 Hall-of-Famer born in Panama
91 System starter
92 Grp. making case studies?
93 Reduces
95 Wise guys
96 Edmonton skater
98 Hit the tarmac
102 Produce protection
103 Singer Neville
104 Stewart and Washington
106 Siam suffix
107 Acapulco gold
108 "The Leap Luck Club" by Amy Tan
111 __ free
112 Geom. point
113 Lovey
114 "Oh, uh-huh"
115 Suffix with ball or bass
116 Wine combiner
117 O'Hara estate
118 Publisher Henry
120 Jamaican sectarian
123 Hendrix hairdo
124 Mexican art
125 Cheapskate
128 "The Second Gratitude" by Walker Percy
131 Earnest
132 Oldest permanent settlement in Ohio
133 Right, in a way
134 Steamed
135 Natural tint source
136 Joined

DOWN

1 Bankers' errors
2 "Oklahoma!" girl
3 Not flashy
4 Marine eagles
5 Makes the calls
6 B.O. sign
7 "Tardy at Eight" by George S. Kaufman
8 It's said with a snap of the head
9 Tommy gun
10 Pres. Bush, to the Joint Chiefs
11 "__ santé"
12 Emmy-winning actress Metcalf
13 26 for Fe: Abbr.
14 __ favor
15 Amoeba feature
16 Comparable to a cucumber
17 Gab
18 "Aspiration Man" by Gore Vidal
19 Previous to
20 __ Plaines
23 D.D.E.'s oversight, once
26 Grow, in a way
31 Leaky
34 Feline ennead
35 Neck of the woods
37 Breathing sound
39 Riyadh resident
40 Host
42 D.M.V. part
43 Mickey and Huck
44 Woe of Genesis 12:10
45 Siouan tribesmen
49 Dazzling eyeful
51 Miss America accessory
53 Word of regret
55 "The Pekoe Towers" by J. R. R. Tolkien
57 Percentage
61 Full of chinks
62 Holds back
63 King of Judea
64 Old-womanish

65 "Much Ado About Virtue" by William Shakespeare
66 Bury
67 So far
68 Parody
69 "__ well"
70 Cross
72 Pointed
74 "An Individual Not Taken" by Robert Frost
76 Street performers
78 Food processor
81 Not live
82 Spanish wool
84 Locale for 1999 solar eclipse watchers
86 __ tricks
87 Track event
88 Put down
90 Nag
92 Budget rival
93 Stage piece
94 Frigid finish
95 "If He Walked Into My Life" musical
97 "__ a roll!"
99 Going to seed
100 Put off
101 Nuts
103 Spartan
105 Pay tribute to
108 "Dear John" letter writer
109 Community club
110 Erin Moran TV role
116 __ the races
117 Circus performer
119 Fairy tale start
121 Banking convenience
122 Roe source
123 About
124 Bring to tears
125 Nine-digit no. issuer
126 Word before ear or horn
127 Embarrassed
129 __ Gardens
130 Vietnam's __ Ranh Bay

by Randolph Ross

ACROSS

1 "Prima Ballerina" artist
6 Hill of law
11 Chester Arthur's middle name
15 Marvel Comics superhero
19 Betel nut tree
20 Confined to one part of the body
21 U-shaped instrument
22 How some things strike
23 Using tape on a bulletin board?
26 Part of the eye
27 Charades, basically
28 Most clever
29 Pell-___
30 Be near bankruptcy
31 Early 70's sitcom
32 Logo
34 Kind of twist
38 Some Brahms works
39 They probably don't think much of you
40 Convex molding
41 Furniture material
42 About 1% of the atmosphere
43 Headline about the Rolling Stones' leader's recovery?
46 Noted work?
48 Way out
52 Order at the George & Dragon
53 Sea bordering Kazakhstan
54 Huge
55 Come into one's own
57 Certain chord
59 Library material
60 Memory
61 A-mazing animals
64 It involves many sharp turns
65 Big paperback publisher
66 Hit the big time
67 Chucks
68 Color wheel display
69 Kitchen tool
70 Neighbor of Mont.
71 It's said with a wave of the hand
72 Compass heading
75 Catch
76 Fleece
77 Blows to the head?
80 Wallace cohort
83 Woman from Bethlehem
86 Sit up for
87 Dog treat
90 Brimless bonnet
91 Nixon policy
93 1980's Sandinista leader
94 Director's option
95 Lister's abbr.
96 Gloomy
97 Having less shading
99 Game resembling pinball
104 "Civilization" director Thomas
105 Soft drinks revealed?
107 She found success with Caesar
108 Purcell's "___ and Welcome Songs"
109 #2 Bill Withers hit of 1972
110 Like some stocks
111 Acetylacetone form
112 Common mixer
113 It may reflect well on you
114 Driving problem

DOWN

1 "Hi and Lois" family pet
2 Old railroad name
3 Contracts
4 One more than sieben
5 Towering desert plants: Var.
6 Certain gene
7 Silent votes
8 Here, but not here
9 Serving of 52-Across
10 Atlas Mountains locale
11 Pop star Morissette
12 Université preceder
13 Synagogue chests
14 Kitty
15 Cardsharp's technique?
16 Shantytown composition
17 Food that may be folded
18 Spheres
24 ". . . ___ You Ain't My Baby?" (1944 hit)
25 Pavarotti's football feats?
33 What Mr. Brown can do, in a Dr. Seuss title
34 Tomato variety
35 Ungodliness
36 Viva ___
37 Source of a bugle call
38 "Do ___!"
39 Centimeter-gram-second unit
41 Wrapped up
42 Advance amount
44 One taking orders
45 The Depression and others
47 Org. with many rules
49 Kind of thermometer
50 Hungry look
51 Lean (on)
54 Fancy home
55 Previously
56 Simple
57 "The Breakfast of Charlatans"?
58 Teen party
59 "We're constantly attacked" and "the stockades are rotting"?
61 Punishment unit
62 Janis's comic strip mate
63 Get-up-and-go
64 Influence
65 Philistine
67 Locks
68 Language with mostly monosyllabic words
71 Covered with many small figures, in heraldry
72 View electronically
73 Stage presentation
74 Italian duchess Beatrice d'___
76 Red or black, e.g.
78 Incubator activity
79 Cow, maybe
81 Hot time: Abbr.
82 Bombs
84 Like the oceans
85 Beat in yardage
87 Lace site
88 Affixable, in a way
89 It may be laid on thick
90 Mother ___
91 What thunder may do
92 Make permanent
94 Like many gardens
98 Fuss
99 Fleshy fruit
100 Favorite one
101 Palm used for basketry
102 Tree trunk bulge
103 Ghoul
106 Small peg

by Raymond Hamel

RARE BIRDS

ACROSS
1 Drams
5 Step on it!
10 Anjou alternative
14 Acted like a baby
19 Flu source
20 ___ legomenon (word that appears only once in a manuscript)
21 ". . . ___ dust shalt thou return"
22 "Step on it!"
23 Bird with a devoted following?
26 "___ of Winter" (1992 Eric Rohmer film)
27 Endures abuse
28 Cowardly bird?
30 Not taboo
32 Word in alumni notes
33 Kind of flute
34 What's place, in a comedy routine
36 Howls
38 Masterful
42 Paradigm of easiness
44 ___ polloi
45 Nasty fall?
47 Be extremely expectant
48 Zapping
52 Bird barber?
56 ___ Smith
57 Climb
58 Exchanged items, maybe
59 Look up to
60 Carson National Forest locale
61 They may be left hanging
63 Creature mentioned by Marco Polo

66 It's in 19-Across
67 Embarrassed bird?
70 Tony winner Neuwirth
71 Letters that please 42-Down
72 Six-time Super Bowl coach
73 Stand for
74 Part of many a disguise
76 Fabric finish?
77 "Death in Venice" author
78 They use horse-shoe crabs as bait
79 Bird with a severe drinking problem?
85 Swear by
86 Mt. Apo's locale, in the Philippines
87 Piecrust ingredient
88 Cologne cubes?
90 Bambi's aunt
91 Quarterback Humphries
92 Make out
94 Ravel wrote a piano concerto for it
98 1995 British Open winner John
100 You might say it when you get it
102 1954 Edgar Award winner
105 Celebratory bird?
111 "Steps in Time" autobiographer
112 1938 hit "I ___ Anyone Till You"
113 Bird on the links?
115 Moon of Uranus
116 "Women and Love" author
117 Library lack
118 Like some ears and elbows

119 70's–80's sitcom title role
120 Breeze (through)
121 Like wheat and barley
122 Show wild instability

DOWN
1 It took effect on Jan. 1, 1994
2 Father of biblical twins
3 Healthy-looking bird?
4 It has a lustrous face
5 Certain Muslim
6 Jet Propulsion Laboratory site
7 It has long arms
8 Dance partner
9 Lay out
10 Base caller
11 Clock or cat preceder
12 Pack
13 "The Private Eyes" co-star
14 Perot prop
15 Some boat motors
16 Kind of testimony
17 Perry's progenitor
18 Unnatural blonde, e.g.
24 Slithering strikers
25 Land in un lac
29 Golfer Geiberger and others
31 "In" place
35 Honeymoon haven
36 47-Across catcher
37 Sports Illustrated's 1974 Sportsman of the Year
39 Part of a vamp's costume
40 First Lady before Eleanor

41 Pliable leather
42 Backers
43 Tuition check taker
45 Domestic
46 "Der Blaue Reiter" artist
47 Studies
49 Poet Sor Juana ___ de la Cruz
50 Navigation abbr.
51 Sneaker
53 Branch of sci.
54 French orphan of film
55 "Once in Love With Amy" songwriter
60 1960 chess champion
61 Wedding planner
62 Arab name part
63 Bird on a night flight?
64 Moon of Uranus
65 Plane producer Clyde
68 Rain drain locale
69 Cherokee Natl. Forest locale
70 Wax unit?
72 Town on the Vire
75 Bit of a bray
76 Like some warehouses
77 Producer: Abbr.
79 Drilling expert: Abbr.
80 Horse bit
81 Charlottesville sch.
82 Yodeler's place
83 Bit of hope
84 Audiophile's purchase
89 Bonn boulevard
92 Father of Phinehas
93 Harmonizes, briefly

by Nancy Scandrett Ross

94 Cause of weird weather
95 Fastened, in a way
96 Cruz ___, Brazil
97 In the neighborhood
99 Felicitously

100 Adrien of skin care products
101 W.W. II general ___ Arnold
103 Often-missed humor
104 Not yet familiar with

105 "Kapow!"
106 Kumar of "The Jewel in the Crown"
107 His horse had eight legs
108 Karmann ___ (car)

109 Big prefix in banking
110 Sufficient, once
114 Alexander ingredient

1

```
HEMAN ▮ DAYBOOK ▮ SEMINAL
AWARE ▮ ASARULE ▮ TRINARY
YOUMARMYWORDS ▮ RAVIOLI
SKIPROPE ▮ META ▮ GMEN
▮ ITO ▮ THEJOYOFCOOING
TOMTOMS ▮ ELAN ▮ OEIL ▮
ADO ▮ STOCKWELL ▮ TOSSUP
BERRY ▮ AWK ▮ YOKE ▮ GOOSE
LOOOUTBELOW ▮ PIGGYBANS
ANNALS ▮ DEFROSTER ▮ SKAT
▮ DEAL ▮ FIN ▮ REPT ▮
AMAH ▮ REPOSSESS ▮ CLOAKS
SINORSWIM ▮ TAKEYOURPIC
IMAGE ▮ DOES ▮ INV ▮ MYRNA
NISSAN ▮ UNTRODDEN ▮ ODD
▮ DEUS ▮ AUTO ▮ SALINAS
BESTSELLINGBOO ▮ FEN ▮
OREO ▮ SYNC ▮ BETATEST
GUNSHOT ▮ THEJOEWASONME
UPSCALE ▮ REVERSE ▮ ENDUE
STEAMER ▮ ORANGES ▮ RESTS
```

2

```
GROWNOLD ▮ DOH ▮ VWS ▮ FIST
LOTHARIO ▮ ERA ▮ EAP ▮ ALPO
ONTOPOFSPAGHETTI ▮ SLOP
BIOME ▮ TIED ▮ AFTERHOURS
▮ PEDRO ▮ STEREO ▮ STE
ABOVEGROUND ▮ SSW ▮ ACE
MORITA ▮ UTERI ▮ EGAD
PLEBE ▮ FOLLOWINGORDERS
LOSE ▮ TAHOE ▮ ONANDON ▮
ITT ▮ NHLTEAM ▮ DIAPER
FIE ▮ BELOWSEALEVEL ▮ ELI
YESIAM ▮ LAXNESS ▮ TIP
▮ TEESHOT ▮ HITIT ▮ VETO
UNDERDISCUSSION ▮ DORIS
SOAR ▮ GIANT ▮ DELIST
ERR ▮ UPN ▮ AHEADOFTIME
RST ▮ ARABIA ▮ ALLEN ▮
BEFORELONG ▮ BAIL ▮ UPTON
AMOR ▮ PRECEDINGMESSAGE
SERB ▮ PER ▮ NUT ▮ HANDAXES
ENDS ▮ YDS ▮ TDS ▮ TREATIES
```

3

```
P R M A N   ■ R C A S ■ B I O G ■ M O S T
A O R T A ■ D E L I A ■ A G U A ■ O N C E
L E A R N ■ I V O R Y ■ B U R B ■ N E O N
■ N I E ■ S E V E N T E E N E I G H T Y
M A D A T ■ T A I ■ O A R S ■ K A R A T E
S A M ■ T A I L S ■ M U S ■ A M E L I A
G R R ■ E L L S ■ C H A T ■ P I L F E R
R E S T F U L ■ P O O L H A L L
■ N O A M ■ T O R M E ■ L E A H ■ F E B
A B O M B S ■ I S E E ■ P I N A ■ E C O
D U R E R ■ M E T R O A R E A ■ V E E R Y
E S T ■ A G A R ■ W H I R ■ R E D B U D
S H H ■ Y A L E ■ K N E L T ■ O N E L
S I D E R E A L ■ C O O L E S T
H A R A S S ■ P A R D ■ T O N I ■ A P E
A R A R A T ■ P I K ■ A R L E N ■ T E C
S E N T R A ■ I C O N ■ L I D ■ K E T C H
H O W L I T T L E W E K N O W ■ L E E
I L I E ■ I R O N ■ A L I D A ■ I R M A S
S A T S ■ O I S E ■ L A C E R ■ N I P P Y
H E H S ■ N O E S ■ E N O S ■ G E T O N
```

4

```
S T I R ■ M A S S E ■ B E R G S ■ P E C S
I O N A ■ A L C A N ■ E W E R S ■ A D I N
G R A N T S P A S S O R E G O N ■ P I T A
H A N D I C A P ■ A T L A W ■ T A S E R
T H E S E ■ C A T S K I L L N E W Y O R K
■ P G A ■ R O S E ■ R Y A N S ■
S E R G I O ■ H A W ■ T R A I L S ■
P L A I N V I E W N E B R A S K A ■ M B A
A K I N ■ E T A L ■ P R I M P ■ M E I N
T O N ■ B R I T ■ N O O N ■ G L I T Z Y
■ F R E N C H L I C K I N D I A N A ■
C H A I N S ■ A S H E ■ E U R O ■ P H D
H A L O ■ C O R E A ■ A G F A ■ S H O R
I L L ■ C O U N C I L B L U F F S I O W A
■ G I V E T H ■ E T S ■ F E R R E T
■ D E E R E ■ V E T O ■ T E N ■
H O L Y C R O S S A L A S K A ■ T H O S E
A R I S E ■ H E A L S ■ I C E R I N K S
R A T E ■ P A W N E E R O C K K A N S A S
E D E R ■ B R E T T ■ A N K L E ■ T E T E
M O S S ■ S A R A S ■ P O S E D ■ S T E N
```

6

Puzzle 5

```
S I T O N I T █ S L O P P Y █ C R O C K S
C O R N I C E █ T O W H E E █ A N Y O N E
T W A S T H R E E W E E K S █ S A L M O N
V A Y A █ █ I N R E █ N E I G H █ E X T
█ █ █ L E S █ T O R S O █ R I A L S █
A F T E R C H R I S T M A S A N D A L L
I L O █ T R U E D █ L E R O Y █ M I A O U
R A W D E A L █ B O N E R █ F O R T E S
E R I E █ M A T T E █ A S T E R N █ E W E
D E T A T █ H A U T E █ █ M A I T R E D
█ █ T H R O U G H T H E H O U S E █
B U S H I D O █ C A R A T █ H A S T O
I R A █ R A P T O R █ L E G I T █ S E A S
T B I R D S █ O N E A L █ C O R E T T A
S A L E M █ T R E A D █ T B O N E █ A U G
█ N O T A S I N G L E T H I N G F I T M E
█ R E N E E █ I N R E D █ A T M █
N O S █ T R O T S █ O R E O █ P L A N
Y O U B E T █ N O T E V E N A B L O U S E
S P I R A L █ A R I S E N █ T E A R G A S
E S T A T E █ N I C E S T █ H A S T E N S
```

Puzzle 6

```
Y E G G █ W H O A █ C O N S █ T U R B O S
A R E A █ H O P I █ O P A H █ A N O I N T
W I L L P O W E R █ C A R O L S I N G E R
█ T A B O O █ N A T O █ C L A S S █ F L O
A R T A P P R E C I A T I O N █ G O O K
P E I █ █ O Y E R █ A S M A D █ R O V E
T A N G I B L E █ E M U S █ S E D A T E D
█ █ E D R E D █ D O R I S █ R E C █
C O I N B O X █ P O L O █ T H E B E L L S
A G R E E S █ H A U L █ B O O K █ P O O H
S L I T █ P A T T Y M E L T █ E R G O
T E S H █ M O V E █ B I T E █ T E R R O R
A D H E R E T O █ C O D A █ P A T I E N T
█ █ R O W █ C A L L S █ A R T O O █
S L E A Z E S █ R O T H █ T O A N D F R O
H A S P █ D O G M A █ I O N A █ L E X
A T T Y █ R O C K Y P R O M O N T O R Y
M H O █ T E E T H █ I S E T █ H E A R A
P E N N Y A R C A D E █ L I L Y W H I T E
O R I E N T █ H I L L █ S M E E █ O N E L
O S A G E S █ A R I D █ E E G S █ E S S O
```

```
P L A C A R D S ■ C R A M ■ O F F T O
I O L A N T H E ■ ⑫H O U R N A I A D
M O T L I E S T ■ S M U D G E ■ A R N I E
P S A L M⑪ ■ L A I R D ■ D①D E A L S
■ V E E ■ W E I R D L Y ■ L I S L E S
S D I ■ S H A M A N S ■ S H A M ■ E D A
H A S⑩ L A T I N I ■ S C E N E②
O R T E G A ■ S T A G E N A M E ■ O P S
D N A T E S T ■ S C H L E P ■ I F A L L
■ S O H O ■ T E L E S I S ■ R A E
C A⑨ ■ R E T O L D ■ E L D E R S ■ ③B S
A L P ■ G R O S S E S ■ R E U S ■
R A I S E ■ T A M O R A ■ S L E E P O N
■ S N L ■ S A L T I N E S S ■ A R T E R Y
⑧S I D E S ■ A P P I A N ■ ④T H S
A L B ■ T Z A R ■ S T E E R E D ■ C E E
L E E L E E ■ P L A N N E R ■ C E L
T H R O W⑦S ■ A U N T S ■ ⑤A L I V E
A M A N A ■ I N T R O S ■ C O M B I N E R
R A T E R ■ D E E P⑥ ■ B R A I D I N G
S N E R D ■ S A S S ■ C O N N E C T S
```

```
H I G H S ■ N E L L ■ P E G S ■ T H A N E
I D I O T ■ A L O E ■ A C R E ■ R O P E S
T I N S E L T O W N ■ T H A T S A W R A P
■ T R I O ■ S T P ■ O N H A N D ■
A B S E N T ■ M O P E D ■ O S A G E S
L E T S O U T ■ L O U R D E S ■ P H O N E
E T A S ■ P I M E N T O ■ T A O ■ A V A
P O R E ■ M A D E ■ D R I L L S ■ L I L
H O R S E D ■ S T Y G I A N ■ M E D L E Y
S K I ■ D O N H O ■ A G E N D A ■ R I D S
■ N O O N E ■ P L Y ■ I N F U N
J I G S ■ A C A C I A ■ D A K A R ■ E D S
O N R U S H ■ H O T S P O T ■ C O R S E T
S H O ■ P U R I S T ■ E E R O ■ E T R E
H A L ■ L E O ■ M A R S A L A ■ F A I L
E L E N A ■ C A N A S T A ■ A D D E N D A
R E S E T S ■ B A N T U ■ H A R D E R
■ S T A S I S ■ I R E ■ S O S A ■
P R E S E N T D A Y ■ B R A N C H B A N K
C H O I R ■ D E L E ■ E L B A ■ E L S I E
T O N E S ■ S S S S ■ D E E P ■ R E P A Y
```

Note: Reading counterclockwise, the circled letters spell ROCKIN'
AROUND THE CHRISTMAS TREE.

9

```
PUMAS   PAPADOC   FLOAT
SHALOM  AIRLANE  GLANCE
SOMEPEOPLELIKETOICEIT
THECHAMP  UNE  OUTSIDE
    INS  PARTY  RLS
SPINET  MONEY  SEA  SHIP
WINO  POUT  OARS  CINE
ANDSOMEPREFERTOHEATIT
POI  CELS  INDUS  DRONE
STATURE  TITTER  SWANKY
  ALIGNED  RANATAB
PERMIT  ENAMEL  PARSING
IMAMS  PATHE  GILD  DOA
NOMATTERHOWYOUSLICEIT
ETON  ARTS  AMAH  PASO
DENY  TKO  SCRIM  SEALER
  MTS  SLANT  SYD
ISEEYOU  NAV  KINGDOMS
FEWPEOPLEYEARNTOEATIT
AMEERS  OVERDUE  DIVINE
TIRES  CARNAGE  NECKS
```

10

```
SLAMS  DAH  WHEE  CLOT
PINATA  EMOTIONS  LACE
INKJET  FIREPROOF  ACER
COLORBLINDNESS  LINEAR
YSER  AAA  EDDY  BOA  RNA
  BITING  AROMATIC
ABBAS  RCAS  RAZORBLADE
CLARE  DEBT  RHOMBUS
HOTBED  LEASE  IRS  LAP
IOTA  OTHERS  MEDO  CARR
EMER  CRU  NSA  LEK  OBIE
SERA  TAMS  EXCISE  NODS
TRY  COM  HATER  REVUES
  CARRYIN  REFS  TERSE
HONORBOUND  SELA  CYSTS
INERTIAL  PANCHO
PET  ELD  SERB  MTA  RTES
POWELL  INDOORBASEBALL
INOR  SIDEISSUE  TREBLE
ETRE  BERCEUSE  SILOED
SAKS  MATT  NED  ETONS
```

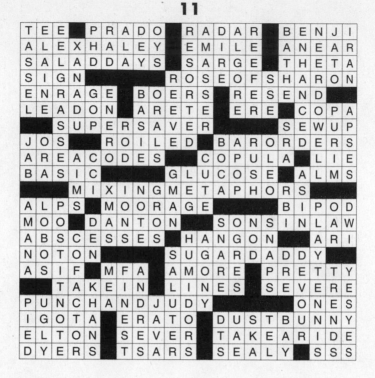

T	E	E	■	P	R	A	D	O	■	R	A	D	A	R	■	B	E	N	J	I
A	L	E	X	H	A	L	E	Y	■	E	M	I	L	E	■	A	N	E	A	R
S	A	L	A	D	D	A	Y	S	■	S	A	R	G	E	■	T	H	E	T	A
S	I	G	N	■	■	■	■	R	O	S	E	O	F	S	H	A	R	O	N	■
E	N	R	A	G	E	■	B	O	E	R	S	■	R	E	S	E	N	D	■	■
L	E	A	D	O	N	■	A	R	E	T	E	■	E	R	E	■	C	O	P	A
■	S	U	P	E	R	S	A	V	E	R	■	■	■	S	E	W	U	P	■	■
J	O	S	■	■	R	O	I	L	E	D	■	B	A	R	O	R	D	E	R	S
A	R	E	A	C	O	D	E	S	■	C	O	P	U	L	A	■	L	I	E	■
B	A	S	I	C	■	■	■	G	L	U	C	O	S	E	■	A	L	M	S	■
■	■	M	I	X	I	N	G	M	E	T	A	P	H	O	R	S	■	■	■	■
A	L	P	S	■	M	O	O	R	A	G	E	■	■	■	B	I	P	O	D	■
M	O	O	■	D	A	N	T	O	N	■	S	O	N	S	I	N	L	A	W	■
A	B	S	C	E	S	S	E	S	■	H	A	N	G	O	N	■	A	R	I	■
N	O	T	O	N	■	■	■	S	U	G	A	R	D	A	D	D	Y	■	■	■
A	S	I	F	■	M	F	A	■	A	M	O	R	E	■	P	R	E	T	T	Y
■	■	T	A	K	E	I	N	■	L	I	N	E	S	■	S	E	V	E	R	E
P	U	N	C	H	A	N	D	J	U	D	Y	■	■	■	O	N	E	S	■	■
I	G	O	T	A	■	E	R	A	T	O	■	D	U	S	T	B	U	N	N	Y
E	L	T	O	N	■	S	E	V	E	R	■	T	A	K	E	A	R	I	D	E
D	Y	E	R	S	■	T	S	A	R	S	■	S	E	A	L	Y	■	S	S	S

■	P	A	P	A	■	A	W	A	C	S	■	R	S	V	P	S	■	P	T	A
T	H	E	A	X	■	V	A	L	L	I	■	C	A	I	R	O	■	E	O	N
B	A	R	R	E	L	O	F	F	U	N	■	A	R	S	O	N	■	C	R	Y
I	R	A	■	L	A	I	T	■	B	U	S	■	D	I	M	■	I	K	E	■
R	A	T	E	■	I	D	S	■	F	A	T	L	O	T	O	F	G	O	O	D
D	O	O	M	E	D	■	B	A	T	A	A	N	■	S	U	L	F	U	R	■
S	H	R	E	D	O	F	D	E	C	E	N	C	Y	■	■	L	O	T	T	E
■	■	■	R	U	N	L	A	T	E	■	E	X	A	C	T	O	R	■	■	■
M	E	D	I	C	■	A	L	S	■	I	N	S	■	T	O	O	S	O	O	N
U	B	O	L	T	■	G	L	E	N	N	E	■	A	T	T	N	■	U	F	O
L	E	S	■	■	R	A	Y	O	F	H	O	P	E	■	■	■	B	T	U	■
E	R	E	■	R	D	A	S	■	T	R	I	K	E	S	■	R	U	L	E	S
S	T	O	V	E	I	N	■	S	E	A	■	E	M	T	■	I	R	E	N	E
■	■	F	E	L	T	T	I	P	■	H	E	A	T	I	N	G	■	■	■	■
F	A	R	G	O	■	■	L	O	A	D	O	F	N	O	N	S	E	N	S	E
O	M	E	G	A	S	■	L	O	B	A	T	E	■	■	V	E	N	O	U	S
G	R	A	I	N	O	F	T	R	U	T	H	■	H	B	O	■	T	S	P	S
■	A	L	E	■	M	A	R	■	T	A	O	■	O	A	K	S	■	E	P	A
I	D	I	■	P	A	G	E	D	■	B	U	N	D	L	E	O	F	J	O	Y
F	I	T	■	E	L	I	A	N	■	U	S	U	A	L	■	F	L	O	S	S
S	O	Y	■	P	I	N	T	A	■	S	E	N	D	S	■	T	U	B	E	■

13

J	E	S	U	■	S	A	U	L	■	■	C	H	O	P	■	■	A	C	M	E
I	V	E	S	■	U	L	N	A	■	S	L	O	W	E	D	■	R	H	E	A
M	E	T	E	R	M	A	I	D	■	C	E	L	L	A	R	D	O	O	R	S
I	N	A	R	U	T	■	■	D	R	E	A	M	S	■	O	R	A	C	L	E
■	■	■	L	E	A	P	■	I	N	N	S	■	S	P	A	R	K	E	D	
C	E	N	T	E	R	P	I	E	C	E	S	■	R	A	P	T	■	■	■	
I	L	I	E	■	■	E	N	C	A	S	E	■	E	R	E	■	S	H	O	O
S	I	N	S	■	D	R	N	O	■	R	A	Z	O	R	C	L	A	M	S	
C	A	E	S	A	R	S	A	L	A	D	■	L	O	Y	■	A	U	R	A	L
O	N	S	A	L	E	■	■	G	A	L	E	N	A	■	M	E	T	R	O	
■	■	■	L	I	Q	U	O	R	L	I	C	E	N	S	E	■	■	■		
I	M	A	G	E	■	U	N	D	I	E	S	■	■	P	U	C	C	I	S	
Z	E	L	I	G	■	O	S	E	■	S	P	I	D	E	R	P	L	A	N	T
O	D	O	R	E	A	T	E	R	S	■	N	A	V	Y	■	I	L	K	A	
D	E	E	D	■	N	E	W	■	A	S	P	I	R	E	■	F	I	L	L	
■	■	■	A	D	E	N	■	M	I	S	T	E	R	C	O	F	F	E	E	
H	O	N	O	U	R	S	■	O	P	T	S	■	S	T	O	P	■	■	■	
A	P	O	G	E	E	■	P	A	L	A	T	E	■	C	I	C	A	D	A	
S	E	W	E	R	W	O	R	K	E	R	■	S	O	C	C	E	R	M	O	M
P	R	I	E	■	S	H	O	E	R	S	■	T	H	E	Y	■	A	B	L	Y
S	A	N	S	■	■	O	W	N	S	■	A	M	E	X	■	G	I	L	L	

14

M	A	S	T	■	A	D	A	M	■	S	C	U	M	■	S	A	S	H	A	Y
A	R	L	O	■	W	O	R	K	S	H	A	R	D	■	O	C	T	A	V	E
S	C	O	T	C	H	W	I	T	H	A	B	A	S	S	C	H	A	S	E	R
C	O	T	E	R	I	E	■	A	D	I	N	■	A	L	E	R	T	■		
■	■	M	I	L	L	E	R	G	E	N	U	I	N	E	D	R	A	F	T	
M	A	P	■	B	E	L	L	E	■	■	S	S	T	■	■	S	L	U	R	
U	C	L	A	■	I	N	U	S	E	■	H	A	L	F	■	U	N	A	■	
G	U	I	N	N	E	S	S	O	N	T	A	P	■	S	A	L	I	E	R	I
G	R	E	N	O	B	L	E	■	M	A	R	A	T	■	Z	I	P	G	U	N
S	A	D	■	T	O	E	■	C	A	R	■	T	A	W	■	C	O	O	N	S
■	■	■	J	A	N	D	B	O	N	T	H	E	R	O	C	K	S	■		
S	H	E	I	K	■	S	O	B	■	I	A	N	■	R	I	O	■	O	R	A
C	O	A	L	E	R	■	W	R	I	N	G	■	A	S	A	F	A	V	O	R
R	O	S	T	R	U	M	■	A	C	O	U	P	L	E	O	F	B	U	D	S
A	R	T	■	S	T	E	M	■	K	N	E	E	L	■	■	C	L	E	O	
G	A	B	S	■	R	B	I	■	■	T	I	S	C	H	■	E	O	N	■	
S	H	O	T	O	F	C	A	N	A	D	I	A	N	C	L	U	B	■		
■	S	U	C	R	E	■	A	T	O	N	■	H	O	L	L	O	W	S		
P	I	T	C	H	E	R	O	F	O	L	D	M	I	L	W	A	U	K	E	E
A	V	O	C	E	T	■	N	I	N	E	S	E	V	E	N	■	F	I	R	E
T	E	N	O	R	S	■	E	X	E	S	■	G	Y	P	S	■	F	E	E	D

15

S	T	A	R		H	O	S	P	I	C	E		T	R	A	D	I	N	G
H	A	B	I	T		E	N	T	I	T	L	E		R	E	T	I	N	A	E
A	L	A	M	O		F	E	A	T	H	E	R		I	L	O	S	T	I	T
V	O	T	E	R	S		A	S	H	E	N		G	A	I	N		E	L	I
E	N	E		T	E	T	C	H	Y		C	H	I	L	E		E	R	S	T
			T	O	A	S	T		K	H	A	N		V	I	M			
H	O	M	E	I	C	E		A	W	N	E	D		M	E	N	O	R	A	H
A	L	O	N	S	O		D	R	I	E	D		R	E	D	S	T	A	R	T
R	E	D	S	E	A		R	I	D	E		S	E	T		P	E	R	M	S
E	S	S	E		S	P	A	D	E	D		T	A	R		A	D	A	Y	
			S	T	A	G	E				A	L	I	G	N			
	H	I	R	E		S	O	S		M	U	N	I	C	H		G	I	N	A
T	O	N	I	C		C	U	T		A	N	D	S		E	A	R	N	E	D
M	A	R	V	E	L	A	T		P	R	O	E	M		T	H	I	E	V	E
C	R	E	E	D	A	L		F	O	S	S	E		S	T	A	N	Z	A	S
		R	E	V		W	A	S	H			G	E	O	I	D			
P	I	N	S		A	B	O	R	T		W	A	R	M	E	R		G	E	M
O	N	O		C	L	A	N		P	A	I	N	E		S	C	U	R	R	Y
P	A	R	B	O	I	L		F	O	R	E	V	E	R		U	S	E	R	S
U	N	T	A	M	E	D		A	N	I	L	I	N	E		T	A	B	O	O
P	E	E	L	E	R	S		N	E	E	D	L	E	S		F	E	R	N	

16

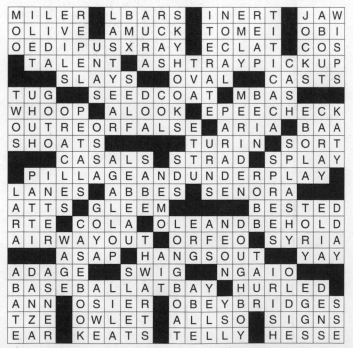

M	I	L	E	R		L	B	A	R	S		I	N	E	R	T		J	A	W
O	L	I	V	E		A	M	U	C	K		T	O	M	E	I		O	B	I
O	E	D	I	P	U	S	X	R	A	Y		E	C	L	A	T		C	O	S
	T	A	L	E	N	T		A	S	H	T	R	A	Y	P	I	C	K	U	P
		S	L	A	Y	S		O	V	A	L			C	A	S	T	S	
T	U	G			S	E	E	D	C	O	A	T		M	B	A	S		
W	H	O	O	P		A	L	O	O	K		E	P	E	E	C	H	E	C	K
O	U	T	R	E	O	R	F	A	L	S	E		A	R	I	A		B	A	A
S	H	O	A	T	S						T	U	R	I	N		S	O	R	T
		C	A	S	A	L	S		S	T	R	A	D		S	P	L	A	Y	
	P	I	L	L	A	G	E	A	N	D	U	N	D	E	R	P	L	A	Y	
L	A	N	E	S		A	B	B	E	S		S	E	N	O	R	A		
A	T	T	S		G	L	E	E	M						B	E	S	T	E	D
R	T	E		C	O	L	A		O	L	E	A	N	D	B	E	H	O	L	D
A	I	R	W	A	Y	O	U	T		O	R	F	E	O		S	Y	R	I	A
		A	S	A	P		H	A	N	G	S	O	U	T			Y	A	Y	
A	D	A	G	E		S	W	I	G		N	G	A	I	O			
B	A	S	E	B	A	L	L	A	T	B	A	Y		H	U	R	L	E	D
A	N	N		O	S	I	E	R		O	B	E	Y	B	R	I	D	G	E	S
T	Z	E		O	W	L	E	T		A	L	L	S	O		S	I	G	N	S
E	A	R		K	E	A	T	S		T	E	L	L	Y		H	E	S	S	E

17

```
B U S H ■ B U B ■ H A A G ■ S C O O P ■
A B O U T ■ E L I G I B L E ■ W I N N I E
C O M M A N D T O A D O G S L E D T E A M
H A M I T U P ■ L I E U ■ T A L E ■ A F T
■ T E D ■ M O R O N S ■ P A S T R Y ■
■ L I E ■ S A G S ■ C O P S E ■ P L A N
G A I T S ■ T H Y ■ C L I O O R E R A T O
A G E I S T S ■ N O E L ■ G E T T O
B U R E A U ■ R E E L O U T ■ W Y S T A N
S A S S ■ T H E R M O ■ O S I P ■ E R E
■ S T U B B O R N B E A S T ■
Y E R ■ T U T U ■ F A M I N E ■ B S M T
A R A R A T ■ S T R A P I N ■ S C O T I A
D R O O L ■ R U S E ■ S T A B I L E
D O U B L E A G E N T ■ B E E ■ L T C O L
A R L O ■ C L O V E ■ C A G E ■ L A K
■ T A H I T I ■ O H I O A N ■ I S A
C A M ■ B E B E ■ A U E L ■ F E L L I N I
W H A T O L I V E R T W I S T W A N T E D
T E J A N O ■ E N T R Y F E E ■ N A T A L
■ M A V E N ■ N O S E ■ F A R ■ G O R E
```

18

```
W O L F ■ B O N A M I ■ D E L L ■ T A T A
E M I R ■ O V I S A C ■ E P E E ■ E V A N
F A C I A L E X P R E S S I O N ■ L A N G
T R E A S U R E S ■ B O I L ■ A M E N D S
■ R I S E S ■ R A N C O R ■ O C T E T
B I D ■ S E A ■ B A G G A G E C L A I M ■
U S E S ■ S T A I D ■ R O D S ■
L A C E S ■ L O A D E D Q U E S T I O N
K A L A H A R I ■ R E D O U N D ■ N R A
S C A L A W A G ■ P A R E ■ C A M R Y
■ R U N N I N G C O M M E N T A R Y ■
A G A P E ■ I O U S ■ R O U L E T T E
A N N ■ H E N R E I D ■ I M P L O R E S
A U T O S U G G E S T I O N ■ A L I S T
■ P A N G ■ M A G I C ■ A B L E
■ C O U N T E R O F F E R ■ S H H ■ E A R
C H I L D ■ D E M U R S ■ U S A I R ■
H A L E S T ■ V A N E ■ I N U N D A T E S
E R I N ■ B L A N K E T S T A T E M E N T
A L E C ■ S E M I ■ S A L I N E ■ B E V Y
P Y R E ■ P I P S ■ T W E E T Y ■ O N Y X
```

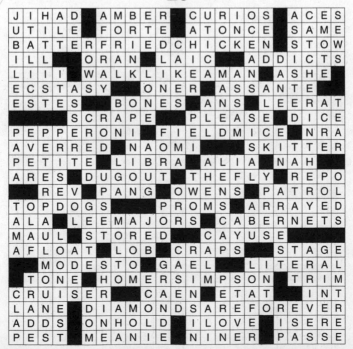

C	A	L	F	■	D	U	E	■	B	R	A	N	C	H	■	G	A	M	E	R
I	D	E	A	L	I	S	T	■	R	E	V	I	L	E	■	O	P	I	N	E
D	E	G	R	A	D	E	R	■	A	V	A	T	A	R	■	L	A	N	D	S
E	L	O	■	G	E	R	E	■	C	E	N	T	S	O	F	F	C	O	U	P
R	A	F	T	E	R	S	■	T	H	A	T	I	S	■	O	P	E	R	E	■
■	M	I	R	O	■	S	O	I	L	■	■	■	A	R	R	■	■	■	■	■
S	T	U	N	■	T	H	E	D	A	■	T	W	I	S	T	O	F	L	E	M
K	I	T	E	S	■	A	R	A	L	■	H	A	T	H	■	J	A	V	A	■
Y	E	T	■	E	S	S	A	Y	■	T	O	K	A	Y	■	S	O	B	I	G
■	■	T	A	T	■	■	A	R	M	E	N	■	■	P	R	O	T	O	■	
S	A	I	N	T	G	E	O	R	G	E	A	N	D	T	H	E	D	R	A	G
A	G	R	E	E	■	P	O	L	E	S	■	■	U	A	W	■	■	■	■	■
L	A	R	G	E	■	O	R	B	E	D	■	B	I	L	G	E	■	O	L	D
E	M	E	R	■	B	A	I	T	■	S	E	M	I	■	D	R	U	I	D	■
M	A	G	I	C	J	O	H	N	S	■	T	R	A	P	P	■	O	T	I	S
■	■	H	I	E	■	■	L	I	E	N	■	H	A	L	O	■	■	■	■	■
■	S	C	O	R	N	■	P	A	T	E	N	T	■	B	E	N	E	F	I	T
I	L	L	F	I	X	H	I	S	W	A	G	■	A	R	N	O	■	S	R	I
N	A	I	F	S	■	A	C	T	I	V	E	■	G	O	O	D	D	E	A	L
R	I	V	E	T	■	L	O	A	N	E	R	■	T	O	L	E	R	A	T	E
E	N	E	R	O	■	S	T	R	E	S	S	■	S	D	S	■	Y	S	E	R

J	I	H	A	D	■	A	M	B	E	R	■	C	U	R	I	O	S	■	A	C	E	S
U	T	I	L	E	■	F	O	R	T	E	■	A	T	O	N	C	E	■	S	A	M	E
B	A	T	T	E	R	F	R	I	E	D	C	H	I	C	K	E	N	■	S	T	O	W
I	L	L	■	O	R	A	N	■	L	A	I	C	■	A	D	D	I	C	T	S	■	
L	I	I	I	■	W	A	L	K	L	I	K	E	A	M	A	N	■	A	S	H	E	
E	C	S	T	A	S	Y	■	O	N	E	R	■	A	S	S	A	N	T	E	■		
E	S	T	E	S	■	B	O	N	E	S	■	A	N	S	■	L	E	E	R	A	T	
■	■	S	C	R	A	P	E	■	P	L	E	A	S	E	■	D	I	C	E	■		
P	E	P	P	E	R	O	N	I	■	F	I	E	L	D	M	I	C	E	■	N	R	A
A	V	E	R	R	E	D	■	N	A	O	M	I	■	S	K	I	T	T	E	R		
P	E	T	I	T	E	■	L	I	B	R	A	■	A	L	I	A	■	N	A	H		
A	R	E	S	■	D	U	G	O	U	T	■	T	H	E	F	L	Y	■	R	E	P	O
■	R	E	V	■	P	A	N	G	■	O	W	E	N	S	■	P	A	T	R	O	L	
T	O	P	D	O	G	S	■	■	P	R	O	M	S	■	A	R	R	A	Y	E	D	
A	L	A	■	L	E	E	M	A	J	O	R	S	■	C	A	B	E	R	N	E	T	S
M	A	U	L	■	S	T	O	R	E	D	■	C	A	Y	U	S	E	■				
A	F	L	O	A	T	■	L	O	B	■	C	R	A	P	S	■	S	T	A	G	E	
■	M	O	D	E	S	T	O	■	G	A	E	L	■	L	I	T	E	R	A	L		
■	T	O	N	E	■	H	O	M	E	R	S	I	M	P	S	O	N	■	T	R	I	M
C	R	U	I	S	E	R	■	C	A	E	N	■	E	T	A	T	■	I	N	T		
L	A	N	E	■	D	I	A	M	O	N	D	S	A	R	E	F	O	R	E	V	E	R
A	D	D	S	■	O	N	H	O	L	D	■	I	L	O	V	E	■	I	S	E	R	E
P	E	S	T	■	M	E	A	N	I	E	■	N	I	N	E	R	■	P	A	S	S	E

21

Grid 21:

```
ROUTES  THEBUG   SCOOPER
INSANA  RAMONE   ALFREDO
THECOMMUNISTMANIFESTO
ZERO  PEA    TAILEND
YRS  BARNS   OMNI  GAILS
   NINETEENEIGHTYFOUR
ARDEN   SIN    NEO  TINA
GARAGES  NOTBEEN  THRUM
AMAPOFTHEWORLD  CHEEPS
TIMS  FAA   PIA  SHIN
ESS  SONGOFSOLOMON  GAP
   CURD   ARP  ROM  PELE
TSHIRT  BRAINDROPPINGS
ATONE  KASTNER  TSELIOT
LOWE  NIL   HES   NOELS
CRIMEANDPUNISHMENT
  YEARN  IANA  SUITE  BAR
   INASNIT   STY  EURO
5001NIGHTSATTHEMOVIES
GILLNET  IONISE  ORELSE
SEABASS  ENTERS  NORTON
```

22

Grid 22:

```
BASS  CHAMP  LSTS  INLET
ETTU  HELIO  ACHT  NOUNS
ERAS  ALIGN  SHEEPTRICK
FISHANDSHIPS  REALIZES
SAHIB  TOTER  FELL
   LOON  SIFTS  ESCAPE
  GRIER  MUSICALSHARES
LEAH  ECLIPSE  OTHELLO
ENNE  GAOL  RUHR  NOES
SODACANS  DECLARED
SABRINATHETEENAGEWISH
   TODIEFOR  SIGNAWAY
AHAB  ITSA  AONE  LISP
PALOOKA  UNARMED  ELSE
SHOPPINGBLOCK  ODDLY
EATSAT  ULTRA  AGNI
   SPIT  ADDLE  MONKS
SHORTCUT  SHEIKTOSHEIK
CASHPHRASE  MAAMS  GALE
ANOUK  SRAS  ILLAT  OTOE
BASES  ESTE  ASIDE  DOST
```

```
☀DAYPUNCH ■ CAPT ■ ASPIRE
REMEASURE ■ ORLY ■ SPARES
OBSTRUCTS ■ SOAPOPERA☆S
OAT ■ CAL ■ RIMIER ■ CESTA
FRED ■ LEASE ■ ADDICTS ■
■ REF ■ ITLL ■ SUGARIEST
MADCAP ■ LOADS ■ PILASTER
TRACERS ■ STENO ■ NFL ■ HAY
STMARYS ■ HELENES ■ LABS
■ IOS ■ IRES ■ TENET
☾RIVER ■ ☀☾AND☆S ■ ☀RISES
CONES ■ ILIE ■ ODE ■
HAVE ■ ANIMATO ■ CANASTA
IDE ■ BED ■ TETON ■ TEDIOUS
LINSEEDS ■ EERIE ■ SERUMS
DETERGENT ■ BOIL ■ DEL ■
■ ENSNARE ■ ANNUL ■ STEP
AMATI ■ DROLLY ■ PAS ■ RKO
TOTHE☾ALICE ■ SHIRTTAIL
APIECE ■ AKIN ■ TANGERINE
NEEDED ■ TADA ■ SHOOTING☆
```

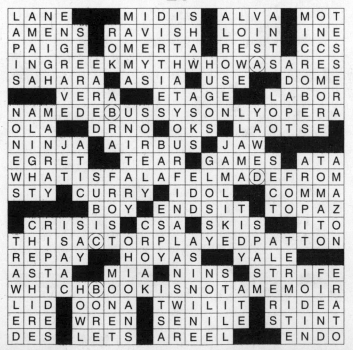

```
LANE ■ MIDIS ■ ALVA ■ MOT
AMENS ■ RAVISH ■ LOIN ■ INE
PAIGE ■ OMERTA ■ REST ■ CCS
INGREEKMYTHWHO(A)SARES
SAHARA ■ ASIA ■ USE ■ DOME
■ VERA ■ ETAGE ■ LABOR
NAMEDE(B)USSYSONLYOPERA
OLA ■ DRNO ■ OKS ■ LAOTSE
NINJA ■ AIRBUS ■ JAW ■
EGRET ■ TEAR ■ GAMES ■ ATA
WHATISFALAFELMA(D)EFROM
STY ■ CURRY ■ IDOL ■ COMMA
■ BOY ■ ENDSIT ■ TOPAZ
■ CRISIS ■ CSA ■ SKIS ■ ITO
THISA(C)TORPLAYEDPATTON
REPAY ■ HOYAS ■ YALE ■
ASTA ■ MIA ■ NINS ■ STRIFE
WHICH(B)OOKISNOTAMEMOIR
LID ■ OONA ■ TWILIT ■ RIDEA
ERE ■ WREN ■ SENILE ■ STINT
DES ■ LETS ■ AREEL ■ ENDO
```

25

```
A L A S K A   S B A   A S T R O   S P A
R E P A Y S   E A S T   O C H E R   O R R
F O R N O W   A T T Y   N O E L S   S U M
      I T A   C H A P T E R I I   D O N A
B O N B O N B O O B O O   P R E F A C E D
O K I E   L A I   R A I   F E D O R A
W A L L A W A L L A Y O Y O   T A U S
L Y E   V I C   S I T I N   C O P S
      M O N K S   S T D   H U A R A C H E
P E C A N   B E A L E   M A R K   W O O L
O A H U   D I N N E R P A R T Y   P U S S
P R I M   U R S A   B O O K I   P A S T A
E S C A P A D E   C I I   S C R E W
      H U L L   S H U L A   A I R   A G E
      P I N A   M U U M U U F R O U F R O U
S E C O N D   I B M   T O I   I G O R
T R A N S I T S   P A G O P A G O D O D O
A R N O   C A R D S H A R P   A P E
B I C   M I M E O   A L A I   S A L T E D
L E A   S E P A L   S E C S   P R I O R Y
E R N   G R A D E   N E H   S T O O G E
```

26

```
P R A H A   G R A B   A C A D S   A R R E T
E U L E R   M A U N A   R A M I S   L E E R Y
S T A R T   A B B A S   C H E A T   A S S N S
T H E B U L L B Y T H E H O R N S   B E T S
      R I T E S   M O O R E   M A M
H I R E   C O D   P L E N T Y   L A M B D A S
U S U R I E S   F A C E   T O N A L I T Y
T H E M O N E Y A N D R U N A W A Y   E S O S
      A U S   O D E S   S A B I N E S   M R T
C P A   S O C K E D   A U T O   S A L S A
A R L O   R O I   A B R A M S   R U N N E R
V I L L A   O N F I V E P L A C E   M E T R O
A G E I S M   G R O A T S   A R M   E L I O
      N O T O F   O N U S   P A L A I S   E N T
S P F   I D I A M I N   A I D A   G P S
L O I S   E F F E C T A F T E R S H A P E U P
A L L U P S E T   R A T S   O T T A W A S
W O M B A T S   V I P E R S   X I I   N E W T
      T R Y   L E N A S   D A R E R
      F I R E   H O L D D O W N O V E R O F F I N
R O D A N   O C C U R   E E R I E   W I L M A
E R E C T   P A R C E   D R I E S   A D O P T
G M A T S   S L O T S   S O A R   N O R S E
```

27

```
R O A D I E   A S I M O V   P A L A T E S
U P L A N D   P H R A S E   I P A N E M A
B R O W N I E P O I N T S   N O S T R I L
E Y E D   T A L E S E   P I E C H A R T S
    L O O S E D   A M E N D     C A S A
S E M I D R Y     S T A R S   O B I
O M A N I   M A S H E D   T A P E D E C K
F U D G E F A C T O R   B Y L A W   R O I
T S E   A R T U R   M A L T L I Q U O R
    T A N K E D   M I N E O   T U C K S
  S W I N G     I Z A A K   S C A T S
S W A M I   A R O A R   C A T C H Y
C A K E M A K E U P   M A C H O     G T E
A L E   A M I S S   B A R M I T Z V A H S
R E D O L E N T   D R Y D E N   B I Z E T
    U S N   A T L A S     S H A N A N A
M O L T   D R A I N   F A K E R Y
C H I P S H O T S   D E A R I E   L A N A
G A S O H O L   M I N T C O N D I T I O N
E R A S U R E   A L E U T S   E R O D E D
E A S T E N D   N O W I S E   R E P E L S
```

28

```
T H O U   O P T   C H O O   R E A C T O R
R O A N   S L A M D U N K   O I L L I N E
O N K P   P I K E S P E A K O R B O A S T
D I S A G R E E D     C P O   E I S N E R
    I N E R T I A   A I D E   N E T T Y
A L L D A Y S O A K E R S   Q U O D
D O U B T     T I N     N U S   S T A B
O G R I S H   G O O D C L E A N P H O N E
B O I L   Y S E R   H A U L   L O R N E
E S E L   D O N   S T A I R   T I P T O P
    O R I E N T A L R O G U E
I B E R I A   R U A R K   S E C   T O D D
S A T I N   B A L I   B I L K   E R O O
B L A C K W A L L N O T E S   S K E I N S
N E T H   E L S   A A A   A T O N E
    T K T S   H O T C R O S S B O N E S
S A S H A   A S I F   T U N E O U T
A L M O N D   A R Y   P E T U L A N C E
N O I F S A N D S O R B O A T S   L A R A
Y O T E A M O   C R Y U N C L E   E N O S
O P E N S E A   H E E D   T E D   R A C Y
```

R	A	M	P	S		C	A	T	E		T	O	P	I	C		S	T	A	Y
A	R	I	A	N		A	L	V	Y		A	V	I	L	A		C	O	M	A
J	U	S	T	I	N	C	A	S	E		P	A	U	L	B	E	A	R	E	R
A	N	T	I	D	O	T	E		H	E	E	L	S		O	R	M	O	N	D
		N	E	H	I		C	O	L	D	S		C	O	O	P				
A	R	C	A	R	O		P	A	L	A	U		G	O	S	S	I	P	E	R
G	A	L	E		W	A	R	R	E	N	P	E	A	C	E		E	D	U	
I	D	I		M	O	E		A	T	A		R	I	N	S	E				
R	I	F	T		W	A	N	D	A	L	U	S	T		G	I	N	N	E	D
L	I	F	E	L	O	N	G		L	I	N	E		R	E	S	T	Y	L	E
		H	E	A	R	D		S	E	M	I	S		O	N	E	A	L		
G	R	A	N	D	M	A		W	R	I	T		C	O	R	N	C	O	B	S
R	A	N	E	E	S		P	A	T	T	Y	C	A	K	E		T	A	L	E
E	N	G	R	S		M	A	N		A	L	I			F	A	T			
A	C	E		M	A	R	S	H	A	D	I	M	E	S		M	E	S	H	
T	H	R	U	W	A	Y	S		I	R	O	N	S		A	B	O	R	T	S
		T	A	N	S		S	T	E	V	E		O	L	E	S				
S	E	G	U	R	A		P	O	S	S	E		I	N	T	H	E	A	C	T
T	E	R	R	Y	C	L	O	T	H		B	E	S	S	S	E	L	L	E	R
A	K	I	N		L	E	N	T	O		A	C	N	E		S	L	I	D	E
T	S	P	S		E	N	D	O	W		R	O	O	T		T	E	T	E	S

I	M	P		F	I	L	M		I	R	A	Q			I	N	V	E	S	T
M	A	I	N	I	D	E	A		V	E	N	U	S		S	O	A	S	T	O
P	I	P	E	D	O	W	N		A	N	G	I	E		N	A	S	C	A	R
A	L	E	V	E	L		H	A	N	D	L	E	W	I	T	H	C	A	R	E
C	I	T	E	S		F	O	R		S	E	T	A	T		S	O	L	E	
T	N	T		S	E	L	A		O	R	E	S			A	D	A			
	G	E	T	T	H	E	E	B	E	H	I	N	D	M	E	S	A	T	A	N
	E	A	R	L	S		W	A	R	T		S	E	N	N	E	T	T		
K	I	S	S	M	E		D	I	N	A	H	S		P	O	D				
A	L	I	T		D	U	G	O	N	G		E	E	L	S		R	E	L	Y
R	I	N	G		T	A	N	G	L	E	S	U	P		O	R	E	O		
L	E	E	R		P	E	S	T		O	R	E	L	S	E		M	I	N	K
		O	A	R		P	T	B	O	A	T		F	R	E	E	Z	E		
I	N	H	U	M	E	R		R	U	S	T		S	C	R	O	D			
K	E	E	P	Y	O	U	R	E	Y	E	O	N	T	H	E	B	A	L	L	
E	E	R		P	L	E	A		S	I	A	M			A	A	H			
	D	A	C	E		E	D	D	I	E		E	C	O		R	E	C	T	O
A	L	L	H	A	N	D	S	O	N	D	E	C	K		M	I	N	O	R	S
S	E	D	A	T	E		E	N	F	I	N		S	T	E	P	O	N	I	T
O	S	I	R	I	S		A	M	E	N	D		B	A	S	E	L	I	N	E
F	S	C	O	T	T		E	R	A	S		Y	U	A	N		C	E	L	

31

```
GASP   TAMALE      CRIPPLE
OVER   ARUGULA   BOUNTIES
FIXESDAMAGES   INTHECAN
ELECTS     EMILE    AROSE
RADIO   DISREGARDSNOTES
     POLISH   NNW   OLD
ADS   PAGEANT   PRO   TREE
BEHEST   DISPLAYSVEILS
BAIL   INTEL   AYN   HELDUP
ALPS   SOU    ARROW   NEELY
    WITHDRAWSDEPOSITS
LORNA   STRIP    LEE   HARE
AREOLE   LES   SAYSA   OWED
INCREASESCUTS   BANANA
COKE   TIS    NASTIER   YOM
     LIT   BAH   TENETS
OBTAINSRELEASES   FARSI
CRONE    AGORA    AUGEAN
TAKESFOR   FOLLOWSLEADS
EVENTIME   TITANIC   SITE
TENDONS    COMETH   TROT
```

32

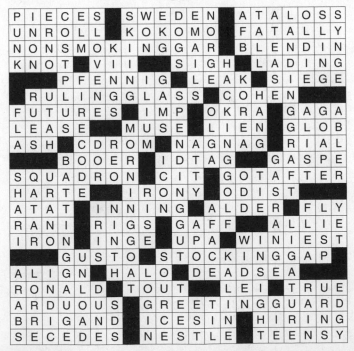

```
PIECES   SWEDEN   ATALOSS
UNROLL   KOKOMO   FATALLY
NONSMOKINGGAR   BLENDIN
KNOT   VII    SIGH   LADING
    PFENNIG    LEAK   SIEGE
   RULINGGLASS    COHEN
FUTURES   IMP   OKRA   GAGA
LEASE    MUSE   LIEN   GLOB
ASH   CDROM   NAGNAG   RIAL
    BOOER   IDTAG    GASPE
SQUADRON   CIT   GOTAFTER
HARTE    IRONY   ODIST
ATAT   INNING   ALDER   FLY
RANI   RIGS   GAFF    ALLIE
IRON   INGE   UPA   WINIEST
    GUSTO   STOCKINGGAP
ALIGN   HALO   DEADSEA
RONALD   TOUT   LEI   TRUE
ARDUOUS   GREETINGGUARD
BRIGAND   ICESIN   HIRING
SECEDES   NESTLE   TEENSY
```

33

```
M A L T   T O D A T E   M A R     W A G S
A M I R   A L I N E S   A H A B   I N R E
N O🔔A U R E A T E S   🔔A T L A N T I C
U R A L S   O N E T E N     C A P S I Z E
R A W E S T     🔔O N A   C H I T   W A D
E L S E   K A P U T   E T H E R   L A🔔E
      C O S I M A     H I T     E R A S
C A M P U S E S   L A B O R   P C T
A M I E S   C A Y   C A R A M E L   D S T
M A R A T     N A D E R   C E R E🔔U M S
P L A C A R D   P O T🔔Y   R E V E R I E
🔔I G E R E N T   W A S I T     E V E R T
S E E   D E A R E S T   N U S   R U S K S
      A S K   U L E E S   N O B L E S S E
A M B I     T A E   A V I A R Y
N E E D   F I N E D   G A S P E   C R A M
N R A   M I N T   O P A L     R E L I V E
A R T W O R K   C A M E O S   C A V I L
🔔I N I O P E R A   P O R T O🔔O R O A D
E L I S   O R T S   A R I O S O   A L T E
E L K E   🔔E S   S E E S A W   🔔I E D
```

34

```
F R A U   A S M A D     P E C S   B E S T
E A R P   L E A V E N   S T L O   A L P O
T H E B I G C H I L I   T H E F A R M E R
E S S E N   A L E C S   N A I L D O W N
      A T T I L A T H E H O N E Y
N E C T A R Y   E E R O     C L I P
E C O   C I A O   V J S   S E A M A N
S H O R T O R D E R C O O K I E   N E V A
T O T O   O L E O S   O D D B A L L S
    P S I S   I N N   R A G A   D O T
H A V E O N E F O O T I N T H E G R A V Y
A B E   O V E R   A G O   O S S A
M A R I N A T E   S C O T T   G A E L
A T O M   D O E S N T R I N G A B E L L Y
S E N A T E   D U O   T A R A   T K O
  D A N E   L O S T   L A M P O O N
    P I C K U P T H E T A B B Y
M A I D E N L Y   S I E V E   O T H E R
I N T H E D E L I   C H I C A G O H O P I
S O T O   I W I N   K A T H I E   O L I N
S N O W   A S E A   T A S T E   N E C K
```

```
C A B A N A ■ C A N N E S ■ ■ M A F I A S
A L A M O S ■ O R I O L E ■ W O M A N L Y
R O B O T S ■ L A N D E R ■ H O I S T E D
I H A V E N O O B J E C T I O N S T O ■ ■
B A S E L ■ T R Y A ■ ■ T Y E S ■ ■ ■ ■
■ ■ ■ L I R A ■ P A S T O R ■ B I T E
S P E D ■ L O N G T E D I O U S P L A Y S
T O L I F E ■ T E H R A N ■ ■ L U M P S
A R I E L ■ A S T R O ■ K I L L E R B E E
Y E S M A A M ■ I O N ■ R A I D S ■ ■
S S E ■ ■ J O H N B ■ K E A N E ■ ■ E S E
■ ■ S P A C E ■ ■ S N L ■ C D R A C K S
T H E N I X O N S ■ H O D G E ■ O B O E S
H E R O S ■ ■ L E A P E R ■ N E L L I E
I A L W A Y S F E E L F R E S H ■ E I N S
S T E S ■ A L L W E T ■ ■ A W L S ■ ■ ■
■ ■ T R U E ■ ■ S E T A ■ A S S A I
■ W H E N I W A K E U P A T T H E E N D
A S I A T I C ■ M I L I E U ■ R A V I N E
N O T D O N E ■ B E A T E N ■ A R E N A S
I C H I N G ■ ■ I L L E S T ■ P A R E N T
```

```
L A H R ■ E T H I C ■ M I D A S ■ C U S S
E L E E ■ R A I S E ■ A L A S T ■ A T I T
C U R T J E S T E R ■ T O N G A ■ T A T A
A L T R U I S M ■ T W I S T A N D S H U T
R A Z E D ■ E E G ■ I N T E R C O M ■ ■
■ ■ A A S ■ ■ R U S E ■ ■ D E L E T E D
F U N D I N G F A T H E R S ■ S L O W E R
U L E ■ C O A R S E ■ O O M ■ W Y L E
G A S H ■ W R A P ■ B A L L A S T ■ L E A
U N T I M E L Y ■ B U L L E T I N B A R D
■ D A D A ■ O R R I S ■ A D U E ■ ■
F R E E Z I N G P I N T ■ R H E T O R I C
R I D ■ E N D U R E S ■ L O A D ■ N A N A
O P I E ■ ■ S S A ■ M A O R I S ■ V C R
D E N I M S ■ T H E C A S T I S C L E A R
O N A T E A R ■ N O P E ■ H O E ■ ■
■ H E R E W E G O ■ R E O ■ T A L E S
Q U I E T A S A M U S E ■ A N E C D O T E
T S A R ■ N A G E L ■ M I S S T H E B A T
I N S O ■ A L O A F ■ T R E E D ■ R O T H
P A I R ■ C E N T S ■ S A L T S ■ S S S S
```

37

```
T A S K ■ O T I C ■ ■ M O V I E ■ ■ C F C
G E T A ■ T E S L A ■ A P A C E ■ A U R A
I S A Y ■ E N A I T C H E L A L L S T A R
F O L G E R S ■ C A I R N ■ R E I S S U E
■ P E E A I T C H D E E S T U D E N T ■
■ ■ M E R ■ O R E ■ ■ E I S ■ ■ H O L
A B A B ■ O N E ■ N A S A L ■ S E C E D E
E M T E E V E E H O S T ■ L O R E L E I
S T E E L E ■ S O T T O ■ C A N O E I S T
■ ■ A I R S ■ B A R C L A Y ■ S E N S E
T R I G ■ A L L B R O K E N U P ■ N E A R
H O N E S ■ Y E S I D I D ■ P Y L E ■
E M A N A T E D ■ Z O N E D ■ G U N F O R
G E N T L E R ■ E M G E E E M G R A N D
A R I S T A ■ H O S E S ■ N A Y ■ E V A S
P O M ■ ■ T E L ■ ■ S T R ■ I P O
■ ■ A I T C H E M E S S P I N A F O R E ■
N O T S U R E ■ S A R A I ■ I N A R A G E
C E E P E E A R T R A I N I N G ■ T B A R
O N L Y ■ S P I E L ■ D A N G S ■ E L L A
S O Y ■ T E D D Y ■ L E S T ■ R Y E S
```

38

```
■ A R R ■ C A R O M ■ I M A M S ■ U T A H
A L A E ■ A L E U T ■ N O R M A ■ N O R A
S I N G I N I N T H E G R A I N ■ K E E N
C E L I B A T E ■ O D O R ■ D A N A N G
E N A M E L ■ G O U T O F A F R I C A
N O T E ■ A P O D ■ L I L I T H ■
T R E N T ■ N A T ■ S A L A R Y ■ H O N
■ T H E G L O V E D O N E ■ D R I V E
E R G ■ E L E A ■ A M A S ■ D R E I S E R
V A R ■ M O L D ■ T I M E S ■ E M I G R E
I S O N ■ P A I R ■ R U B S ■ S O L I
C H O I C E ■ N E P A L ■ B R A D ■ W A D
T E M P U R A ■ A U T O ■ D A L I ■ N Y S
E R A S E ■ G A L L A B O U T E V E
E S T ■ F A R M E D ■ M E T ■ A S T R O
■ T H A L I A ■ I N D Y ■ C R I B
■ T H E K I N G A N D G I ■ E M A I L S
T O E C A P ■ R E I N ■ S C R A P P L E
E S T A ■ P L A N E T O F T H E G A P E S
S C O T ■ E E L E D ■ R E L I C ■ D E T S
T A P E ■ R A L L Y ■ E B O A T ■ E D S
```

```
J A M S   T A M I L   S H A D S   P A L E
A S A P   E R I C A   H A Z E L   I B E X
Y O G I   S A L E M   A D O L E S C E N T
  F I N D S B A D I N D I V I D U A L S
    D E E S     N E E     S P Y
S T A L E R   T H A W   R M S   R U S S A
N A M E D A S H U T T L E A T L A N T I S
A X E     T E T E   O N C U E   E R R S
P I N E T R E E S   L A O   B O A   I R E
    L O B E D   R A D I I     S O N A R
I N C O M I N G R E T U R N S S O U G H T
M O A N S     E A T U P   S T I N T
A M S   K O S   S R S   S T A T E S M A N
G E T S   R I C K I   C O E N     E C O
E A R T H S P R I M A R Y A D V O C A T E
S T O R E   S Y N   L E A D   A L A N I S
    E R A     A P E     E L A L
  U S U A L L Y S T O P S A L L F O E S
P R E S S T I M E S   S A T I E   R A K E
O G L E   E M C E E   U N I T Y   I R I S
W E L L   R E A D A   P E T E S   E N D S
```

```
B U T I D   L O O K F   C R A G   S T I R
O M A N I   I T A L O   P O C O   H O L E
A P I N G   E S K E R   A U T O   E R L E
S I P   R E D   L I A R   S U N G   P U N
T R A   E S O   E N N E   S P A R S E S T
S E N D S A W A Y   A P S E   B E N D E R
    U S I N G   U N S E A T   W O O D Y
B O E R     T O N G   M U U M U U
O F F O N A T   P A L S   R A P T U R E
N L F   E V A D E   E M B A N K   S P A N
G A O   D I N E R S   U L S T E R   H I C
O T R A   A G L A R E   A P H I D   I S A
S E T R A T E   O X E N   E T A B L E S
    C L E N C H   I N K Y     E L S E
S T O A T   T R A I T S   E L I D E
C O R N E R   O R B S   S T O V E P I P E
R E V E R S E S   E T A T   V A T   M A V
A N I   S T A S   T A T A   E N O   B Y E
W A L L   O V I D   G A L A S   U N I O N
L I L A   R E N O   E R A S E   R O B L E
S L E D   E D G E   R I G H T   A H E A D
```

41

```
APTLY   WENT   TRURO    STAG
PASEO   IDEA   WEBER    HELL
BREAKINGINTOSONG        ONTO
     FORGINGAHEAD      BODES
LIP   HEME   SNORT   CATERS
ONE   ALARM   GUV   CHAIR
BATSMAN   AMORETTO   NABS
BHUTAN   EXES   ARPEGGIO
IONE   DAVIT   JON   INTEND
ELIA   MIL   DOUG   NTH
DEAL   KILLINGTIME   EFTS
   ICI   NANA   TEA   MAIL
WALNUT   EEK   HOREB   OLLA
EXEGESES   DOSS   ROOSTS
BEST   COSTFREE   VARNISH
   SHAHS   RAJ   AMANA   TAE
SHEEDY   FETOR   ALAN   YTD
MORSE   POACHINGEGGS
UTAH   HOLDINGUPTHELINE
REPO   ELIOT   ODIE   RURAL
FLEW   PEONY   REED   YEATS
```

42

```
BUSCH   MARI   JOVE   DONA
IGLOO   CADIZ   AXED   ERAS
THUMBSARIDE   VEROBEACH
   REBELLED   HAYS   APPLE
LASSIE   BULGE   EASIER
ILO   ESPO   ERIC   ANNOY
LOVESTORY   ASHCAN   ENOS
AHEM   ROOMSTOLET   DODO
CARO   UNSNAP   KORAN   BET
   TOPO   MADEDO   ATILT
ELMERS   GAITERS   GROSSO
QUEST   SUREST   COAT
UND   SEPIA   TARPON   IRAS
AGIO   VULGARTERM   NEIL
LEAN   ENDORA   LOTTOGAME
   SPOOR   NEWT   JEER   PEW
   ENDSUP   ASONE   SLOPES
GARDE   SITS   MUCILAGE
ITSASHAME   WARTSANDALL
FLOG   EGAN   ATSEA   DELES
TINA   PEST   HOED   ONSET
```

43

```
C A S H I N S ■ C H I R A C ■ W A G N E R
O N E O C A T ■ H E L E N A ■ A R R I V E
R O C K Y M U S I C I A N S ■ R E A G A N
E S T E ■ E M T ■ K A P U T ■ D A P H N E
■ A S P I E ■ S I L A S ■ E T S
A C T O N ■ E N E M Y ■ T E L ■ I V Y
T R I C K O R T R E A T Y ■ L A T I S H
M O R T A R ■ S Y N C H ■ P I R A N H A S
S W E A R A T ■ S H E B A ■ G L E A N S
■ V A L E ■ W A T E R Y L O O ■ D E T
B A B E ■ M I A ■ I S A ■ M E S S
A G E ■ S C A R Y F A C E ■ D E C O
B A L B O A ■ I S O L A ■ S T A P L E S
A T L A N T I S ■ A T B A T ■ C H E E T A
E Y R I E S ■ B L O O D Y T H I R S T Y
C C C ■ E L I ■ S T O R E ■ E S S E S
C U E ■ B E E P S ■ S O N A R
P A R L O R ■ A L I A S ■ N A G ■ A D U E
I N V O K E ■ P A N C A K E B A T T E R Y
K E E N A N ■ E N C I N O ■ L I N E A G E
E S S A Y S ■ D E E D E D ■ E N T E R E D
```

44

```
C L O G S ■ A H E M ■ T H A W ■ R A P T
R A V E L ■ S E T A E ■ H U L A ■ O L I O
T B O N E S T E A K S ■ E D B R A D L E Y
T E P I D ■ E S M E ■ A S S I S T S
O R B I T E R ■ G M A T ■ A N T O N
M A U L E D ■ X R A Y V I S I O N ■ C O S
E B B E D ■ L E E D S ■ S T A R E D O W N
N I B S ■ G O N G ■ L O O N Y ■ O F N O
S N L ■ M O N O ■ L I M N ■ S A F E R
E R O S E ■ U S E M E ■ H U B E R T
A R B I T E R ■ N A D E R ■ T O P L E S S
B E R A T E ■ C R O S S ■ A P E E K
R E A L S ■ P L A N ■ B R E R ■ L A P
A L I T ■ D A Y A N ■ C U T S ■ W A D E
D I N O S A U R S ■ T S A R S ■ P A T E R
E N S ■ H Y D E P A R K N Y ■ M U S C L E
T A T A S ■ M A Y S ■ T E E T H E S
O C E A N I C ■ E P I C ■ N O T B E
R I G H T M I N D ■ N A T U R A L F O O D
C I A O ■ E T R E ■ S P E N T ■ O U T T O
A I D E ■ R Y A N ■ S A N E ■ S L O B S
```

45

```
PARE█ATTIC█LARDS█VASE
AMEN█ROONE█ATBAT█ORYX
RIND█PEARLSSWINE█LANE
ICEAGE█DETECT█IVTUBES
SAWLOGS█MIRA█ASIAN███
███LOGIC█CALMTHESTORM
OLD█FINAL█APE██SEGUE
LOOKYOULEAP█HUMP█ELBA
MANN█SIGNUP█PEAGREEN
OTHERS█CATNAP█SBA███
SHOWSPHOTOGRAPHSSHOWS
███VIE█ONEIDA█THENHL
SKINPEEL█SNARLS█ILIE
WINO█SLOP█THEOTHERONE
AWASH█FAS█SMEAR█WET
NINEAQUARTER█AARON███
███BLURT█AXER█MADEOFF
PULLTAB█ANCHOR█NEWCAR
SHUE█CARSCHASING█AERO
SOLE█KNUTE█BIJOU█RAGS
THUD█SEMIS█SNORE█KNOT
```

46

```
COSTAR█CABS█BRAY█AMBS
ARCANE█ALOE█LAVA█NELL
MIAMIADVICE█AKIN█TRUE
POL█SLEIGH█SNEAK█ICED
ELITE█RANCHADDRESSING
REAR█BAR█OIL█YEA█FOE
███IGOT██FEUD██TAUS█
ADMISSIONIMPOSSIBLE█
SPILLS█RIO██CAPONE██
PRAY█CONMEN██RHODIUM
EIN█STOCKADOPTION█RNA
CLAMORS█RATOUT██RACK
███ALIENS██CPR█UNIQUE
ADJUSTFORTHEFUNOFIT█
█CRAB█LUAU███NINE█
RAE█LOX██NBC█CIT█STAG
ADAGEOFAQUARIUS█STORE
DEMO█LITUP█EATOUT█ORR
IMIN█ALLA█WOMENSADLIB
SING█LEAR█ALBS█SLEEVE
HAGS█ASST█REST█RENDER
```

47

```
D C C A B   ■ D O L L S ■ P O L E M I C S
A H O R A   R E X A L L ■ A N A L O G U E
V A L I D   A M A N D A ■ T E N S P O T S
I S L A M   C O L D S T O R A G E ■ T O A
D E E ■ A S I T I S ■ H I C ■ S T U M
■ G E N E S E S ■ C O Y O T E S T A T E
■ J E N N E T S ■ M O N E T ■ T H O ■
■ A S T E R S ■ B A L L S ■ T R A M C A R
A L T E R S ■ F U L L Y ■ B E A N P O L E
S O U R S ■ M A R L A ■ S L A D E ■ M A L
C U D S ■ C O R N E R S T O R E ■ A F R O
E S E ■ G O N G S ■ S T A C Y ■ S T O M A
N I N T E N D O ■ S T O R K ■ F L O R I D
D E T E N T E ■ F O U N T ■ B R A N T S
■ ■ P I E ■ C R U D E ■ B R A V E S T ■
C O M I C S T R I P S ■ K E E N E S T ■
A R I D ■ ■ O U T ■ S N E A K S ■ A P E
N I L ■ C O M M O N S T O C K ■ H O T E L
T A K E A N A P ■ T E E T H E ■ I S I T I
E N E R V A T E ■ W A L T E R ■ P L O T Z
D A R E S N O T ■ T R E Y S ■ ■ S O N Y A
```

48

```
L A V A ■ M A S S E ■ P E N C E ■ N C A A
A S I S ■ E L T O N ■ O C E A N ■ A H A B
B A C K G R O U N D ■ S H O R T S T O R Y
S P E A R G U N ■ E A T O N ■ R A T I O S
■ ■ F E E D ■ B A R B ■ T A V E R N S
F O S T E R ■ M O R T A L ■ A C E R ■
A S H E N ■ H O U S E G U E S T ■ B A R
I T O R ■ P O U R ■ C A K E ■ R U S E
T I P ■ C H A R G E C A R D ■ C A C H E
H A W T H O R N ■ E R L E S ■ G A W K E D
■ I R O N Y ■ R I O ■ G R I L L ■
C A N A P E ■ A V I S O ■ T R A N S E P T
A U D I S ■ D E E P F R E E Z E ■ D I E
A T O N ■ G O O N ■ U R G E ■ R O N A
N O W ■ U P S T A N D I N G ■ V O W E L
■ ■ E T T U ■ S C O R N S ■ S O U N D S
Z E A L O T S ■ C U E S ■ L U L L ■
I N S I T U ■ A M E N S ■ L A R G E S S E
L E T T E R H E A D ■ S T E P F A T H E R
C R E E ■ A E R I E ■ E R A S E ■ T O N I
H O P S ■ L Y O N S ■ R A K E D ■ E T T E
```

```
W A K E D   S C R A P   O T T E R   A R S
A P E R Y   A R E N A   B R I N E   P E T
B O L L A   S O P O R   S E A O F L O V E
A L L E N   H O O D S   C A R L   I S E E
S L Y   S A N S E I   U T A   T A T A R
H O M E B O Y S   F O R E S T H I L L S
  C L O P S   S O A R E D   E A S E S
A L G A L   W O R L D   D A R E
T O I L E T   E V A   R U E R   M I A
L O L   R E T A I L S   U N L I T   I N T
A T L   O L I V E B R A N C H E S   N P R
S E I   S L E E T   A B O L I S H   T U E
T D S   S I R S   A V E   T I N C T S
  B R A N   K I T E S   R O O S T
  A R A I L   S P A C E R   G O T I N
E M E R A L D C I T Y   F I R S T D A Y
L U S T S   R O C   S A L A M I   I V E
O S H A   M Y R A   T R I L L   S A T E S
P E A B R A I N S   A R E T E   H E I R S
E M P   D I C E S   R O G E T   A R O S E
D E E   A L E R O   E W E R S   H O N E S
```

```
P I T A S   T E A C H   P A T A C A K E
I R I S H   A T S E A   M A R I N A T E D
N O T T I N G H I L L   A B B E Y R O A D
A N T O N I A   S T S   L A S   T I N Y
T I L   S A L   I T A L   A W E
A C E S   C O P   C O V E N T G A R D E N
  O P I N E D   N A T U R E S   A G O
P A D D I N G T O N   S I A M   L Y O N
I L I A C   A N O N   V A M O O S E
K I O S K S   R H E I N   P E T I T
E A R   L O N D O N L O C A L E S   L O S
  M E N U S   D E V I L   S H T E T L
G A P E D A T   S A G A   A U D I O
R U E D   T M E N   E A T O N P L A C E
A D E   D I E S E L S   R E M I S S
B I L L I N G S G A T E   S E X   A R C H
  I D A   A V I V   L O W   E L O
S W A N   R U T   F O B   E N A B L E S
L I M E H O U S E   F L E E T S T R E E T
O P E N E N D E D   E V E N T   T E N S E
T E N S P E E D   D E F O E   S A T E D
```

51

```
S P E D   C L A S S     B O P   A M A T I
I A M A   S Y L P H S   E R R   S I R E D
F R O M ▸ T O F O O T ▸ S O R   T A I L S
T O T A L   N A I V E   S O D I U M
E L E G I E S   L E A D   N U P T I A L
R E S E N T   G A L L I C   C E E   T A O
    D E E   A G E   A R L E N   C L I P
E N G     A B E D   M I L D   N O O N E
L E E W A R D     B O N O   B E R G E N
M A T I N E E   S P O N G Y   A G O G
S T A N D S   P A R A D E D   S A N E S T
  ▸ S E T   O V E R ▸ S   U T T E R L Y
V I S T A S   P A S S     M E E T O N ▸
A N T O N   S U B S   S C O W     S T E
S C A N   A P P L E   C O D   E B B
T A R   A L E   E R R A N D   T E A B A G
  S T O P G A P   S O B S   W H E R E T O
    R O A R E D   A R O S E   T E N O R
D O U B L E ▸ E R   C O M P A S S ▸ I N G
A V A I L   E V E   H U M A N S   E C C E
H O W T O   D E W   S E N S E   D E E D
```

52

```
R E T A K E   V I S E   C R A G S   W A R E S
A R A R A T   I N K A   H A B I T   A L I S T
J I M M Y C R A T E R   A R O M A   P E S T O
A C E   O H O   W I L L I A M M Y N I C K E L
S A R A   P H O N E I N   B E S E T   S E E
    R O M E O   L U G S   S I C
F R A N K L I N R E C I P E   P O T   O M E N
L A N O L I N   O M I T   T W I R L   R I D E
O C A L A   D W I G H T W H E R E O N E I S
R E I D   P R O S T   R E O S   T I N C T
A D S   C R O W   C O O L S   D E T E S T S
  T H E O D O R E S O L E V O T E R
M I D R I F F   F E D U P   C Z A R   R A Y
O R I O N   O F F A   D A R E S   L O D E
B E N J A M I N A I R H O R N S   N A D I A
I N G A   I D Y L L   O R E O   C H A R I E R
L E O N   N I X   M A R T I N B R A V E N U N
    S E C   A S I N   O I L E D
S P A   D E I O N   R E M A R K S   O D D S
M I L L A R D F I L M R O L E   I A M   R I P
A X I O M   L A M I A   J A M E S N O M O R E
R A N G E   E G A D S   O M A N   T W I N G E
T R E S S   D E L O S   S O P S   I N D E E D
```

53

MAST FACES OMAR ERRED
ALTO AROMA CARA NAIVE
YOUMAKEMEFEELBRANDNEW
SECEDE REEL SEEING
KID SASSOON BOSOMS
ADO OHIO TOEIN RYES
SINK TURNTO VETS BEA
KEYEDON GROAN AHEMS
INONE THRILLS DEMILLE
NEUTER UNFED REAPPLY
POORS DANTE
ABASHED HAPPY ARCHER
VERMEER NEMESES ELOPE
ARECA TIEUP ALSATIA
TIA SCAN LEGATE MDCC
SETH NAMES ATIT ISH
SHEBAT SURVIVE WAG
LEARNS MAIN TINGOD
FEELSLIKETHEFIRSTTIME
APSES PIPE JUNTA ETAL
MISDO SPAR ALTER DYNE

54

REHEAT SELKIRK STASH
OTELLO TREADON SHASTA
NURSER ANATOLE MONTEL
AIRAPPARENT FLOURGIRL
HOYT BELL TIRE
OVA RELAPSE SASE
SIXAM REBIND VEX RAPT
SELLERS BEARBONES BAR
ADELEH ADROIT DONATE
ATOWN LOGES LATEN
NEIGHSAYER MAINEEVENT
ALBEE SMEAL NORMA
MISSAL ENNEAD GARCIA
ETE DIRTYLYRE HOTRODS
DENT DES ATEASE EERIE
AMOR TEARING DOA
NANA IATE ACOW
MORNINGDO THYMEKEEPER
ONSALE ONLEAVE ABRADE
MOOTED BEATLES RETRIM
ASNER EDMEESE TREATY

55

E	G	G	S	O	N	■	T	A	K	E	■	J	I	B	E	■	E	M	I	R
L	A	R	E	D	O	■	E	L	I	A	■	O	G	R	E	■	M	A	N	E
D	R	A	G	O	N	F	L	I	E	S	■	S	N	A	K	E	B	I	T	E
■	■	M	O	R	A	L	E	■	L	E	G	I	O	N	■	G	A	T	E	D
C	H	E	■	■	G	A	M	■	B	L	E	A	R	■	S	E	N	A	R	Y
H	O	R	S	E	O	P	E	R	A	■	S	H	E	E	P	S	K	I	N	■
U	R	C	H	I	N	■	T	A	S	■	■	■	R	O	T	■	■	■	■	■
M	A	Y	A	N	■	S	R	T	A	■	F	A	I	R	■	A	V	I	A	■
■	■	■	D	A	I	S	■	■	M	O	N	K	E	Y	B	A	R	S	■	■
R	O	O	S	T	E	R	C	O	G	B	U	R	N	■	M	A	R	A	T	■
E	L	M	W	O	O	D	■	A	M	O	■	N	A	C	R	I	T	E	■	■
A	D	E	A	R	■	D	O	G	I	N	T	H	E	M	A	N	G	E	R	■
P	I	G	I	N	A	P	O	K	E	■	E	E	R	Y	■	■	■	■	■	■
S	E	A	N	■	M	E	W	S	■	G	L	A	D	■	T	I	L	T	S	■
■	■	■	U	P	S	■	■	■	O	E	R	■	B	E	F	O	R	E	■	■
■	R	A	T	P	A	T	R	O	L	■	O	X	T	A	I	L	S	O	U	P
R	E	M	A	P	S	■	A	B	I	R	D	■	I	R	S	■	■	S	E	T
A	G	I	L	E	■	S	I	E	V	E	D	■	N	A	T	A	L	E	■	■
T	I	G	E	R	L	I	L	Y	■	H	A	R	E	B	R	A	I	N	E	D
I	N	O	N	■	A	L	E	E	■	A	M	E	S	■	O	R	N	E	R	Y
O	A	S	T	■	T	O	D	D	■	B	E	D	S	■	S	P	A	D	E	S

56

Q	U	A	H	O	G	■	U	N	S	A	Y	■	H	O	T	W	A	T	E	R
U	N	R	I	P	E	■	P	O	L	L	O	■	A	R	E	A	C	O	D	E
A	W	A	K	E	N	■	D	O	U	B	L	E	D	O	M	I	N	O	E	S
S	I	R	E	N	■	F	A	N	G	■	K	A	T	Z	■	T	E	T	R	A
A	S	A	■	F	I	A	T	■	■	S	O	C	K	■	D	E	L	L	■	■
R	E	T	U	R	N	R	E	C	E	I	P	T	■	O	I	L	■	D	E	E
■	■	■	S	A	V	E	■	U	L	N	A	■	■	T	I	S	■	■	■	■
■	C	R	E	M	E	S	■	P	A	R	S	E	■	P	E	E	K	S	A	T
R	A	I	D	E	R	■	■	M	I	S	S	M	I	S	S	O	U	R	I	■
A	T	M	■	T	O	P	S	■	■	E	T	O	N	■	T	A	B	L	E	■
F	A	M	O	U	S	F	A	C	E	■	S	O	L	O	S	O	L	V	E	R
F	L	I	R	T	■	A	C	A	T	■	■	P	E	N	T	■	E	N	C	■
L	A	N	G	U	A	G	E	L	A	B	S	■	■	D	E	C	R	E	E	■
E	N	G	A	R	D	E	■	P	L	A	I	T	■	H	E	L	O	T	S	■
■	■	■	N	N	E	■	■	I	N	D	Y	■	O	N	E	R	■	■	■	■
A	M	C	■	S	P	Y	■	T	I	G	E	R	S	T	I	C	K	E	T	S
S	A	L	T	■	T	O	G	O	■	■	P	E	S	T	■	R	O	T	■	■
I	L	I	A	D	■	N	O	O	K	■	A	B	E	L	■	R	A	N	D	Y
D	O	C	T	O	R	D	O	L	I	T	T	L	E	■	N	O	D	E	A	L
E	N	H	A	N	C	E	D	■	N	A	I	A	D	■	A	D	E	S	T	E
S	E	E	S	T	A	R	S	■	G	O	T	B	Y	■	B	E	S	T	E	D

```
L A R A M  ■ H E M P  ■ S O U L  ■ D E F E R
E L I S A  ■ E P E E  ■ A N N A  ■ A G A T E
W E D S N A P P E R  ■ W A I V I N G M A D
■ G S U I T  ■ S T I L T S  ■ S U C C E S S
■ ■ C L E M  ■ S L E E T S  ■ M E R  ■ ■
U N W H O L E  ■ D E R A T  ■ R A W E R
N E E  ■ W I N G M A S T E R S  ■ S T O V E
I W A S  ■ E L I O T  ■ H A G A R  ■ E M E R
T E R A  ■ R O T T E D  ■ K E R B S  ■ B R A
S L I N G S  ■ S H A R P  ■ S I N K S I N
■ N Y E  ■ S M E A R  ■ I R E  ■
G I G O L O S  ■ S A L U D  ■ S T A R T S
A N T  ■ D O L E D  ■ M I N U E T  ■ I V A N
M O O S  ■ H A D E S  ■ S T E N O  ■ T I T O
A N G U S  ■ W I D E S H O T G U N  ■ C A R
L E O N E  ■ S T I L E  ■ E T A G E R E
■ D C L  ■ S C A M P S  ■ L I M O  ■
A R E A R U G  ■ A S I A N S  ■ S E P T S
W A Y N E C O A T S  ■ W E I G H T H I K E
E J E C T  ■ D R E I  ■ N A N A  ■ A E R I E
D A R E S  ■ S P E E  ■ S K E D  ■ G R E T E
```

```
A G I R L  ■ O R S O  ■ M D V I  ■ A B A S H
M A T E O  ■ S E A L  ■ I R A N  ■ V E S T A
B R O W N S T O N E  ■ K I N G F I S H E R
■ P O R G I E S  ■ A L I V E  ■ L A M E N T
■ ■ O H N O  ■ R O T E  ■ B I N E  ■ ■
R A G T A G  ■ J A Y W A L K E R  ■ A B B E
B U R E N  ■ V A L S E  ■ I N T H R E E D
I R A  ■ D E A N S  ■ C U T E S Y  ■ L A D
S A S S  ■ F L O O D G A T E S  ■ D E L T A
■ S P I R E S  ■ E L M E R  ■ T R I B E S
■ P H O N E S  ■ T R A P S  ■ H E A D O N
M A O I S M  ■ V O I C E  ■ B A S S E T  ■
A P P L E  ■ W I L D E R N E S S  ■ R T E S
R E P  ■ C R A D L E  ■ E S T A B  ■ O L E
C R E A T U R E  ■ O H B O Y  ■ I M M I X
S S R S  ■ S N O W S T O R M  ■ B R A S S Y
■ P A S S  ■ H A I L  ■ B O D Y  ■
E S S E N E  ■ G A S S Y  ■ D I S C O E D
B L A C K S M I T H  ■ W O O D C A R V E R
B E R T H  ■ A V I A  ■ A X L E  ■ G A I L Y
S W I S S  ■ D E F Y  ■ R O T S  ■ E L L I E
```

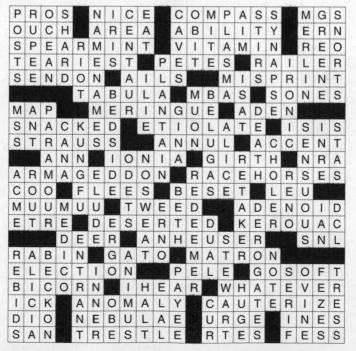

59

```
E N T E R   C L A R A   A T T A   S H A G
F E R R I   O I L E R   M O O S   T E R I
F L I N G S T A T U S   P A N K I L L E R
A S S I S I   R O P E D   S T E N O P A D
C O T E   D D S   N E S T O R S   S S S
E N E   W E E   R I A L   S I B
    C H A N R E A C T I O N   G R A S S
A P P L E   T A L C   H E R A   N A T T Y
M A R A T   I S L I P   R E P A I N T E D
O R E M   S T E E L   E A T E N
  A D J   S T A N R E M O V E R   E M T
  B A U M S   A U D E N   A P O P
D O T M A T R I X   T R E A T   A S T R A
S L O P S   O D E S   A L L I   M E S S Y
C A R E S   C O N C O L L E C T O R
    R A M   O O P S   E H S   S S A
A R I   C O C O N U T   S D I   A H A S
L I V E R I E D   T I A R A   E A S E U P
P L O T E R R O R   C H E F O F S T A T E
H E R R   E I R E   A M B E R   S E V E N
A S Y E   S A S S   L E A S T   T R E S S
```

60

```
P R O S   N I C E   C O M P A S S   M G S
O U C H   A R E A   A B I L I T Y   E R N
S P E A R M I N T   V I T A M I N   R E O
T E A R I E S T   P E T E S   R A I L E R
S E N D O N   A I L S   M I S P R I N T
    T A B U L A   M B A S   S O N E S
M A P   M E R I N G U E   A D E N
S N A C K E D   E T I O L A T E   I S I S
S T R A U S S   A N N U L   A C C E N T
  A N N   I O N I A   G I R T H   N R A
A R M A G E D D O N   R A C E H O R S E S
C O O   F L E E S   B E S E T   L E U
M U U M U U   T W E E D   A D E N O I D
E T R E   D E S E R T E D   K E R O U A C
    D E E R   A N H E U S E R   S N L
R A B I N   G A T O   M A T R O N
E L E C T I O N   P E L E   G O S O F T
B I C O R N   I H E A R   W H A T E V E R
I C K   A N O M A L Y   C A U T E R I Z E
D I O   N E B U L A E   U R G E   I N E S
S A N   T R E S T L E   R T E S   F E S S
```

H	A	D	J	I	S	■	C	R	U	S	A	D	E	■	B	A	T	H	E	D
A	M	O	E	B	A	■	B	A	N	A	N	A	S	■	U	N	R	U	L	Y
W	I	T	H	I	N	G	E	N	U	I	T	Y	A	N	D	G	U	I	L	E
■	S	H	U	D	D	E	R	■	■	L	O	A	■	O	G	R	E	S	S	■
■	■	■	E	Y	E	■	G	L	E	N	N	■	T	E	Y	■	■	■	■	■
S	P	E	R	M	■	M	O	O	D	Y	■	G	I	T	■	B	A	C	H	■
M	I	N	T	■	F	A	R	O	■	■	D	O	E	■	E	B	R	O	■	■
I	N	V	E	N	T	I	V	E	N	E	S	S	A	N	D	F	L	A	I	R
T	O	O	■	O	H	O	S	■	G	O	W	N	S	■	O	L	S	E	N	■
S	T	I	M	S	O	N	■	A	D	O	N	I	S	■	B	R	I	E	R	Y
■	■	A	T	L	A	R	G	E	■	■	I	N	K	H	O	R	N	■	■	■
A	B	L	A	R	E	■	E	O	C	E	N	E	■	O	N	E	I	D	A	S
K	E	A	N	U	■	C	H	R	O	N	■	E	T	N	A	■	R	I	A	■
I	H	I	D	M	Y	H	O	A	R	D	S	O	S	L	Y	L	Y	I	L	L
T	A	R	P	■	I	A	N	■	P	O	S	Y	■	■	E	L	E	M	■	■
A	N	D	A	■	E	R	E	■	M	A	I	Z	E	■	N	A	L	D	I	■
■	■	■	A	L	L	■	C	A	R	N	E	■	A	N	I	■	■	■	■	■
■	G	R	A	N	D	E	■	O	R	T	■	A	B	E	T	T	E	D	■	■
B	E	B	L	E	S	S	E	D	I	F	I	K	N	O	W	W	H	E	R	E
O	R	I	E	N	T	■	D	E	N	U	D	E	S	■	T	I	A	R	A	S
W	I	S	E	T	O	■	A	D	E	L	I	N	E	■	S	T	R	O	B	E

B	S	A	■	C	H	A	S	■	S	M	A	R	T	■	G	R	U	F	F	■
R	A	G	■	H	A	S	H	■	E	A	D	I	E	■	R	E	P	L	A	N
A	P	I	S	A	T	H	E	A	C	T	I	O	N	■	I	N	T	O	T	O
S	I	T	A	R	S	■	B	L	U	T	O	■	R	E	T	O	R	T	S	■
S	E	A	T	O	■	N	A	P	L	E	S	U	L	T	R	A	■	E	E	E
I	N	T	E	N	S	E	■	H	A	L	■	N	A	E	■	L	E	N	N	Y
E	T	E	■	■	T	A	T	A	R	■	M	U	Y	■	S	A	C	■	■	■
■	■	■	C	L	A	R	A	S	■	S	A	M	O	S	A	■	R	E	A	M
A	C	C	O	U	T	E	R	■	T	U	X	■	P	O	S	■	L	I	S	A
G	A	R	A	G	E	D	■	P	E	N	I	T	E	N	T	■	L	S	U	■
G	R	A	T	E	R	■	S	T	A	R	M	A	N	■	I	O	N	I	A	N
I	O	N	■	O	N	T	A	R	I	A	N	■	H	O	M	I	N	I	D	■
E	L	B	A	■	M	A	R	■	I	S	L	■	G	A	P	I	N	G	L	Y
S	E	A	T	■	E	T	E	R	N	E	■	B	E	R	A	T	E	■	■	■
■	■	R	O	D	■	T	O	G	■	G	R	E	A	T	■	■	C	U	M	■
B	A	I	Z	E	■	I	T	S	■	P	O	O	■	S	H	A	N	A	N	A
O	T	S	■	G	E	N	O	A	M	O	T	O	R	S	■	T	E	N	O	N
C	H	A	I	R	E	D	■	A	P	A	C	E	■	B	E	A	T	I	T	■
C	A	U	D	A	L	■	E	N	N	A	W	H	E	R	E	A	T	A	L	L
E	N	C	O	D	E	■	M	O	I	R	A	■	D	E	E	S	■	T	E	E
■	D	E	L	E	D	■	S	L	A	T	Y	■	Y	O	R	E	■	A	D	S

63

Grid 63:

L	A	B	R	A	T	■	A	N	N	E	A	L	■	F	R	I	S	K	E	D
A	N	Y	O	N	E	■	L	O	A	T	H	E	■	L	I	N	E	A	G	E
C	I	T	I	E	S	■	A	R	C	H	E	D	■	O	C	T	A	V	A	L
E	T	E	■	W	H	E	N	T	H	E	M	A	N	W	H	O	M	A	D	E
S	A	S	S	■	■	A	B	H	O	R	■	■	O	I	L	■	■	■	■	■
■	■	O	H	A	R	A	■	■	E	B	O	N	Y	■	■	D	I	A	L	■
T	H	E	F	I	R	S	T	D	R	A	W	I	N	G	■	M	E	C	C	A
S	E	P	T	E	T	■	E	R	O	D	E	D	■	■	E	M	E	R	Y
A	R	O	O	■	I	N	S	O	L	E	■	E	T	A	■	L	O	D	E	S
R	E	D	N	O	S	E	■	N	A	S	A	■	A	N	T	O	N	■	■	■
S	S	E	■	S	T	E	V	E	N	■	W	R	I	G	H	T	■	B	R	A
■	■	M	I	S	D	O	■	D	A	N	A	■	L	I	T	H	I	U	M
M	E	L	E	E	■	S	A	T	■	B	I	D	D	E	R	■	A	N	N	O
B	L	E	A	R	■	■	B	E	A	N	I	E	■	S	A	I	G	O	N
A	B	E	T	S	■	B	O	A	R	D	G	O	T	I	T	W	R	O	N	G
S	A	K	S	■	H	O	U	R	S	■	■	R	A	Y	E	D	■	■	■
■	■	■	A	R	C	■	T	A	T	A	S	■	■	O	I	N	K	■
W	H	A	T	D	I	D	H	E	G	O	B	A	C	K	T	O	■	M	O	M
A	U	R	E	O	L	E	■	R	A	R	E	S	T	■	A	R	M	A	D	A
S	L	E	N	D	E	R	■	A	V	I	A	T	E	■	M	E	A	G	E	R
P	A	S	T	O	R	S	■	T	E	S	T	E	D	■	S	L	Y	E	S	T

64

Grid 64:

A	B	A	T	E	S	■	C	L	A	R	E	T	■	S	C	A	M	P
S	E	V	I	L	L	A	■	T	R	I	R	E	M	E	■	P	A	N	E	L
T	H	E	M	O	U	S	E	H	A	S	M	I	C	E	■	A	R	E	N	A
O	E	R	■	N	E	S	T	E	D	■	M	E	T	S	■	O	M	A	N
R	A	S	P	■	T	H	E	L	O	U	S	E	H	A	S	L	I	C	E
■	D	E	A	L	S	■	E	M	P	■	E	N	T	I	C	E	D
■	■	S	U	R	E	S	T	■	A	D	D	A	■	D	E	N	■
■	W	H	Y	C	A	N	T	A	G	R	O	U	S	E	■	M	A	R	L
M	A	Y	S	■	S	A	U	R	■	M	I	L	■	■	A	U	G
C	H	U	T	E	D	■	B	R	E	E	D	B	A	B	Y	G	R	I	C	E
K	I	N	E	T	I	C	■	G	L	O	■	A	R	O	U	S	E	S
A	N	D	M	O	T	H	E	R	G	O	O	S	E	■	S	O	B	E	R	S
Y	E	A	■	U	V	A	■	M	A	L	E	■	B	R	N	O
■	S	I	A	M	■	B	E	G	E	T	S	H	E	R	G	E	E	S	E
■	N	A	T	■	N	U	D	E	■	L	E	G	E	N	D	■
S	T	E	E	L	I	E	■	G	A	R	■	M	O	I	R	A
W	H	Y	C	A	N	T	T	H	E	M	O	O	S	E	■	N	A	B	S
I	R	E	D	■	A	C	R	O	■	B	R	I	E	F	S	■	C	U	E
P	I	L	O	T	■	H	A	V	E	L	I	T	T	L	E	M	E	E	S	E
E	V	I	T	A	■	E	L	E	V	E	N	S	■	S	T	O	R	M	E	D
S	E	D	E	R	■	S	A	L	A	D	S	■	E	G	R	E	S	S

65

```
DIALER  SAT  ALL    MOPUP
ASLOPE  HORATIO  SALINA
MADCAP  ANIMATE  ALIENS
  DOH  CHEXANDBALANCES
BORA  SAD  INA   TOY  ERA
IRAN  PROSEANDCONS   AVG
DAYDREAMT   GOOP   KNEE
   KENT  EMBLEM  AMID
LATENT  PROLE  PALENQUE
ASHY  GENOA  SONAR  UMA
ICY  FAREANDSQUARE  IBM
RAM  AGIRL  DAUNT   HERO
SPECTATE   REDID  BHUTAN
   APER  DOURER  HAIG
ZENO   FIRN   ELIASHOWE
IND  WHINEANDDINE  AVON
PCS  HEN  ROE  PED  NERD
COPSEANDROBBERS   DRS
ORATED  ROULADE  UNCLES
DECALS  AMNESIA  SHRINE
EDENS  WED  ETD  SLYEST
```

66

```
ACROSS  CHAFF   DIPPIER
CLARKE  RESULT  UTRILLO
HENRYWRINKLER  DOONEIN
TWI  BEAM   NOSEOUT
   JODIEFROSTER  DOJOS
CODEX   AIRE  NAMESAKE
ORES  SHARONSTONER  CAN
NIBS  WARMTO  ORCS  SKYS
MORE  EIN   RAH  LAPSE
ALAS  DRESSLER   COPA
NEW  WESLEYSNIPERS  RAM
  RAIN  ANTEDATE  ALLA
SKIRT  MOL   GUM  MAYS
EENY  CORA  SECEDE  UNDO
TAG  PHOEBECRATES  SCAN
UNERRING  LAIR   PEERS
PUREE  SONDRALOCKER
  PARTNER   WREN  PGA
COLOMBO  VIRGINIAMAYOR
CRISPIN  ACCUSE  TABLET
IDLESSE  HAVER  SNEERS
```

```
WEST  ICI   HARARE  TEAM
ONER  NOSE  IRANIS  RAJA
ROTE  SQUEALOFAPPROVAL
SCAMPI  ZELDA     EVERT
THEBASQUESARELOADED
    LUTE        LAMPS
ANGEL  DUHS  AIMAT  ZEBU
SCARAB  MAO  NOAHSQUARK
HAWS  ALEVE  ITSA  UNTIE
YAK  BROKEUP     DEISTS
   PAQUINRELIEVERS
RAZORS     ZOMBIFY  TAN
ABOMB  PTAS  CASIO  HOPI
FINEQUARTS  AGE  GAELIC
TEES  CRASS  LENT  BADGE
    SLICE      ABED
  QUEASYASONETWOTHREE
AMUSE    APISH  USUALS
QUALMSFORTHEPOOR  NOES
UNIT  HAWAII  NUNN  TUNA
AIDA  EASTER  STE  SLAY
```

```
PRAWNS  CAGED  ASTA   THAW
ABLOOM  ORONO  WWII   ERASE
LIFETI(ME)(ME)MBERSHIPS  NOWIN
     ILLSAY   COMIN(GA)(GA)INST
REFT  EBON  TAO   ERG
EL(IL)(IL)LYANDCOMPANY  NIPPON
SPEEDS    ANAEMIA  INARUT
CRASS  PARTII  ANNE  GNOTE
UAW   ADE  CNNHEADLI(NE)(NE)WS
EDAMS  NONO  OLA  SON  TIT
ROY(AL)(AL)BERTHALL  MMES  ROTS
   PEELE  STAIN  ILENE
ROTH  RIDS  SCENESFRO(MA)(MA)LL
ITO  RLS  TAE  WACO  ENDUE
SING(IN)(IN)THERAIN  RUR   DNA
KO(IN)G  SEER  CYCLED  BLEEP
ISEULT  BLEMISH    SAINTS
TERSER  BE(AR)(AR)ESEMBLANCETO
    AAA    TRA  AEON  EDEN
CLAU(DE)(DE)BUSSY   OSCARS
HAZER  A(MI)MISSINGSOMETHING
EVILS  CATT  SALEM  MUUMUU
FAZE   IKES  OBESE  OBTAIN
```

69

```
RAPID █ HOPE █ NERD █ DUSKS
OMANI █ AMEN █ OBIE █ ONTOP
BUCKETSEAT █ TOMFOOLERY
ELI █ CAEN █ REINS █ FRONDS
DENMARK █ PARTY █ MIMOSA █
█ TOAST █ ARIA █ IOTAS █
█ STAGNANTPOND █ TEPEE
RPM █ REEDS █ URGED █ SLIM
ERATO █ TWO █ ATLASES █ AGT
PELICAN █ SHOOT █ LAUGHS
█ HARTFORDCONNECTICUT █
REPEAT █ URALS █ RALLIED
HAR █ LEONARD █ WEE █ SANER
ETON █ RHYME █ TIGER █ GNU
ASPIC █ BOARDINGPASS █
█ LIMON █ ENDS █ DUETS
█ THETOY █ TANKS █ LINEOUT
ARUBAN █ TENSE █ EAST █ OBI
BULLDOZING █ RAMSHACKLE
RECUE █ IDOL █ EDIT █ NOTER
AREEL █ PERE █ DOTS █ SPOTS
```

70

```
ACTS █ AREEL █ GLEE █ SPRAY
WARP █ ROLLO █ LUGS █ CRIME
ELIA █ GOLAN █ OLIO █ AUDEN
█ LARRYKINGSSUSPENDERS
ALKALIS █ SASS █ HATE █
█ ISLE █ LILY █ CAGY █ CPR
ASSNS █ SINS █ SAGE █ SHOE
DOUGLASMACARTHURSPIPE
ALI █ ENTIRE █ EONS █ WIPED
MEND █ GAL █ SIP █ LIN █
█ GEORGEBURNSSCIGAR █
█ ROY █ ORO █ OHO █ LEEK
EMAIL █ CANS █ DEMONS █ ACE
SALVADORDALISMUSTACHE
MULE █ OWNS █ ESSE █ ANTON
ELY █ LUBE █ ATMO █ UCLA █
█ LEGO █ ARGO █ OPHELIA
DOROTHYLAMOURSSARONG
ABOUT █ HORA █ NISAN █ GANG
MOOSE █ ANON █ TOILE █ ULEE
PETER █ TEND █ STEAL █ ELSE
```

71

Puzzle 71

A	S	L	E	E	P	■	H	A	L	L	O	■	■	S	T	A	C	K	■
L	O	U	V	E	R	■	A	R	M	E	N	I	A	■	O	R	I	O	N	S
B	O	N	A	C	O	N	T	E	N	T	I	O	N	■	B	I	R	D	I	E
S	T	A	N	■	T	A	C	T	■	T	O	T	A	L	■	A	B	A	C	I
■	■	T	O	T	H	E	T	U	N	A	T	E	N	B	U	C	K	S
C	O	C	A	I	N	E	■	A	C	S	■	W	A	L	D	O	■
A	B	A	C	K	■	E	S	T	E	■	S	P	I	N	E	■	N	E	O
H	O	W	C	I	L	I	A	M	E	■	T	O	R	S	O	■	E	D	N	A
N	E	S	T	■	I	N	R	E	■	D	I	N	O	■	B	L	U	E	S
■	■	M	A	N	N	A	W	A	R	■	W	I	S	E	A	C	R	E
O	S	B	O	R	N	E	■	R	I	V	E	T	■	L	E	A	N	T	O	S
T	H	E	B	E	A	S	T	■	P	I	S	A	M	I	N	D	■
R	U	L	E	D	■	R	E	E	D	■	M	O	A	N	■	B	E	A	U
O	L	A	Y	■	S	N	E	R	D	■	D	E	C	C	A	C	A	R	D	S
S	A	T	■	G	L	U	E	S	■	P	O	R	K	■	A	L	G	A	E
■	H	I	L	U	M	■	B	O	P	■	S	A	V	I	O	R	S
T	H	E	B	A	R	B	A	R	A	S	E	V	I	L	L	E	■
R	O	B	E	D	■	S	C	O	O	T	■	I	D	I	O	■	B	U	S	H
A	W	A	R	D	S	■	T	U	B	A	T	O	O	T	H	P	A	S	T	E
M	I	L	I	E	U	■	S	E	A	G	U	L	L	■	A	S	I	D	E	S
■	E	L	A	N	D	■	B	E	T	A	S	■	S	I	T	A	R	S

72

Puzzle 72

D	A	H	S	■	B	A	R	E	S	■	A	C	T	S	■	P	O	S	E	R
E	B	A	N	■	E	C	O	N	O	■	T	R	E	K	■	I	L	E	N	E
T	I	M	O	N	A	H	A	L	F	■	R	I	S	E	■	E	A	R	T	H
E	D	U	C	A	T	E	D	■	A	R	I	E	L	W	A	R	F	A	R	E
R	E	P	O	T	■	S	M	U	■	H	A	R	A	S	S	■	P	E	A
■	N	A	H	■	A	P	R	I	L	S	■	K	O	S	H	E	R
O	P	H	E	L	I	A	P	A	I	N	■	C	R	E	P	T	■
V	I	I	■	I	R	R	■	P	O	R	T	I	A	D	E	A	L	E	R
E	N	S	■	E	A	T	■	M	E	S	H	I	N	G	■	N	I	E	C	E
R	E	P	S	■	B	E	G	U	N	■	O	E	D	■	B	E	N	T	O	N
■	A	P	O	L	L	O	S	■	■	D	E	L	U	D	E	S	■
T	E	N	A	C	E	■	R	T	E	■	F	O	R	U	M	■	D	D	A	Y
S	A	I	N	T	■	N	I	E	L	S	E	N	■	I	S	R	■	O	R	A
P	U	C	K	I	N	G	O	R	D	E	R	■	G	O	O	■	W	O	W
■	E	L	I	O	T	■	C	A	S	S	I	U	S	I	N	O	N
T	E	R	R	E	T	■	F	A	T	L	I	P	■	T	E	D	■
A	L	E	■	R	O	C	O	C	O	■	E	L	K	■	T	O	B	I	T
B	A	N	Q	U	O	S	H	O	U	R	S	■	O	N	E	T	O	O	N	E
L	I	E	U	T	■	C	O	L	A	■	T	I	T	U	S	A	D	R	U	M
A	N	G	I	E	■	A	S	I	T	■	A	C	C	T	S	■	I	N	S	P
S	E	E	D	S	■	R	E	N	E	■	T	E	H	E	E	■	T	E	E	S

B	A	L	E	R	S	■	L	A	S	C	A	L	A	■	■	P	O	A	C	H	E	D
A	D	O	R	E	R	■	A	C	T	I	V	A	T	E	■	O	N	S	H	O	R	E
D	O	W	N	F	O	R	T	H	E	C	O	U	N	T	■	R	E	C	I	P	E	S
L	A	K	E	S	■	A	E	O	N	■	T	R	O	O	P	■	C	O	N	E	■	■
O	N	E	S	■	L	I	F	O	■	A	R	I	■	O	R	E	O	■	F	A	A	■
A	N	Y	■	M	I	S	O	■	F	R	E	E	F	O	R	A	L	L	■	O	R	R
N	I	E	■	O	V	E	R	L	I	E	■	■	A	T	O	L	L	■	T	R	A	M
S	E	D	A	T	E	■	D	O	N	A	T	■	M	O	U	E	■	S	I	T	B	Y
■	■	■	L	O	S	■	I	O	N	■	E	R	I	E	S	■	S	H	A	H	■	■
H	A	G	A	R	■	I	N	K	S	T	A	I	N	S	■	S	T	A	R	E	A	T
E	N	O	S	■	A	N	N	E	■	O	F	M	E	■	O	P	E	R	A	B	L	E
R	I	O	■	M	I	T	E	R	■	D	O	O	■	G	N	O	M	E	■	E	L	S
O	L	D	T	I	M	E	R	■	M	A	R	S	■	R	E	O	S	■	I	S	I	T
D	E	F	A	M	E	R	■	B	E	T	T	E	R	O	F	F	■	A	R	T	S	Y
■	■	O	P	E	D	■	C	A	R	E	W	■	E	C	O	■	A	B	A	■	■	■
P	A	R	E	S	■	M	A	G	I	■	O	I	L	E	R	■	L	A	N	D	E	D
R	I	N	D	■	A	A	R	O	N	■	■	M	A	R	T	H	A	S	■	E	S	E
O	R	O	■	J	U	M	P	F	O	R	J	O	Y	■	H	O	M	E	■	C	T	R
P	E	T	■	I	S	E	E	■	■	O	O	N	■	O	E	N	O	■	T	A	R	A
■	■	H	O	L	T	■	R	A	S	T	A	■	A	F	R	O	■	M	A	Y	A	N
S	T	I	N	T	E	R	■	T	H	A	N	K	S	F	O	R	C	O	M	I	N	G
S	I	N	C	E	R	E	■	M	A	R	I	E	T	T	A	■	A	V	E	N	G	E
A	N	G	E	R	E	D	■	■	D	Y	E	W	O	O	D	■	M	E	R	G	E	D

D	E	G	A	S	■	A	N	I	T	A	■	A	L	A	N	■	T	H	O	R	■
A	R	E	C	A	■	L	O	C	A	L	■	L	Y	R	E	■	H	O	M	E	■
W	I	T	H	H	O	L	D	I	N	G	T	A	C	K	S	■	U	V	E	A	■
G	E	S	T	U	R	E	S	■	K	E	E	N	E	S	T	■	M	E	L	L	■
■	■	■	A	I	L	■	A	R	N	I	E	■	E	M	B	L	E	M	■	■	■
R	E	V	E	R	S	E	■	T	R	I	O	S	■	E	G	O	I	S	T	S	■
O	V	O	L	O	■	C	E	D	A	R	■	A	R	G	O	N	■	■	■	■	■
M	I	C	K	S	W	E	L	L	■	S	O	N	G	■	■	D	O	O	R	■	■
A	L	E	■	A	R	A	L	■	V	A	S	T	■	E	M	E	R	G	E	■	■
■	■	T	R	I	A	D	■	F	I	C	H	E	■	R	E	C	A	L	L	■	■
L	A	B	R	A	T	S	■	P	O	L	K	A	■	B	E	R	K	L	E	Y	■
A	R	R	I	V	E	■	H	U	R	L	S	■	T	O	N	E	S	■	■	■	■
S	L	I	C	E	R	■	A	L	T	A	■	S	H	O	O	■	■	S	S	E	■
H	O	O	K	■	■	B	I	L	K	■	E	A	R	W	H	A	C	K	S	■	■
■	■	S	A	F	E	R	■	N	A	O	M	I	■	■	A	W	A	I	T	■	■
B	I	S	C	U	I	T	■	T	O	Q	U	E	■	D	E	T	E	N	T	E	■
O	R	T	E	G	A	■	R	E	C	U	T	■	E	T	C	■	■	■	■	■	■
D	O	U	R	■	S	T	A	R	K	E	R	■	P	A	C	H	I	N	K	O	■
I	N	C	E	■	C	O	K	E	S	O	U	T	O	F	H	I	D	I	N	G	■
C	O	C	A	■	O	D	E	S	■	U	S	E	M	E	■	N	O	P	A	R	■
E	N	O	L	■	S	O	D	A	■	S	H	E	E	N	■	G	L	A	R	E	■

NIPS · SCALE · BOSC · COOED
ASIA · HAPAX · UNTO · HURRY
FANTAILEDPIGEON · ATALE
TAKESIT · YELLOWWARBLER
ACCEPTED · NEE · ALTO
· ONSECOND · BAYS · ABLE
ABC · HOI · HAIL · DROOL
NUKING · RAZORBILLEDAUK
GRANNY · GOUP · IONS
ESTEEM · TAOS · FILES · ROC
LAOS · SCARLETIBIS · BEBE
SRO · SHULA · MEAN · SHADES
· ATOR · MANN · EELERS
DOUBLEBARFINCH · RELYON
DAVAO · LARD · EIS · ENA
STAN · ESPY · LEFTHAND
· DALY · AHA · IRALEVIN
WHOOPINGCRANE · ASTAIRE
HADNT · CHIPPINGSPARROW
ARIEL · HITE · NOISE · BENT
MINDY · SAIL · AWNED · YOYO

The New York Times
Crossword Puzzles

The #1 name in crosswords

Available at your local bookstore or online at nytimes.com/nytstore

Coming Soon!

Daily Crossword Puzzles Vol. 72	0-312-35260-3	$9.95/$14.95 Can.
Biggest Beach Crossword Omnibus	0-312-35667-6	$11.95/$15.95 Can.
Easy Crossword Puzzles for Lazy Hazy Crazy Days	0-312-35671-4	$6.95/$9.95 Can.
Weekend Away Crossword Puzzle Omnibus	0-312-35669-2	$11.95/$15.95 Can.
Weekend at Home Crossword Puzzle Omnibus	0-312-35670-6	$11.95/$15.95 Can.
Sunday Crossword Omnibus Volume 9	0-312-35666-8	$11.95/$17.95 Can.
Backyard Crossword Puzzles	0-312-35668-4	$6.95/$9.95 Can.
Fast and Easy Crossword Puzzles	0-312-35629-3	$6.95/$9.95 Can.

Special Editions

Brainbuilder Crosswords	0-312-35276-X	$6.95/$9.95 Can.
Fitness for the Mind Crosswords Vol. 2	0-312-35278-6	$10.95/$14.95 Can.
Vocabulary Power Crosswords	0-312-35199-2	$10.95/$14.95 Can.
Will Shortz Xtreme Xwords	0-312-35203-4	$6.95/$9.95 Can.
Will Shortz's Greatest Hits	0-312-34242-X	$8.95/$12.95 Can.
Super Sunday Crosswords	0-312-33115-0	$10.95/$15.95 Can.
Will Shortz's Funniest Crosswords Vol. 2	0-312-33960-7	$9.95/$14.95 Can.
Will Shortz's Funniest Crosswords	0-312-32489-8	$9.95/$14.95 Can.
Will Shortz's Sunday Favorites	0-312-32488-X	$9.95/$14.95 Can.
Crosswords for a Brain Workout	0-312-32610-6	$6.95/$9.95 Can.
Crosswords to Boost Your Brainpower	0-312-32033-7	$6.95/$9.95 Can.
Crossword All-Stars	0-312-31004-8	$9.95/$14.95 Can.
Will Shortz's Favorites	0-312-30613-X	$9.95/$14.95 Can.
Ultimate Omnibus	0-312-31622-4	$17.95/$25.95 Can.

Daily Crosswords

Fitness for the Mind Vol. 1	0-312-34955-6	$10.95/$14.95 Can.
Crosswords for the Weekend	0-312-34332-9	$9.95/$14.95 Can.
Monday through Friday Vol. 2	0-312-31459-0	$9.95/$14.95 Can.
Monday through Friday	0-312-30058-1	$9.95/$14.95 Can.
Daily Crosswords Vol. 71	0-312-34858-4	$9.95/$14.95 Can.
Daily Crosswords Vol. 70	0-312-34239-X	$9.95/$14.95 Can.
Daily Crosswords Vol. 69	0-312-33956-9	$9.95/$14.95 Can.
Daily Crosswords Vol. 68	0-312-33434-6	$9.95/$14.95 Can.
Daily Crosswords Vol. 67	0-312-32437-5	$9.95/$14.95 Can.
Daily Crosswords Vol. 66	0-312-32436-7	$9.95/$14.95 Can.
Daily Crosswords Vol. 65	0-312-32034-5	$9.95/$14.95 Can.
Daily Crosswords Vol. 64	0-312-31458-2	$9.95/$14.95 Can.
Volumes 57-63 also available		

Easy Crosswords

Easy Crossword Puzzles Vol. 7	0-312-35261-1	$9.95/$14.95 Can.
Easy Crossword Vol. 6	0-312-33957-7	$10.95/$15.95 Can.
Easy Crossword Vol. 5	0-312-32438-3	$9.95/$14.95 Can.
Volumes 2-4 also available		

Tough Crosswords

Tough Crosswords Vol. 13	0-312-34240-3	$10.95/$14.95 Can.
Tough Crosswords Vol. 12	0-312-32442-1	$10.95/$15.95 Can.
Tough Crosswords Vol. 11	0-312-31456-6	$10.95/$15.95 Can.
Volumes 9-10 also available		

Sunday Crosswords

Sunday in the Park Crosswords	0-312-35197-6	$6.95/$9.95 Can.
Sunday Crosswords Vol. 30	0-312-33538-5	$9.95/$14.95 Can.
Sunday Crosswords Vol. 29	0-312-32038-8	$9.95/$14.95 Can.
Sunday Crosswords Vol. 28	0-312-30515-X	$9.95/$14.95 Can.
Sunday Crosswords Vol. 27	0-312-20414-4	$9.95/$14.95 Can.

Large-Print Crosswords

Large-Print Crosswords for Your Bedside	0-312-34245-4	$10.95/$14.95 Can.
Large-Print Will Shortz's Favorite Crosswords	0-312-33959-3	$10.95/$15.95 Can.
Large-Print Big Book of Easy Crosswords	0-312-33958-5	$12.95/$18.95 Can.

Large-Print Big Book of Holiday Crosswords	0-312-33092-8	$12.95/$18.95 Can.
Large-Print Crosswords for Your Coffeebreak	0-312-33109-6	$10.95/$15.95 Can.
Large-Print Crosswords for a Brain Workout	0-312-32612-2	$10.95/$15.95 Can.
Large-Print Crosswords to Boost Your Brainpower	0-312-32037-X	$11.95/$17.95 Can.
Large-Print Easy Omnibus	0-312-32439-1	$12.95/$18.95 Can.
Large-Print Daily Crosswords Vol. 2	0-312-33111-8	$10.95/$15.95 Can.
Large-Print Daily Crosswords	0-312-31457-4	$10.95/$15.95 Can.
Large-Print Omnibus Vol. 6	0-312-34861-4	$12.95/$18.95 Can.
Large-Print Omnibus Vol. 5	0-312-32036-1	$12.95/$18.95 Can.
Previous volumes also available		

Omnibus

Lazy Sunday Crossword Puzzle Omnibus	0-312-35279-4	$11.95/$15.95 Can.
Crosswords for a Weekend Getaway	0-312-35198-4	$11.95/$15.95 Can.
Supersized Book of Easy Crosswords	0-312-35277-8	$14.95/$21.95 Can.
Crossword Challenge	0-312-33951-8	$12.95/$18.95 Can.
Giant Book of Holiday Crosswords	0-312-34927-0	$11.95/$15.95 Can.
Big Book of Holiday Crosswords	0-312-33533-4	$11.95/$16.95 Can.
Lazy Weekend Crosswords	0-312-34247-0	$11.95/$15.95 Can.
Crosswords for a Lazy Afternoon	0-312-33108-8	$11.95/$17.95 Can.
Tough Omnibus Vol. 1	0-312-32441-3	$11.95/$17.95 Can.
Easy Omnibus Vol. 4	0-312-34859-2	$11.95/$17.95 Can.
Easy Omnibus Vol. 3	0-312-33537-7	$11.95/$17.95 Can.
Easy Omnibus Vol. 2	0-312-32035-3	$11.95/$17.95 Can.
Easy Omnibus Vol. 1	0-312-30513-3	$11.95/$17.95 Can.
Daily Omnibus Vol. 15	0-312-34856-8	$11.95/$17.95 Can.
Daily Omnibus Vol. 14	0-312-33534-2	$11.95/$17.95 Can.
Daily Omnibus Vol. 13	0-312-32031-0	$11.95/$17.95 Can.
Sunday Omnibus Vol. 8	0-312-32440-5	$11.95/$17.95 Can.
Sunday Omnibus Vol. 7	0-312-30950-3	$11.95/$17.95 Can.
Sunday Omnibus Vol. 6	0-312-28913-8	$11.95/$17.95 Can.

Variety Puzzles

Acrostic Puzzles Vol. 10	0-312-34853-3	$9.95/$14.95 Can.
Acrostic Puzzles Vol. 9	0-312-30949-X	$9.95/$14.95 Can.
Sunday Variety Puzzles	0-312-30059-X	$9.95/$14.95 Can.
Previous volumes also available		

Portable Size Format

Crosswords for Your Lunch Hour	0-312-34857-6	$6.95/$9.95 Can.
Café Crosswords	0-312-34854-1	$6.95/$9.95 Can.
Easy as Pie Crosswords	0-312-34331-0	$6.95/$9.95 Can.
More Quick Crosswords	0-312-34246-2	$6.95/$9.95 Can.
Crosswords to Soothe Your Soul	0-312-34244-6	$6.95/$9.95 Can.
Beach Blanket Crosswords	0-312-34250-0	$6.95/$9.95 Can.
Simply Sunday Crosswords	0-312-34243-8	$6.95/$9.95 Can.
Crosswords for a Rainy Day	0-312-33952-6	$6.95/$9.95 Can.
Crosswords for Stress Relief	0-312-33953-4	$6.95/$9.95 Can.
Crosswords to Beat the Clock	0-312-33954-2	$6.95/$9.95 Can.
Quick Crosswords	0-312-33114-2	$6.95/$9.95 Can.
More Sun, Sand and Crosswords	0-312-33112-6	$6.95/$9.95 Can.
Planes, Trains and Crosswords	0-312-33113-4	$6.95/$9.95 Can.
Cup of Tea and Crosswords	0-312-32435-9	$6.95/$9.95 Can.
Crosswords for Your Bedside	0-312-32032-9	$6.95/$9.95 Can.
Beach Bag Crosswords	0-312-31455-8	$6.95/$9.95 Can.
T.G.I.F. Crosswords	0-312-33116-9	$6.95/$9.95 Can.
Super Saturday	0-312-30604-0	$6.95/$9.95 Can.
Other volumes also available		

For Young Solvers

New York Times on the Web Crosswords for Teens	0-312-28911-1	$6.95/$9.95 Can.
Outrageous Crossword Puzzles and Word Games for Kids	0-312-28915-1	$6.95/$9.95 Can.
More Outrageous Crossword Puzzles for Kids	0-312-30062-X	$6.95/$9.95 Can.

 St. Martin's Griffin